Volunteers in the School Media Center

VOLUNTEERS IN THE SCHOOL MEDIA CENTER

Linda Leveque Bennett

Libraries Unlimited, Inc.   Littleton, Colorado

1984

Copyright © 1984 Linda Leveque Bennett
All Rights Reserved
Printed in the United States of America

No part of this publication may be reproduced, stored in a retrieval system, or transmitted, in any form or by any means, electronic, mechanical, photocopying, recording, or otherwise, without the prior written permission of the publisher.

LIBRARIES UNLIMITED, INC.
P.O. Box 263
Littleton, Colorado 80160-0263

Library of Congress Cataloging in Publication Data

Bennett, Linda Leveque, 1946-
   Volunteers in the school media center.

   Bibliography: p. 229
   Includes index.
   1. Instructional materials centers--United States.
2. Volunteer workers in education--United States.
I. Title.
LB3044.B46 1984   371.1'4124   84-20176
ISBN 0-87287-351-X

Libraries Unlimited books are bound with Type II nonwoven material that meets and exceeds National Association of State Textbook Administrators' Type II nonwoven material specifications Class A through E.

To

Mrs. Eunice F. Melder

and

The Volunteers of
St. Luke's Episcopal School Library

"These Americans are a peculiar people. If in a local community a citizen becomes aware of a human need which is not being met, he thereupon discusses the situation with his neighbors. Suddenly a committee comes into existence. This committee thereupon begins to operate on behalf of the need. And, *mirabile visu* a new community function is established. In the meantime, these citizens have performed this act without a single reference to any bureaucracy or to any official agency."

Alexis de Tocqueville

Table of Contents

Foreword xiii
Preface xvii
Acknowledgments xix

1 – IMPACT OF A VOLUNTEER PROGRAM 1
Impact on the Budget 1
Impact on Services 3
Impact on the Librarian, the Staff, and the Children 3
Impact on the Coordinator 5
Impact on the Volunteer 5
Notes 6

2 – APPREHENSIONS 7
Job Insecurity 7
Problem Masking 9
Lack of Control 10
Exploitation 11
Costs 12
Volunteers: Yes or No? 13
Notes 14

3 – PREPLANNING 16
The First Glimmer 16
Establishing a Committee 17
Instituting a Needs Assessment 18
Formulating the Program 19
Evaluation 20

4 — THE VOLUNTEER COORDINATOR..........................24
- The Initial Decision..24
- Central Coordinators..25
- Independent Coordinators.....................................31
- Liaison Coordinators..36
- Establishing a Style of Supervision............................36

5 — ATTRACTING VOLUNTEERS.............................40
- Reasons People Volunteer.....................................41
- Systems of Authority..43
- Types of Campaigns...48
- Financing Volunteer Recruitment..............................73
- Notes...74

6 — SCREENING AND PLACING THE VOLUNTEER...............75
- The Central Coordinator and the Interview....................75
- The Building-level Coordinator and Placement.................89

7 — TRAINING AND IMPLEMENTATION........................98
- Policies and Rules...98
- Authority..104
- Training in Universal Tasks..................................105
- Understanding the Schedule..................................122
- Special Programs..122
- Reassessment..132
- Substituting...133
- Notes..134

8 — PREDICTING AND ALLEVIATING PROBLEMS...............135
- The Role of the Coordinator.................................135
- Interpersonal Problems......................................138
- Problems with Responsibility................................142
- Problems with Time Management............................144

9 — RECOGNITION..155
- Recognition of Volunteers...................................155
- Recognition of the Coordinator..............................163

10 – EVALUATION AND MODIFICATION 164
Methodology and Goal Setting 164
Evaluation of Personnel 165
Evaluation of the Program 174

Appendix A: Guidelines 181

Appendix B: Sample Evaluations 185

Appendix C: Sample Manuals 197

Appendix D: Responses to Survey of Volunteers 215

Bibliography 229

Index 233

Foreword

Although early studies of library volunteers are few, one could say that libraries originated as a direct result of voluntary contributions. In starting libraries, the great men and women of America gave of their resources in a multitude of ways. In 1840 Alexis de Tocqueville described with admiration "the extreme skill with which inhabitants of the United States succeed in proposing a common object to the exertions of a great many men, and in getting them voluntarily to pursue it."

In tracing the history of library volunteers, one must return to the beginning of the public library movement in New England. According to *The Dictionary of American History*, that movement began in 1636, with the establishment of the Harvard College Library, composed of three hundred volumes, a gift of the estate of the Reverend John Harvard. The Reverend Thomas Bray introduced parochial libraries in 1696, and by 1699, he had begun twenty colonial libraries. Although these libraries were for ministers only, they did serve as public libraries. In 1700, their existence encouraged the enactment of the first American library law. It was passed by the General Assembly in South Carolina to regulate the use of one of Bray's libraries, referred to as a "Provincial Library." The *Dictionary of American History* also refers to the "subscription library" founded by Benjamin Franklin in Philadelphia in 1732, as an outgrowth of a voluntary literary association that later became the American Philosophical Society. In 1812, the Philadelphia Academy of Natural Sciences was founded. Arthur Schlesinger identifies this association as composed of amateurs, i.e., volunteers, who "established libraries and museums," among other activities. It was not until 1833, that the first free public library supported by public funds was founded, in Petersborough, New Hampshire. With the passage of legislation in 1848, Boston was able to establish the first tax-supported library. In 1895 the New York Public Library was formed with the merger of the foundations established by James Lenox, Samuel Tilden, and John Jacob Astor.

The American Library Association was organized in 1876, and *The Library Journal* began publication. The specific goals of the organization were to improve the quality and effectiveness of libraries, to make libraries more accessible to all people, and "to improve professional standards of libraries and librarians." Unfortunately, a side effect of the last goal was to create an attitude of superiority among many professionally trained librarians that would make it difficult for library volunteers to be appreciated. Nevertheless, by 1876, the free public library was firmly woven into the fabric of American society along with free public education.

From the 1870s on, a national network of volunteers was formed through the efforts of the Women's Clubs across the country. Initially, members addressed the issues of women's suffrage, child labor laws, and consumer needs. For more than a century, the Women's Clubs produced large numbers of volunteers from the many homemakers who were traditionally unemployed. It was not until 1920 and 1921, respectively, that the League of Women Voters and the Junior League, both well-known organizations today, were organized. Today all of these groups comprise hundreds of thousands of volunteers who have given quality support to education, and particularly school libraries.

Charlotte Mugnier, in her book on the library paraprofessional, notes that during the first half of the twentieth century, "a librarian was a professional by virtue of incumbency" because few persons had been trained in librarianship. During the 1940s and 1950s, librarianship was divided by the American Library Association into two classifications: professional and clerical. Eventually the policy of the fifth year bachelor's degree and the present requirement of a master's degree emerged as minimum standards for professional librarianship. The role of the "paraprofessional" was clearly defined, but any job description for the nonsalaried "library volunteer" was noticeably absent. During this period of history, trained librarians were filling many positions. They actively discouraged the use and the recruitment of library volunteers.

In 1953, the nationwide school volunteer movement began in Bay City, Michigan. Elfrieda McCauley describes it in her 1976 article as an attempt of American citizens to compensate for "teacher shortages, overcrowding, and the demand for individualized instruction" in the public schools. Concurrent staffing problems arose in the libraries. Student library aides were no longer readily available because of changes in the school curriculum and changes in scheduling practices that gave them less free time. The door was open for library volunteers because the number of trained volunteers was simply insufficient. Alice Sizer Warner estimates that in 1960-1961, there were "21,625 adult volunteers helping in the school libraries." By 1964, the National School Volunteer Program, Inc., was founded, aided by a grant from the Ford Foundation. The reaction of professional librarians to the influx of volunteers remained less than enthusiastic.

Other school-centered volunteer organizations were born. In 1969 the Volunteers in Education program was funded in five states by the United States Office of Education. In 1970 The Center for Urban Education recruited volunteers for inner-city schools. The approval of use of Elementary and Secondary Education Act (ESEA) Title II funds for the establishment of school libraries was significant. Library volunteers could be used to staff these new libraries.

Not until 1971 was tacit approval of the use of library volunteers given by the American Library Association, in its publication of "Guidelines for Using

Volunteers in Libraries." Volunteers were said to provide a "new outlook, a different perspective, added talents, and a different concept."

The professional schools of librarianship were less responsive, however. In a 1972 study of fifty-five approved schools of library science in the United States and Canada, Alice Sizer Warner received only thirty-four responses. Despite the enormous growth in numbers of school library volunteers, the schools reported little positive interest in them and some outright rejection of their use in libraries.

A breakthrough in practice came in Connecticut in 1975. In a transaction reported by the *School Library Journal*, a consortium of three agencies agreed to put aside concerns over professional library positions being filled by volunteers and to use Title II funds to start sixty-seven libraries in schools in Connecticut still lacking central libraries. One of the agencies approving use of volunteers in staff positions was the Connecticut School Library Association.

The use of volunteers began to be more acceptable. By 1976, the number of volunteers in education, according to Elfrieda McCauley, had mushroomed to "more than 2.5 million and was still growing." Of these volunteers, she estimated 250,000 to be serving in school media centers.

In conclusion, the history of library volunteers has almost come full circle. From places of authority and respect in the founding of libraries during colonial times, volunteers slipped into positions of subservience to governmental guidelines and professional training standards. With the financial difficulties facing libraries today, however, volunteers are again in demand. There is little reason to believe that this need will subside. On the contrary cuts in financial aid to schools, such as those made necessary by Proposition 2½ in Massachusetts in 1981, will make library volunteers valued partners in public service.

Mrs. Bennett's book provides a practical guide to follow in designing, implementing, and funding a program for library volunteers. It was my pleasure to work in the same school with her for three years. At St. Luke's Episcopal School in San Antonio, Texas, I was fascinated with her ability to recruit large numbers of volunteers, children and adults alike, and to manage them with warmth and efficiency. The annual book fair was a sight to behold! Her "chicken day" fund-raising project was a great success, so much so that I copied the idea in designing "hamburger day" to fund a preschool gifted program at the school. Linda Bennett is clever, witty, infinitely patient, and incredibly attentive to the small, but significant, details of management of library volunteers. Her suggestions will make sense to the reader, and following them will mean success for new volunteer programs.

Mary Jensen Crist

Preface

It is a pleasure to share with the reader ideas about the use of library volunteers. While offering the accessibility of a manual, this book is written in essay style to allow for in-depth consideration of those topics which concern everyone who wishes to be involved with volunteerism in libraries. The book is designed to cover all areas of interest from the planning stage through the evaluation process.

Although this book is primarily designed for the use of school library media specialists, most of it is applicable wherever volunteers are used. The first chapter discusses in some detail the need for volunteers and the benefits of using their services. The following chapters propose an orderly approach to implementing a volunteer program. Those who are working with such a program already will find it easy to locate ideas which may smooth out a problem or two.

Working with volunteers has provided some of the most interesting, pleasant moments of my career; it is the hope of sharing these moments which prompted this book.

Acknowledgments

I am deeply indebted to those who made the creation of this book easier, and to those who supported the project with their time and enthusiasm. Babette Noto, Jan Reed, and Ellie Chapa turned my rather creative typing into readable copy. My family, Ocie Leveque, Janet Malone, and Angela Bennett helped in a multitude of ways.

Kay Nelson, Jan Paprskar, Pat Lobritz, Marie Rastorfer, Carol Reposa, Judy Sharrock, Randy Porter, and Helen Halloran helped with the gathering of information. Theresa Pugh, George Johnson, Dorothy Baird, Yvonne Ross, and Joe Burchard were instrumental in acquiring certain facts, as were the indefatigable reference librarians at Trinity University, especially Craig Likness.

Carol Simons, whose patience helped relieve some of the pressure, has been a great help. Dianne Bailey has been a source of unfailing enthusiasm, as have Maxine Thom, Mary Crist, Mary Alice Potter, Margarete Bain, and Nan Cuba.

I am deeply grateful for the help given by Dr. Lillian Wehmeyer. Her comments and suggestions on the manuscript were invaluable. Dr. Gaston Scott and Donna Schaeffer were also extremely helpful.

In addition, I would like to thank all those who work with volunteers for their time, their effort, and their patience. By such work, we are enabled to share the best everyone has to offer!

1 Impact of a Volunteer Program

Working with volunteers is a fascinating business which will bring great pleasure to those who wish to discover its mysteries. The first step in instituting a volunteer program is the crucial one of decision-making, of deciding whether or not the operation is worth undertaking in a particular school. Needless to say, such consideration should be thorough so that ensuing decisions will be valid and little time will be lost in backing up to reconsider factors not given enough preliminary thought. After careful initial consideration, inquirers will be in a position to make a decision and move on, either to the next step or to some other project. The many advantages of a volunteer program will be considered in this chapter. In chapter 2, we will look at the issues which concern some people when they consider such a project.

There are so many advantages to a volunteer program that it is difficult to describe just a few. The advantages will vary somewhat from school to school, still there are some which are so general that almost everyone will experience them. An improvement in services is certainly to be expected, as is a decided upswing in positive public relations. But perhaps the most encouraging benefits are those which affect the school media center budget.

IMPACT ON THE BUDGET

Expenditures simply keep going up, and balancing a budget gets more and more difficult. Aside from the rising costs of personnel and the increasing price of paper, the changing nature of libraries may be the major spur to rising costs. Libraries today are facing a period of upheaval unequaled since the advent of the first lending library. Pressures from many institutions—from businesses to universities—are forcing librarians to search avidly for the right approach to managing the proliferation of information which characterizes our cultural and scientific progress. School libraries reflect this challenge as they seek ways to provide students with information skills which will last them throughout their lives—while still supplying the basic, traditional library resources and atmosphere.

Clearly, the advent of electronics into the library, especially at the high school level, represents a major impact on the media center budget. Audiovisual equipment and microcomputers are becoming so necessary to the life of the library that their high costs cannot be overlooked. The software to go with the machines can also be a major expense, and should be taken into consideration and students need not only the information provided by the more sophisticated machinery, but also the expertise with which to use it. They need to feel secure in their capabilities before they go to college. Students of today will be expected to have a working familiarity with all sorts of audiovisual equipment and with computers. They will waste many hours needlessly if they do not know how to handle research using more advanced methods than the card catalog and the *Readers' Guide*. The most important need, however, is to teach attitude. Most people are familiar with someone who is capable of accomplishing a certain task but who, because of lack of self-confidence, cannot. By the time students are graduated from high school, they should *know* that they are capable of acquiring every last bit of information from any library, by themselves and with the help of librarians. By the time students have completed their secondary educations, they should be so capable in the use of libraries that they can concentrate on topical study, not on the method by which they locate material for that study.

In addition to these more sophisticated techniques for information retrieval, the school library is finding that it needs to spend a higher and higher percentage of its budget on nonfiction, specifically on science and social science. In a world which is increasingly influenced by almost daily discoveries of literally world-shaking importance, elementary and high school libraries have an obligation to keep students well informed and to help guide them to a realization of the important place science holds in our lives.

To do all this without sufficient funding usually means either to do an incomplete job of it or to borrow from other crucial programs. Rather than succumb, the library should seek ways to circumvent the loss. Volunteers can help:

According to Sannwald and Hofmann in an article in *Library Journal*, the Ventura County, California, public libraries were faced with a 13 percent reduction. In a choice between closing over half of the branches or using volunteers, Ventura County opted for volunteers. During the course of the first year of the program, 440 citizens donated 13,170 hours of service to the library.[1] That sort of response would shore up any program and allow resources to be redirected.

In today's economy libraries sometimes are distressed to the point of having to close unless they can find some way to divert funds into other channels where untenable cuts would otherwise have to be made. When this is the situation, one way to free funds allocated to clerical help is the volunteer. "Without our volunteers we couldn't have survived the summer," states one librarian,[2] who felt she would have lost her job without the help of recruits. When deciding upon whether or not to embark upon a volunteer program, the professional must consider what the results might be without it. At a workshop held by the New York Metropolitan Reference and Research Library Agency, it was pointed out that some services disappear permanently when funding falls too low.[3] It would be a real disservice to the betterment of the library to fail to recognize the fact that libraries often use volunteers to help solve financial problems.

IMPACT ON SERVICES

In addition to more or less universal expenses, most schools have some special need. Many libraries support active tutoring groups, since, as Connie Haendle says, reading is very obviously the main concern of libraries.[4] Some act as clearing houses for school activities. Others supervise the peripheral activities which support classroom teaching, such as mimeographing teachers' activity sheets and preparing displays in support of special units. Each activity takes funding in time, in money, or in both. Each activity could form the basis of a good volunteer program.

How are libraries handling this pressure for more and better services? Catherine Murray of Cornell University states that Cornell successfully uses nonprofessionals at the reference desk in order to deal with burgeoning public demands for more services. Librarians have found that these carefully trained nonprofessionals are skilled and dedicated and are positive additions to their reference service.[5] While reference is generally considered a professional task, it is better to use volunteers than to eliminate the service.

Elfrieda McCauley acknowledges that volunteers free the schedule of professionals, which makes it possible for them to deal more with individuals. "The elimination of study halls, the advent of advance placement courses, the open-ended school day ... served to decimate the ranks of student helpers traditionally made available to us."[6] She continues: "In Orange County schools, in the vicinity of Orlando, Florida, schools have media specialists, but no paid clerks. There, more than 100 library volunteers work in 65 elementary schools, performing clerical work, operating audio-visual equipment and telling stories—always under the supervision of a professional."[7]

June Needle finds that people with special knowledge of a field can be very helpful in cataloging and in such things as building shelves.[8]

Harold Jenkins states that if units could be manned by volunteers under supervision of a professional, funds for materials could double. While this would not be likely in a small library, certainly services could double, and, in libraries, service is what funds are all about. Jenkins foresees using volunteers to assist in present tasks, but also to make it possible to keep the library open longer, and to provide help in special subjects and in the acquisition of materials in special subject areas.[9]

IMPACT ON THE LIBRARIAN, THE STAFF, AND THE CHILDREN

The use of volunteers in the library is one of the best, most consistent ways to win the hearts of the public. Librarians who bring the community into the school are benefiting the library and its students, the staff of the school, the volunteers themselves, and the community as a whole. Those who come to work in the library will become ardent advocates of library goals. They will learn to understand library problems and accept those which cannot be completely solved, while actively working to change those which can. The support that a group of enthusiastic volunteers gives the librarian is splendid and most uplifting. Since the nature of library work is to a degree a factor in separating the librarian from the teaching staff, and since many of the concerns of the library do not have a counterpart in the classroom, the understanding and reinforcement of workers who are aware of nuances within the library setting are extremely gratifying.

Staff morale is an important facet not to be overlooked. Volunteers provide a support group second to none. The staff can build their confidence in leadership and organizational skills through the use of volunteers and can feel a deep sense of recompense when those volunteers actively recognize their abilities. People who volunteer are generally very positive thinkers; they are eager to find strengths and abilities in those with whom they work. While people generally know when they are doing a good job, it is a real morale-builder to have someone voice admiration.

Another positive aspect of the typical volunteer program is that many volunteers are senior citizens. The public relations potential in helping variant age groups work together is tremendous and, again, will benefit all concerned. In today's typical limited family, children sometimes have little opportunity to interact with those much older than their own parents. What an unexpected pleasure it is to these young people to discover how very interesting much older people can be! The more mature volunteers often relish an opportunity to again work with children much younger than their own now-grown offspring. Both groups will remember that their experiences were made possible through their involvement with a library.

On a more practical note, the use of volunteers can free much-overworked staff to do more complex tasks, or to do them better. Most librarians have had the sense of feeling pressured for time, of wishing they could concentrate just a little longer on some important project, possibly one which is near completion and which could be implemented immediately. A well-organized, active volunteer program can make this and more possible. Not only can present work be accomplished more quickly and possibly in greater depth, but other interesting tasks may be undertaken, tasks for which there is presently no time. The presence of well-trained volunteers means hours of extra time available to the librarian.

Furthermore, volunteers frequently are willing to do things which just are not possible for the librarian, such as picking up or delivering materials during regular work hours, putting up bulletin boards in other parts of the building, manning money-making projects, giving book talks and telling stories in other locations. All these would require the physical presence of the librarian in the library and in another location at the same time. Volunteers make these projects possible.

Moreover, pupils and staff alike will benefit from the special skills and interests of those with whom they work. The addition of volunteers will increase the pool of knowledge from which all can draw inspiration as well as specific help. Who can judge the ultimate impact of one well-done book talk on marine biology, accompanied by materials gathered by an expert in the field? How can one put a value on the joy and pleasure one ardent advocate of folklore can give to a student, a pleasure which could lead to a lifetime of reading?

The use of volunteers truly offers a wider pool of skills from which to draw. Many volunteers have spent years perfecting their skills. When a volunteer whose avocation is art teams up with the art teacher, the quality of displays is likely to be very high.

Another area in which using volunteers can be pleasing to the coordinator is the library story hour. Many librarians do not feel that they do justice to the children they serve at story time. A well-done presentation takes time that most librarians do not have. Volunteers, however, who spend hours during the week preparing for their presentations can produce top-notch performances. Dolls can be dressed to match characters in stories, treasure maps designed, games played which were inspired by the stories. Volunteers who really enjoy their story time will often prepare splendidly, usually at their own expense, if there is extra cost. The satisfaction the children receive and the excellent publicity for the program are very rewarding.

IMPACT ON THE COORDINATOR

Librarians in general, their staffs, and their students are not the only ones who will benefit from a volunteer program. Someone will have the responsibility of coordinating the volunteer program. There will be many special rewards for the central coordinator of a good volunteer program as well. One of the finest is the pleasure of working with a variety of people from all segments of the community.

Moreover, watching the library or department grow and realize aspirations which the librarians have held for years is one of the greatest pleasures imaginable.

IMPACT ON THE VOLUNTEER

Along the same lines, librarians will feel a sense of real accomplishment when they realize how much they are helping their volunteers. Many people use hobbies and outside interests to further or to enhance skills they already had—such as public relations or typing—or look to those activities to offer new experiences, which libraries can certainly do! It is a wonderful feeling to have a volunteer say, "You know, I thought when I went back to work, I'd have to go back to teaching, even though I never really liked it. After working in the library on so many different things, I've discovered that the times I've been really happy have been the times I was working on things involving record keeping and numbers. I've decided to go back to school to get my degree in accounting." Since the library can offer so many different types of work, it presents a perfect opportunity for volunteers to try out their ideas and to discover what is involved in different jobs.

The blossoming of self-worth in volunteers is inspiring. They have many, many opportunities to accomplish feats not normally available to them and to garner immediate recognition for their successes. It would be a rare person indeed who would not react positively to these stimuli. A deep sense of satisfaction will reward the librarian who sponsors a situation which can foster such growth.

NOTES

[1] William W. Sannwald and Catherine N. Hofmann, "Volunteers in Venture County," *Library Journal* 107 (1982): 681.

[2] Ibid., 682.

[3] Leslie Trainer, "Metro Workshop on Volunteers in Libraries Sparks Controversy, Offers Practical Advice," *American Libraries* 7 (1976): 666.

[4] Connie Haendle, "The Community Link: Libraries and the Literacy Volunteers of America," *Wilson Library Bulletin* 50 (1976): 731.

[5] "Letters," *Library Journal* 106 (1981): 83.

[6] Elfrieda McCauley, "Volunteers? Yes," *School Library Journal* 22 (1976): 29.

[7] Ibid., 30.

[8] June Needle, "Peace Corps Librarians in the Developing World," *Special Libraries* 68 (1977): 206.

[9] Harold Jenkins, "Volunteers in the Future of Libraries," *Library Journal* 97 (1972): 1401.

2 Apprehensions

Some professional librarians anticipate disadvantages in a volunteer program. In this chapter we shall examine some of their apprehensions with the hope of dispelling them.

JOB INSECURITY

A recurrent fear of established librarians is that the use of volunteers will be a threat to their job security. They feel that the public might come to believe that anyone with time to give could run a library.[1]

Furthermore, many librarians expect that the volunteers will have high visability while the professionals will be assigned to less conspicuous tasks, and many professionals are afraid that anything which takes them out of the public eye will be deleterious to their positions. As it happens, this is almost certainly true. The public needs to see the librarian interacting with the patron. School librarians need to spend a great deal of their time with the students. Put very simply, in a well-organized volunteer program there is more time to do this. Volunteers can perform more of the routine activities and leave those which require true interaction to the librarian. Even the very public task of checking out books can be done to advantage by volunteers, thus freeing the librarian to mix with the students and deal with their questions and concerns. This is almost impossible to do from the circulation desk, yet a very active library requires that someone be on call, if not actually there, at all times. If librarians remain adamant about being before the public in clerical positions, they can hardly complain when the public perceives them as something less than real professionals. Using volunteers can thus boost the public image of librarians by giving them more time for those aspects of librarianship which require true expertise. Librarians who demand professional standing based on their performance at such tasks as putting the due date in books are being unrealistic. They must offer more and better quality service if they expect to gain status.

There is an additional issue of similar nature. Some librarians are fearful that the volunteer is really a job-hunter in disguise. This fear results from a lack of self-confidence and sense of place in the profession. A certain number of well-trained volunteers may indeed be hired; these should become real assets to the libraries in which they work. Once guidelines have been established as to which jobs are professional only and which are clerical, job-hunting volunteers should be welcomed since the administration will know much more about the quality of their work than about that of almost any person whom they meet during a couple of interviews only. The uneasy professional should remember that the hiring will be done by those who have been determined competent to ferret out high-quality personnel. It is to their advantage not to hire someone who is unqualified to hold a position or who is incapable of doing the work involved. Administrators, while needing to hold firmly to a budget, will not be likely to jeopardize their professional reputations by hiring unfit people as an expression of gratitude for their volunteer work. The central issue is that a nonprofessional, whether volunteer or on staff, is no threat to a professional.

Along another line, some librarians are worried that volunteers will be given the best assignments in order to keep them interested.[2] The experienced user of volunteers will find that the very nature of the volunteer system will work against this. In the first place, working with volunteers in itself is terribly exciting: the new faces, new skills, and new ideas combine in a kaleidoscope of fascinating arrangements which will pull from the staff ideas they never knew they had. The stimulation is marvelous. In the second place, the fact that volunteers do not actually spend much time in the library (compared with a full-time employee) makes it almost impossible for them to accomplish really big projects on their own. Instead, they will usually be limited to brief portions of major endeavors or to regular, repetitive tasks which will give the staff more time for the interesting projects. In the third place, most volunteers are well aware of the limitations of their commitment to the library. They will rarely overcommit themselves, even for an adventurous assignment. They seem to have a built-in sense of quantity control. In brief, most of the types of work in which volunteers can really shine are not those showy, more exciting tasks which help brighten the schedules of the staff. Instead, their attention to the less interesting details will make the librarian's work more varied and enjoyable.

The assumption that job security may depend on avoiding the use of volunteers is really, as was mentioned above, a result of lack of definition of responsibility. The issue of professionalism must be settled before any permanent, acceptable solution can be found. One result of a nebulous view of professionalism may be seen in the contention of a librarian who stated during the metro workshop in New York that the substitution of volunteers at the "lower levels" could allow professionals to "move up" to regional and state offices.[3] This negates what librarians have worked toward for years: an interaction with society which will be felt by every member of the community, and from which every member will benefit. Over-extension and misapplication of this kind can cause a backlash: as an example, one professional concludes that "we must stop chasing the chimera of professionalism; it is keeping us from the work at hand."[4] While it is easy to understand the frustration and impatience which may have spurred this remark, and appreciate the fact that its author had before her the goals of library service, the action would be akin to cutting off the foot to eliminate the ingrown toenail. "The work at hand" can be accomplished with much greater facility once the elusive issue of professionalism is tied down. Having done this, one will eliminate or at least greatly lessen the reason for many fears about job loss. Once librarians must be legally competent, once job descriptions are so precise that even the librarians of the smallest libraries know which of their tasks are professional, then the question of job security will be academic.

The general basis of fear seems to be that some librarians suffer from lack of self-confidence. In line with that a professional from New York asserted during the metro workshop mentioned above that "some librarians are afraid that the volunteer they work with may be smarter" and so do not want a "specialist aide."[5] This fear is at odds with one of the best reasons for using volunteers: to gain the use of special knowledge. Graduates of top-notch library science programs who have been encouraged to make the most of their skills will be less likely to fear the abilities of others than those who feel that their backgrounds and experiences are weak. Those who have been guided to develop executive skills will be eager to use them. They will relish discovery of a nugget of expertise within an otherwise ordinary person, whether that person be salaried or volunteer. Librarians are aware that the vastness of the scope of their work often precludes depth of knowledge in many of the fields covered within libraries. This should be a badge of honor rather than of denigration. How many other fields include every iota of information from every period of time and from every country? No one could reasonably expect to excel in every field of knowledge. Really competent, self-confident people will identify their own weak areas and search out those who are more adept in them. They will utilize that ability and their own knowledge for the benefit of the library. This search may take them to a government office, to a university department head, or to a well-informed volunteer. In each case the librarians will be demonstrating their skill as information specialists by acquiring that information in the fastest way possible. There is no benefit in doing something the hard way when an easier way will result in the same answer. Time spent in fruitless searching could be more profitably spent on other library projects.

PROBLEM MASKING

Attempting to use volunteers to solve all problems in the library is another possibility which worries some. To do this may prevent efforts to analyze the problems and come up with long-term solutions.[6] That would indeed be an error. It is, however, one which can be avoided by a realistic evaluation of needs and a determination from the outset not to gloss over significant problems by using volunteers to "make do." Instead, a well-planned program will make full use of volunteers to enhance existing programs and to create new ones, not to cover up old problems. Any attempt to do so on the part of administration should be met with a clearcut, concise statement from the coordinator about the uses and limits of volunteers.

LACK OF CONTROL

The issue of volunteer control occupies a large percentage of the literature. Many librarians fear that, once accepted, volunteers will not be subject to the same control that staff would. In actuality, volunteers usually perceive themselves as working under greater stricture than employees do.

One element of this fear is that, once volunteers are accepted, they can do as they like without fear of correction or of being dismissed. Coordinators who feel that they cannot let an unsatisfactory volunteer go would indeed be at a great disadvantage. This problem, however, will be exceedingly rare. If there is difficulty with volunteers, changing their jobs or sites of work will usually take care of it. If not, coordinators in a school have a decided advantage over some others, since many schools have other volunteer programs besides the one in the library. Volunteers can be made aware of a great need in another area, and told that, while their work in the library was valued, they have been transferred and their former positions filled. If this is not acceptable, they can indeed be told that the coordinator feels that library work is not right for them, and that it would be better to find work in another field. Delicate, yes. Impossible, no. Thoughts on this subject which came out at the metro workshop referred to in chapter 1 included the statement that volunteers are often more dedicated and reliable than paid staff. Some felt that problems with volunteers are no worse than those with any other employee.[7]

As for the opposite problem of volunteers who take up training time, then quit, "no employer ever knows how long any employee will remain on the job."[8] The coordinator should expect an attrition of about one-third the first year. After that, the rate will go down considerably, since the experienced volunteers will know that they want to work, and will help keep enthusiasm high for the new ones.

Reliability is an issue which justifiably concerns the new coordinator. A properly planned program will allow for some irregularity of schedule. This, combined with a determination to place the volunteer in a compatible situation, even if it means reassigning a job, will result in an arrangement in which those who are unreliable will not have a strong negative effect on the library. The concern is a real one, but it is one which can be handled.

The fact is that, while there are some totally unreliable volunteers (who soon cease to volunteer) and some who are occasionally unreliable, the woods abound with tried and true types who can be depended upon implicitly. In 1972 there were more than one million voluntary associations in America.[9] These must have some way of staying in operation. They cannot depend upon totally unreliable people. A $168,632 profit made by the Greenwich Public School system in using volunteers did not happen because of unreliable people. The 282 percent statewide increase in volunteers in California does not indicate that the volunteers were unreliable. The $900,000 increase in budget from one year to the next, attributed to volunteers, in the Ventura County, California, libraries does not show a severe unreliability rate. Can we not, then, stipulate the existence of some degree of unreliability in some volunteers, but conclude nevertheless that the use of unpaid help is an advantage?

The contention that the enthusiasm of volunteers quickly wanes[10] is probably the result of a volunteer program in which there was not enough pre-planning or one in which volunteer recognition has been minimal. There are two times when absenteeism is high among volunteers: right before Christmas, when shopping and out-of-town guests claim their time, and right at the end of the school year, when everyone is tired and ready for a break. Short of that, enthusiastic coordinators can keep their volunteers happy and eager by their attitude and their approach to the volunteers' duties.

Another fear is that totally unsuitable people would volunteer and must be accepted. One head of a library, originally antagonistic to the program, later defended her volunteers: "We didn't have a lot of 'just anybodies' walk in; we got very intelligent people."[11] On a nationwide basis the average volunteer has had some college and has an inquisitive, adventuresome personality. Rare indeed is the volunteer who is totally inept. As to accepting just anybody who offers to volunteer, a good screening process will eliminate most of the undesirables, and a realization that the coordinator must consider that dismissing the volunteer is an option will take care of the rest.

EXPLOITATION

Another negative feeling about the use of volunteers became apparent during the metro workshop in New York. One vehement opponent to the use of volunteers felt that volunteerism is just another form of exploitation of women, and that the only acceptable volunteer jobs are those that are "change-oriented." Anyone "who feels they must volunteer to pick up job experience is just getting exploited."[12] The speaker contended that women want to work and not volunteer. Some women do indeed want to work. On the other hand, some consciously make the choice to volunteer. While volunteering should not be demanded of anyone as a criterion for being hired, the fact is that one can learn many skills while working in an unpaid position. The issue here, as in the staying home/having a career argument, is choice. Arbitrary statements about what "all" women want are a bit presumptuous and negate the evidence supplied by the Gallup Poll which indicated that sixty-nine million Americans would be willing to give 245 million man-hours a week to volunteer action.[13] It is hard to believe that sixty-nine million people are being coerced. If the term *exploited* is limited to the definition, "put to use, make use of," without the more recent negative connotation, then indeed organizations all over America—and the people they benefit—are exploiting these volunteers. But again, one arrives at the fact that the volunteers are choosing to be "exploited." As far as people desiring to work rather than volunteer, the two are not mutually exclusive. The average volunteer is between 18 and 36 years old, and 70 percent of these unpaid helpers are already working.[14] In other words, these people are volunteering to fill some need that their careers do not satisfy. They need diversity; they need to feel that their contribution helps; they need the growth which comes with dealing with new fields of experience—there are multitudes of reasons for volunteering.

Another argument which seems specious is that volunteering exploits women in particular. This is hard to give credence to, in view of the multitudinous men's organizations which give millions of hours in volunteer time. While some areas of volunteerism are typically undertaken by women, there are volunteer groups which are exclusively male, the fraternal organizations, for example. Women are no more exploited than men, and for both there remains the element of choice.

COSTS

Volunteer help is not free. There are costs to be considered, in terms both of finances and of professional input.

One liability stands out immediately in the mind of most coordinators: they are now responsible for more people. Any laxness on the part of the volunteer, they protest, will reflect negatively on the head. Two things ameliorate the potential negative effect of this factor: the support of the administrator and the nature of the volunteer.

Once principals decide to allow the use of volunteers, they are accepting the fact that there will be some problems. They should hold their coordinators responsible only for their performance in relation to the volunteers. The librarians who have separate individual coordinators working under their direction should require proper training and follow-up. They should require remedial training when unforeseen problems arise and not expect perfection, for there will be problems. The head of the library must accept these without recrimination but expect remediation. In other words, the coordinator should expect support from the administration as the problems are worked through.

The other factor which will lessen negative results is the nature of most volunteers. If anything, they err on the side of caution. Most volunteers listen carefully and ask questions which are pertinent and timely. They want to do a good job and take steps to insure that they do. Volunteers usually live in fear of creating havoc. One of the most difficult tasks of coordinators is to help volunteers feel free enough to risk making a mistake. Once the volunteers can do this, they become more than automatons. They can offer much of value, including their loyalty, which would have a difficult time flourishing in an atmosphere of little trust.

The financial investment in a well-organized program is minimal when compared with the benefits. In the Ventura County, California, program, time and supply expenses totalled an estimated $40,518 the first year. "Training was particularly expensive, we believe, largely because we were unprepared to do it. Also, nearly 200 volunteers dropped out, and whatever training they had received was lost."[15] While most schools will not be involved in anything on this scale, there are lessons to be learned. The first is to be prepared before beginning such an ambitious program. If a program has not been adequately coordinated, there will be financial investment in excess of that which was necessary to accomplish the program. The loss of such a large number of volunteers reflects lack of planning. Many things make a difference: giving recognition, using the volunteers' time wisely, fostering the self-concept of the volunteers, and establishing the program in the eyes of the community specifically enough so that new recruits are reasonably sure what they are signing up for. The most important aspect of all might have needed more preparation: making sure that those who would be working with the volunteers would really support the program. The result in Ventura was still considered a success because it drew in a larger budget for the following year— $900,000 larger. In another public school system, the use of volunteers cost about $9,000 and "a little loving care," and the dollar value of the program at the rate of $3.50 per hour was $177,632.[16]

Small schools will find their outlay minimal, and the help the volunteers give will probably produce results which will justify the expense. Private school libraries in particular will find that volunteers are financially rewarding. One school library had a budget of $400 per year. ("That's what the last librarian made on the book fair.") After five years of an active volunteer program, the budget (now school-supported) was increased to $3,000. Once parents and school board members see the possibilities, they become more willing to give financial support.

While the cost of volunteer programs when compared with benefits is minor, still, one must budget them in. Effective service, volunteer or otherwise, is the result of accurately foreseeing needs and preparing to meet them. The statement that volunteers can be the most expensive way to get a job done[17] can be true—with poor planning. With good planning, using volunteers can be the least expensive. Anything done poorly can cost so much that it might be almost mandatory to eliminate it. However, almost anything can be improved to the point at which it is not only acceptable, but also highly desirable.

VOLUNTEERS: YES OR NO?

The advantages of a volunteer program are many. A representative of the Greenwich Public Schools said, "any other decision (than welcoming the volunteer) would have been futile resistance on my part against an upswelling of popular involvement in the concerns of public education."[18] This eagerness of many people to become involved and to feel that they are helping is nationwide, both within schools and without. "Whose fault is it that we have not come up with ways to enlist the help of those enthusiastic, and often expert, people? There are surely ways to take advantage of the reservoirs of good will and enthusiasm they represent. Why are we so afraid whenever someone shows up at the library to offer to help out?"[19] While not everyone wishes to volunteer, many do, and acquiring volunteers is often just a matter of saying yes.

The use of volunteers has kept open libraries slated for closure, as in Ventura County,[20] or has helped maintain services, as in Ithaca, New York.[21] It can staff kiosk libraries,[22] some of which will probably grow into full-fledged service institutions, demanding professional staffing. Volunteers can help fund the library simply by giving their time. (In Ventura County where 440 people gave 13,170 hours in one year, calculated time at the salary for entry-level clerical workers volunteer work represented $54,260.)[23] They can help by donating supplies and equipment as well as books. In other words, volunteers have a strong potential for supporting libraries.

Volunteers can work as liaison with the community. They can turn the creative energy of civic groups, both men's and women's, into a supportive effort. They can serve as a force for social change, as has happened many times in the past. They can build small programs into large ones which will demand funding and a professional staff. Library operation eventually outgrows volunteers who will insist on a professional librarian.[24] The presence of volunteers can create professional level jobs while helping alleviate the clerical level. Most of all, the use of volunteers can build support for the future. The better people understand libraries, what they stand for and what they need, the more supportive these people will be. This support will be passed on to their children in the form of positive attitudes.

Using volunteers can affect the existing program by saving money which can then be used for books and materials and not for the salaries of clerical help. They can free librarians so that they can turn their attention to more professional tasks, especially those which involve assistance to patrons.

Finally, librarians have in the past been very energetic in recognizing and acquiring funds from many sources.[25] Volunteers are an excellent source.

No matter how dedicated the efforts of librarians, they could fail for lack of support by the people.[26] Librarians are reaching the point where they have to work together with the community if their goals are to be reached. They need to enlist the energies of the people in "small, splendid, efforts."[27] Together, a community can succeed in wonderful things.

NOTES

[1] William W. Sannwald and Catherine N. Hofmann, "Volunteers in Venture County," *Library Journal* 107 (1982): 681.

[2] Noel Savage, "Special Report: Volunteers in Libraries," *Library Journal* 101 (1977): 2431.

[3] Harold Jenkins, "Volunteers in the Future of Libraries," *Library Journal* 97 (1972): 1401.

[4] "Letters," *Library Journal* 106 (1981): 83.

[5] Leslie Trainer, "Metro Workshop on Volunteers in Libraries Sparks Controversy, Offers Practical Advice," *American Libraries* 7 (1976): 666.

[6] Alice S. Warner, "Voluntarism and Librarianship," *Library Journal* 97 (1972): 1242.

[7] Trainer, 667.

[8] Helen C. Goodman, "The Library Volunteer—III: Volunteers in El Paso," *Library Journal* 97 (1972): 1676.

[9] Jenkins, 1400.

[10] Ibid.

[11] Sannwald and Hofmann, 682.

[12] Savage, "Special Report," 2432.

[13] Jenkins, 1400.

[14] Savage, "Special Report," 2432.

[15] Sannwald and Hofmann, 682.

[16] Elfrieda McCauley, "Volunteers? Yes," *School Library Journal* 22 (1976): 29.

[17] Jenkins, 1400.

[18] McCauley, 29.

[19] John Berry, "Listen to the Delegates," *Library Journal* 194 (1979): 1093.

[20] Sannwald and Hofmann, 681.

[21] "Letters," 83.

[22] Noel Savage, "News in Review, 1980," *Library Journal* 106 (1981): 121.

[23] Sannwald and Hofmann, 682.

[24] Warner, 1242.

[25] Jenkins, 1400.

[26] Ibid., 1399.

[27] Ibid.

3 Preplanning

A period of preplanning usually precedes any well-organized volunteer program. Some basic decisions must be made so that the eventual plan will be smooth and those working with it will be able to put it into action very quickly. The earliest step will be taken by the person who suggests the volunteer program. If that suggestion is accepted, a committee is selected to direct the process, which includes goal setting, needs assessment, a study of methods of implementation, and the provision of a method of evaluation. While most of these topics are covered in detail in later chapters, they are a part of the concerns to be dealt with in preplanning.

THE FIRST GLIMMER

Where do ideas for programs such as a volunteer program usually originate? The answer is invariable: from people who see a need or an opportunity.

Nonprofessionals

There are numerous instances in which a parent or other interested nonprofessional sees a need, assesses it, and concludes that an active volunteer program would be the answer to the problem. Initiation of a program may begin with parents who learn that their children did not have time to accomplish all the things they would have liked to in the library because the staff was just too busy. Parent groups consider projects which will be worth their attention and time and often single out the library, since the entire school would benefit from any library program. Initial interest can come from parents who have worked in other volunteer programs and would like to participate in one at a new school, or it can result from a gift to the library which will require time from the staff, time which is just not available. Or interest can come from parents who feel that they would like library work and who approach the librarian with the idea.

Professionals

The librarian is another common source for volunteer programs. Often librarians will assess their situations and find that their programs could be much better with more resources, usually of time. If money for staff time is not forthcoming, these librarians often move to the next step: acquiring the time without money. Librarians are in a perfect position to predict whether or not a given situation could benefit from the use of volunteers. They see the many little details which are not accomplished or not thoroughly accomplished because of time. Librarians also see the myriad benefits that can come from the influx of new ideas and enthusiasm through the use of volunteers. Sometimes librarians will be offered materials or equipment which they long to use but which they realize must be stored unless intensive short-term help is available. Similarly, librarians may have splendid ideas for new projects which will be hopeless without help. The issue of money has been one which has spurred many a librarian to try a volunteer program.

On a higher administrative level, district librarians sometimes see the use of volunteer programs as a method by which they can assure better services to a variety of school libraries. These supervisors are able to assess the general needs of a district and can formulate projects from which all would benefit and to which the entire district could contribute. They often reach the conclusion that extra help would be useful indeed.

Other sources sometimes initiate the idea: principals, who are eager for both the help and the good public relations which will result; teachers, who use volunteers within their own classrooms and wish to use them in connection with units on storytelling or research; and the students themselves, who often see fascinating possibilities.

ESTABLISHING A COMMITTEE

Customarily in starting a volunteer program one will wish to establish a committee to formulate the basic program. This committee should be large enough to include representatives from most of the areas which will be affected by the program and from any area which requires special expertise. Members from influential community volunteer groups or from the students should have a beneficial effect. A member of the parent-teacher association would be a powerful ally. One or more representatives from the teaching staff would be a positive addition, as would one of the library's clerical staff. Needless to say, the librarian of the school will be a member of the group, or, in the case of a school district, librarians should be represented by one or more of their peers. In school districts, the district librarians may also be invited to participate, if they are not the force behind the program already. In every case the goal in selecting the committee is to form a group of people with special insights and abilities.

The attitude of the committee will definitely have an impact on the development of the program. Imagination and capability can result in the perception of opportunities which will be the soul of the project. The committee's ability to plan and implement will affect the degree to which the program succeeds.

INSTITUTING A NEEDS ASSESSMENT

Once the committee has been selected, some members will be assigned to do a needs assessment. This should be relatively formal, even in the smallest library, since putting things on paper in an organized manner will help assure that no important area has been overlooked. This assessment should cover not only all areas of the library which might be affected by a volunteer program but also the wishes of the teachers, the administration, and the students.

Teachers should be canvassed and asked what they would like to see the library accomplish and whether they have ideas which they would like to see implemented. Suggestions might range from having some in-the-classroom presentations to having the students do more research in the library. Teachers might want more frequent or better library instruction for their students. They might want the library to fill a need in the area of literature, by providing games or encouraging book reports. While some teachers may be satisfied with their present relationship with the library, others may view the resource center as the ultimate information source which can provide the students with the opportunity to put their knowledge into practice, and thus may wish to have closer ties. Teachers may want longer hours available to the student. They may wish to institute some special system for checking out a needed item. The assessment should be as broad as possible so that even ideas which would take years to realize are included. The goal is to identify ideas which can become part of both short- and long-range plans.

Administrators have an interest in any widespread program. It is to their advantage to help projects begin well and they can often point out things which would affect the school as a whole. This ability to provide an overview is especially valuable in establishing priorities.

The existing library staff, whether professional or clerical, can contribute greatly to a needs assessment, since they are faced daily with unmet needs and unrealized potential. Bringing them into the decision at this stage will also help allay any feelings of insecurity caused by the addition of volunteers.

Students can provide a candid "grass roots" view of what the library needs. They have a way of seeing the obvious. They also, with their limited experience, will be less tempted to rule out ideas because they have never been tried before. Children can be very self-concerned in a positive way, reaching out for things which can make their environment better. Those doing needs assessment for a school library will wish to take advantage of this freshness.

The needs assessment for the library should also involve a set of thorough task analyses which will cover both existing procedures and potential tasks. The bottom line, of course, is to determine where and how volunteers will help. In dealing with each area, it is necessary to involve both someone who knows in depth what the processes are and someone with enough distance to be able to view the situation with perspective.

Existing procedures should be broken down into units of work where needs may be identified. (Some knowledge of flowcharting would be useful here. An excellent source is James Rice, "How to Accomplish Flowcharting," chap. 14 in *Introduction to Library Automation* [Littleton, Colo.: Libraries Unlimited, 1984], 107-19.) Needs might include ways to do the work more efficiently, or ways to handle items which have never before been dealt with satisfactorily. Certainly as a result of such task analysis ways to use volunteers will become apparent.

Once the needs of the library and its users have been identified, it is time to assess the needs of the volunteer program. These would include space, money, personnel, training, and time from both volunteers and staff. Specifying these needs will make it possible to begin a program which will be as effective as possible very quickly.

The needs of the volunteers themselves must also be taken into consideration. These may include the need to be associated with a quality product, the need for affiliation, esteem, self-actualization, and many other factors. When a work situation is extremely specialized, fewer of the workers' skills are required. This may in some cases lead to frustration and dissatisfaction. Workers typically derive more satisfaction from jobs when they have input into what needs to be done and how it is to be accomplished, so a method of doing this needs to be built into the system.

FORMULATING THE PROGRAM

When it comes to setting up the program, the identification of the library's mission or objectives will be the first step since these objectives determine the nature of a program. The objectives will also determine the extent to which and means by which the library committee will respond to the needs they have established (though the objectives should in no way predetermine the scope of the needs assessment). The managerial process, types of systems used, kinds of materials used, and the type and number of personnel should all be consistent with the objectives of the library. Job descriptions, organizational planning, performance standards, and work rules will all derive from the identification of these basic objectives.

Strongly defined objectives will assure the program of balance. Those involved in one process will be unlikely to interfere with the management of others. Furthermore, objectives are necessary in the formulation of evaluation standards. The objectives will, of course, be constantly revised so that the library is always working toward desirable goals.

In order to proceed in an orderly fashion and to accomplish those things which are considered desirable, it is necessary to incorporate the general objectives of the organization into a concise set of goals, both long-range and short-term. This step takes considerable time and thought.

Short-term goals are those which can be accomplished within a brief period of time—within a month or a year. Long-range goals are those which will take much longer to accomplish and which must be slowly worked toward. In either case all goals must be compatible with the mission of the library.

Furthermore, the committee will decide whether there will be a flat structure of supervision or many layers. The attitude of the committee toward centralization will greatly influence the nature of the program.

Introducing volunteers into a library setting will create a situation which will require a definite and written policy statement. The status of the volunteers must be established as well as the scope of their work. The committee is also responsible for this. Such a statement usually becomes part of the volunteer manual (see appendix C).

The duties of the committee will extend to assuring that there are space and funding available to support the program, or that adequate means of acquiring them are established.

In addition, the committee will establish means by which the coordinator of the program is selected. The responsibilities of the coordinator should be delineated (table 3.1). Although these responsibilities and other requirements will be covered in great detail in chapter 4, it should be noted here that standards must be set up by which to measure potential coordinators, lines of authority and responsibility must be identified, a style of supervision within the library must be established, and the role of the coordinator in the school must be defined. Preplanning committees will identify as within the purview of the coordinator certain aspects of planning, decision-making, executive action, control of services, and managerial functions. Administrative influences which will affect the coordinator will be identified, as will the impact of those influences.

EVALUATION

Lastly, the preplanning committee will wish to create a basic format for evaluation. It is especially important to establish this before work is actually begun so that methods can be devised by which coordinators themselves may be evaluated. An in-depth study of evaluation is provided in chapter 10.

The information in table 3.2, pages 22-23, provides an intensive and helpful approach to decision-making and the evaluation of projects and ideas. Modifying this procedure to meet the needs of a given library will assure a good beginning to the activity of preplanning.

(Text continues on page 24.)

Table 3.1

Responsibilities of the Coordinator

---

1. SETTING OBJECTIVES

2. PLANNING
    Gathering facts and opinions
    Programming

3. MAKING DECISIONS

4. TAKING EXECUTIVE ACTION
    Organizing
    Directing
    Supervising

5. DIRECTING SERVICES
    Methods
    Materials
    Projects

6. EXERCISING CONTROL
    Reading reports
    Inspecting
    Conducting surveys
    Assessing costs

Table 3.2

Evaluation of Purposes and Ideas

What Are Criteria for Decisions?
1. How appropriate is the proposal to the purpose? Consider the purpose and scope of the library's program, as well as of the proposal.
2. Recognize and define the problem as exactly as possible; this is seldom possible at first thought; it may arise specifically or evolve from an array of generalities; it clarifies only with time and study.
3. Where does it fit into present organization and activities? Is it totally new and additional? How would it be influenced by a period of inflation or depression?
4. Does it duplicate a similar activity, present or planned, of some other area of the school? What other idea or project is in competition with it?
5. How pressing is it? Is it immediate or long range?
6. Though action and putting into effect may not be necessarily immediate, it may be vital to start the chain of developments leading to later action.

Procedure for Evaluation (Promptness is desirable)
7. Assign someone to study the problem, i.e., be responsible for the gathering of fact and opinion to place before those who decide.
8. Realizing from the start that the coordinator as leader of opinion must avoid overinfluencing the others; he should, however, not follow what may be poorly formulated ideas.
9. State the problem for all to understand and weigh. This usually requires a series of restatements, each more exact, with previously unforeseen details, ramifications and objections.
10. Gather professional literature, data from other libraries, and nonlibrary parallels.
11. Gather reader opinion and probable reactions.
12. Gather staff opinion. What are repercussions at all parts of the organization, especially those most affected?
13. Gather a frank, critical opinion of small group of top leaders who appreciate the larger aspects, i.e., financial, political, public opinion, staff reactions, etc.
14. Present to supervisor; get his reactions, should it be postponed until completely formulated?
15. Find or foresee the attitude of public officials.

Table 3.2—*Continued*

> Later Criteria and Procedures
>
> If the project or problem has survived to this point it requires still further study:
>
> 16. Analyze and estimate cost factors, immediate investment, whether annual costs will increase, etc.
> 17. List alternative solutions, including "do nothing about it."
> 18. Determine the consequences of each of these.
> 19. Make a comparative evaluation of these sets of consequences.
> 20. Foresee valid and specious objections from inside and outside, and weigh these, perhaps forestalling or counteracting, if a proposal is likely to be adopted, or if a refusal may arouse criticism.
> 21. Get each employee to see what difficulties there may be in foreseeing the resulting reactions of all concerned. These may include opinions of citizens who have never even been in the library.
> 22. Carefully restudy to foresee all the detailed steps and difficulties, persons involved, assignment of responsibilities, and follow-up, in order to formulate a complete statement of pros and cons.
> 23. Balance all of the pros and cons: appropriateness, importance, timeliness, complications, objections, overall educational worth as a library activity, costs.
> 24. Establish a fair priority, compared with other proposals.
> 25. Consider the possibility of a tryout on a small scale.
> 26. Prepare complete instructions as a device to clarify additional details and difficulties.
> 27. If favorably decided, arrange for all constructive factors: staff and reader cooperation; outside publicity; detailed instructions to each person concerned, including provision for supervising and checking on results.
> 28. If there has been negative decision, procedures for explaining reasons to all concerned, especially to those who proposed it.

From PRACTICAL ADMINISTRATION OF PUBLIC LIBRARIES by Joseph L. Wheeler and Herbert Goldhor. Copyright © 1962 by Joseph L. Wheeler and Herbert Goldhor. By permission of Harper & Row, Publishers, Inc.

4 The Volunteer Coordinator

A volunteer system sometimes happens by chance. When it does, there will be improvements in service and moments of glory, but these will be fewer and have less impact than they would have had had the system been actively organized from the beginning. One of the major drawbacks of a project which grows spontaneously is that there is not likely to be a person in charge who has planned time into the schedule for the volunteers and their questions. Either the librarian will guide them sporadically or they will function on their own, more or less without supervision. Most drawbacks can be minimized or even alleviated in a program which has begun by chance once someone takes over its supervision and planning.

THE INITIAL DECISION

Even without a thoroughly planned program, volunteers want a leader, someone who is available and able to answer their questions. Most volunteers are well aware that they represent a limited portion of a larger picture. They want someone who will understand the overall situation and interpret it for them, putting into perspective their own accomplishments. Thus, a coordinator is important to a volunteer system.

Smaller systems usually prefer that each individual library function independently in terms of a coordinator. The large city school system might employ a central coordinator to oversee all member schools. In the case of a central coordinator, it will still be necessary for a person in each library to perform at least limited liaison functions as a coordinator, since someone must be delegated to work with the volunteer at all stages.

The selection of a volunteer coordinator at any level involves many elements, especially a consideration of personality, of attitude, and of available time. Volunteer coordinators are the directors and inspiration of the volunteer system. The people selected for this position will determine the future of the program, so every effort should be made to find coordinators who will be enthusiastic and effective.

Once coordinators are selected, they will need to know what is expected of them and what they can expect of the other staff members. New coordinators will need a clear understanding of the lines of authority and of their place in the system. As was indicated in chapter 3, these things are part of the preplanning stage.

CENTRAL COORDINATORS

Systems of Authority

Central coordinators must know precisely those areas in which they will function and those which will be left to the liaison coordinators who will direct the volunteers within the library, as well as those areas which will overlap.

When central coordinators work directly under the directors of the school systems, they can maintain a certain amount of autonomy not available in systems in which the central coordinator is more or less on a level with the different school principals (see table 4.1, pages 26-27). The former system may provide a false sense of control, however, since the attitudes and desires of principals must be taken into consideration. Principals of schools will affect any volunteer programs under their jurisdiction, at least by the atmosphere which they foster within the school. To leave the principal out of the line of authority is to make assumptions about control which will probably be proven either false or incomplete. It is far better to set up a system which includes principals on the same level as the central coordinators and invite them to offer their ideas.

In systems which involve high school, middle school, and elementary school directors in positions between the central coordinator and the director, it is still better to involve the principals. The coordinator might find that several of the principals prefer not to become actively involved; still, knowing what all the relationships are would make things run more smoothly as different issues arise.

Use of Liaison

It is not recommended that a system be set up in which the central coordinator is directly responsible for volunteers. As was mentioned above, someone designated as a liaison coordinator, working within the individual library, should be the person to work with volunteers on a daily basis. It should be fully established very early in the program if there are any limitations on the functions of the liaison coordinators and whether or not one is superior in authority to the other.

Responsibility is another area which should be considered. Who is responsible for any problems which might arise with the volunteers or other staff members? Some guidelines must be established before problems arise, so that they can be dealt with efficiently and quickly with as little disruption as possible. These guidelines must be devised by mutual consent of those concerned. This may include both coordinators, the librarian, and the library director. Together the two coordinators (central and liaison) can have an

(Text continues on page 28.)

26 / 4 — *The Volunteer Coordinator*

Table 4.1

Systems Suitable for Use of a Central Coordinator

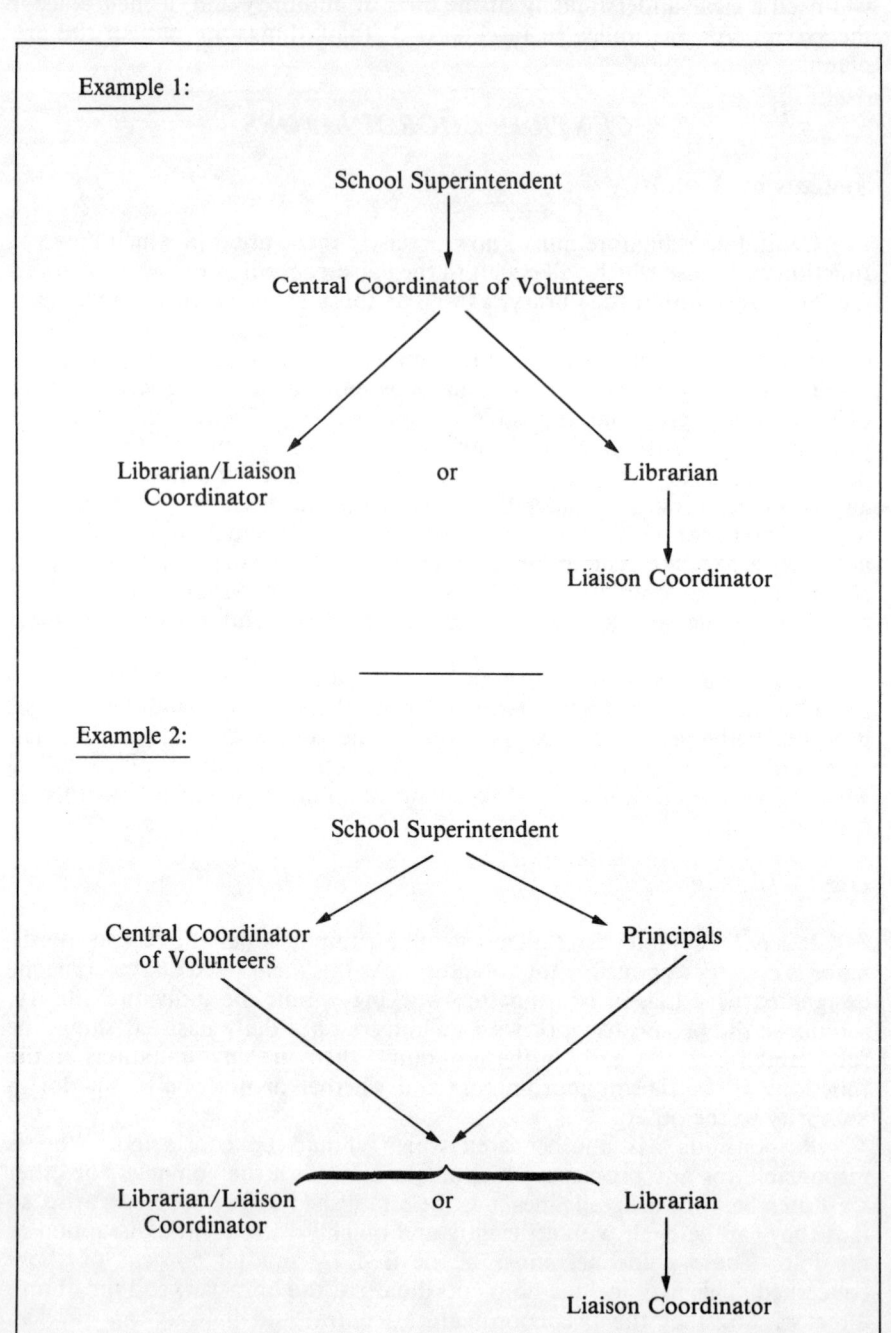

Example 1:

```
                    School Superintendent
                            │
                            ▼
                 Central Coordinator of Volunteers
                   ╱                        ╲
                  ▼                          ▼
         Librarian/Liaison      or        Librarian
            Coordinator                       │
                                              ▼
                                      Liaison Coordinator
```

Example 2:

```
                    School Superintendent
                    ╱                    ╲
                   ▼                      ▼
         Central Coordinator           Principals
            of Volunteers
                   ╲                    ╱
                    ▼                  ▼
              ⎰─────────────────────────⎱
         Librarian/Liaison     or      Librarian
            Coordinator                    │
                                           ▼
                                   Liaison Coordinator
```

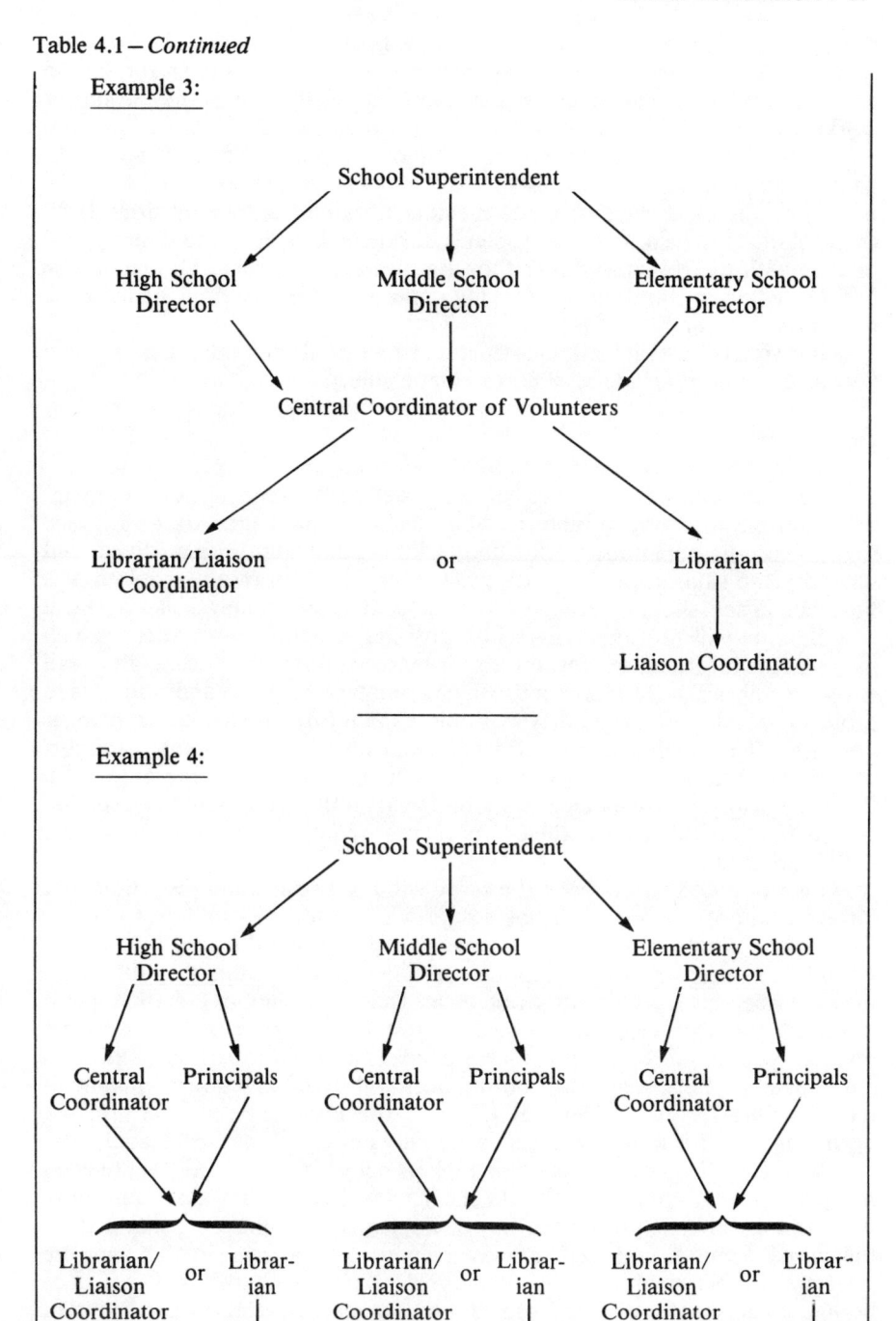

Central Coordinators / 27

Table 4.1 – *Continued*

Example 3:

```
                    School Superintendent
                   ↙         ↓         ↘
      High School      Middle School    Elementary School
       Director          Director           Director
              ↘            ↓            ↙
              Central Coordinator of Volunteers
                   ↙                  ↘
       Librarian/Liaison      or       Librarian
          Coordinator                      ↓
                                    Liaison Coordinator
```

Example 4:

```
                    School Superintendent
                   ↙         ↓         ↘
      High School        Middle School     Elementary School
       Director            Director            Director
        ↙    ↘              ↙    ↘              ↙    ↘
  Central  Principals  Central  Principals  Central  Principals
 Coordinator         Coordinator          Coordinator

 Librarian/    Librar-    Librarian/    Librar-    Librarian/    Librar-
  Liaison  or   ian       Liaison   or   ian       Liaison   or   ian
 Coordinator     ↓       Coordinator      ↓       Coordinator      ↓
         Liaison Coordinator   Liaison Coordinator   Liaison Coordinator
```

excellent program with little additional work load for the library. In order for the volunteers to feel as secure as possible, it would be better for liaison coordinators to have as much responsibility as possible, since they would be working more closely with the volunteer and would thus have a closer relationship as well as a better understanding of most problems. The central coordinators' role would involve counseling and support, since they would have the benefit of the experience of many member librarians and could draw from their solutions to help with the problems of others, but they should rarely deal directly with the volunteers after they are placed in a library. This should be left to the liaison coordinator, working under the supervision of the librarian or library director.

It is vital that organizational structure be established in the beginning, and that its definition include all lines of responsibility.

Duties

Central coordinators' duties consist of determining the needs of all member libraries, attracting volunteers, and placing them in the various schools. Central coordinators must work closely with the many libraries involved, and must develop skills at public relations far above those normally required of a librarian. They should be agents for dissemination of new ideas. Central coordinators will find themselves in a position to acquire and categorize all manner of information concerning volunteerism in libraries. They will encourage librarians to report jobs which volunteers perform and solutions to problems which arise. Then they can shuttle the information to other member libraries. Central coordinators will be responsible for developing a rapport with many librarians, investigating their requirements, and seeking ways to fill them. They might have a much larger budget than the coordinator of a smaller system and thus may have at their disposal more complex means of advertising the libraries' needs.

Central coordinators have the responsibility of spending their time and efforts equitably among all schools who wish to use the volunteer system. Central coordinators must guard against being overly influenced by any one librarian or other school representative in order to be sure that they distribute their services fairly. This does not mean that they should fail to respond positively to those who have a real interest in the program. These highly involved people will be a good source of ideas and will usually be willing to participate in pilot programs. Coordinators will spend much of their time in member libraries, or at least talking with the librarians, especially in the beginning, when priorities and needs are being discussed and evaluated.

Wise coordinators will maintain copious notes, even on needs that they do not plan to service immediately. As the year progresses and more and more programs are effected, new ones may be implemented without repeating all of the initial research, although it may need to be updated. In this way the program will become more and more effective with less and less effort, since both the coordinator and the others who are participating in the program become more experienced as time passes.

Before initiating new programs, central coordinators must carefully gather information and make their plans. They must visit all member schools and interview the head librarians. They must keep accurate notes on needs and wishes. They must respect those librarians who choose not to use volunteers, at the same time encouraging them to consider them at a later date (a few success stories can do wonders).

They must then plan their publicity program or select their publicity director. See chapter 5 for more on this.

Then, before taking action, these coordinators must have a fairly specific strategy for placing their volunteers. They should know needs well enough to be able to match quickly a new volunteer to the appropriate school. They must be able to suggest types of work to the volunteer without promising specific placement. This should be left up to the liaison coordinator in the school. See chapter 6.

Once plans have been made, the program can begin. In order to determine their effectiveness, central coordinators must maintain good communication with their member libraries. Through this feedback they will be able to determine possible changes in areas of responsibility.

Those people selected for the job of central coordinator would ideally be able to devote their entire week to the job. In a less than ideal situation, they must at least have a great deal of time to devote to the project. (Frequently, the person who assumes the role of central coordinator is one who is already a central library director.)

Characteristics

The central coordinator should have a working knowledge of libraries and the logic behind them, enjoy organizing and working with people, be able to work with other professionals without making them feel threatened, and be empathetic. The central coordinator should be caring and have the skills necessary to help alleviate unnecessary worry in others. Any coordinator must be able to assess signals people give out concerning their real feelings, since these will be an important factor in their work. Central coordinators will essentially be working under their own direction, so should be highly self-motivated. They should be able to accept criticism of the program as a means of improvement, and by this attitude encourage thoughtful suggestions from others. If they are going into established programs, they should have the ability to assess the work of their predecessors and have the patience to continue it, making changes gradually and with authority. They should have a firm idea of their role and be able to leave anything not directly under their jurisdiction to the individual librarians of the member schools. People selected as central coordinators should be adept at publicity or be capable of learning quickly. They should seek out any information which might better their program and avoid locking themselves into a system which is not constantly being modified. New coordinators should eagerly seek out and disseminate information to member libraries which could help improve the local programs. They must be enthusiastic both in attitude and manner and must have a very positive view of volunteers in the library, perceiving them as a way to enhance and expand existing programs and as a means to effect programs which have been only dreams to the librarian. A high level of creativity would be desirable, since this could be used in many ways to broaden the program and enhance publicity. Coordinators must be able to budget wisely and fairly both money and time. They must be adept at setting priorities and at accomplishing goals and must not become so enamored of their own enthusiasm that they fail to respect the attitudes of those who do not agree with them. They must be able to transmit enthusiasm to potential volunteers who may be a bit wary of their involvement.

Central coordinators, like others in management positions, should have excellent planning, organizing, coordinating, directing, and controlling skills. Indeed, those who have these abilities at their command will be well on their way to a vibrant program! Good managers maintain a certain distance from the tasks at hand, so that they are able continually to evaluate and accelerate progress in their programs. They know when to lessen this distance and involve themselves directly, thus gaining greater knowledge and the good will of the volunteers.

Some systems have used volunteers to fill the position of central coordinator, often with the duty of supplying volunteer needs of the entire school. This can work well if the volunteers are willing to devote the time required. The main problem might lie in their acceptance by the professionals with whom they will be working. But since their role would be more that of support or liaison than supervision, this might not affect the program. In any case, the attributes necessary for the position would, of course, be required of the volunteer who acts as coordinator as well as being required of the coordinator who is a staff member.

In the case of the central coordinator who is adept at public relations but who has little library background, it must be remembered that most library work requires an attitude which values precision. Talking with librarians about problems they have had with volunteers in the past should give some idea of the types of things which should be considered. New coordinators will find their effectiveness in acquiring good volunteers heightened as they learn more about the nature of libraries.

Value

The value of using central coordinators lies in the time/cost effectiveness. They will become adept much more quickly at public relations skills because more of their time will be spent developing this area. Their work will be more concentrated in the area of volunteerism since they will not have the additional responsibility of a library, although they may have other directive duties.

The main negative factor is that the benefits of the program might be fragmented rather than concentrated. It might be argued that one person cannot devote himself to the betterment of any particular library program when he has so many others to work on. Sometimes the personal relationships and dedication which tend to grow in a more concentrated setting can motivate others even better than great technical skill.

Some situations are better handled with a central coordinator, while others would thrive under an independent building-level coordinator. The problem must be considered carefully, then a commitment made. Either system will take about two years to produce enough data for a realistic evaluation. The plan can be modified, but those working with it should be sure to give the overall program enough time. Any changeover in basic systems will be very costly in terms of time and credibility, and should be made only after careful consideration.

INDEPENDENT COORDINATORS

Systems of Authority

In systems which do not use a central coordinator, the building-level coordinator must assume responsibility. The question of lines of authority will be simplified, with the librarian acting also as coordinator under the principal, or with a separate person acting as coordinator under the librarian, who in turn reports to the principal (see table 4.2).

Table 4.2

Systems Suitable for Schools Using Only Building-level Coordinators

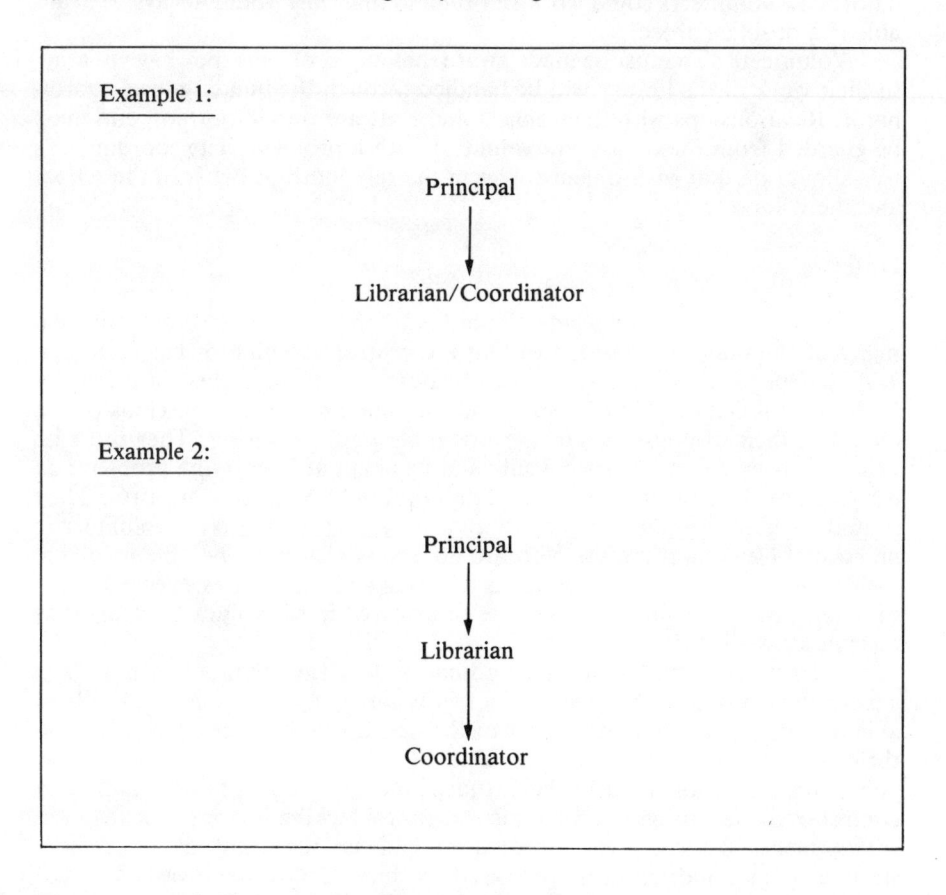

```
Example 1:

                    Principal
                       |
                       ▼
               Librarian/Coordinator




Example 2:

                    Principal
                       |
                       ▼
                    Librarian
                       |
                       ▼
                   Coordinator
```

The responsibilities and authority of the building-level coordinator must be established before any real program is initiated. The staff could be told that if any problems with volunteers arise which are related to their work in the library, the coordinator is the person who is responsible for correcting them. (An in-service on volunteerism is a good idea, since the staff will then be able to put in perspective any inconveniences caused by the volunteers.) Most coordinators will find that the staff is largely pleased by the use of volunteers under the direction of the coordinator; some may want to establish their own volunteer programs.

Building-level coordinators will also find that most staff members are only too glad to leave any problems or disciplinary measures to them. It is absolutely mandatory that the volunteer be the responsibility of only one person. Any criticism, no matter how mild, will be a touchy subject, and will be accepted most readily from the coordinator, who will be established as a friend. This is another reason that a staff member should be used as coordinator. Few volunteers could work full-time so that they would always be available if a problem arose.

Volunteers also must be made aware that any problems they have relating to their work in the library will be handled through the building-level coordinator. Relationships with the teachers and staff are very important, and must be guarded from the occasional volunteer with a problem. The coordinator's role should be that of problem-solver in the relationships between the school and the volunteer.

Duties

Those selected as independent coordinators to serve in a library will have many of the same responsibilities that the central coordinator has (see table 4.3). Independent building-level coordinators should be skilled in using the forces of publicity to their benefit, and they should be very conscious of the means at their disposal to increase favorable public reaction. They must be able to convey directions specifically and be adept at identifying problems as early as possible. Independent coordinators should be tactful but firm. They should be able to maintain control and be willing to dismiss a volunteer if necessary. New coordinators who are librarians also must be able to divide their time well between their duties as librarian and their duties as coordinator of volunteers. They must not become so involved in the volunteer effort that their other work suffers.

Independent building-level coordinators will find that all their efforts benefit their own libraries, which is a highly satisfying situation. They will be able to utilize one hundred percent of the desirable volunteers they attract in their own libraries. They will be able to develop a closeness with those volunteers which will attract others. Independent coordinators will maintain a control over their programs which is sometimes lacking in a more centralized arrangement. While central coordinators can use the needs of others as a starting point, independent coordinators must learn to investigate and interpret their own needs. Independent coordinators must be initiators, self-starters. They will be in almost total control of their programs and so must be the catalysts.

Table 4.3

Functions of Management

PLANNING	—	The course of action to achieve a goal.
ORGANIZING	—	Structure to be used.
COORDINATING	—	Securing cooperation of all concerned.
DIRECTING	—	Action.
CONTROLLING	—	Continuous monitoring and evaluation.

Planning is the highest executive function and the crucial beginning.

PLANNING SAVES TIME!

Adapted from *Finding Time for Success and Happiness through Time Management* by Ivan W. Fitzwater, by permission of Mandel Publications, a division of Management Development Institute. Copyright, 1977, Management Development Institute, Inc.

Characteristics

In libraries using librarian/coordinators, one of the biggest drawbacks is that coordinators must fill two roles at once. They must be full-time librarians with well-run libraries and, at the same time, coordinate progressive volunteer systems. One factor which will alleviate some pressure is that the two functions overlap to a degree. Many facets of normal library life cry out for publicity. Volunteers can learn about library arrangement and locating material as they sit in on regular children's classes. It is easy to teach someone without spending extra time as one does many of the things necessary in a library. On the other hand, librarians will discover almost immediately that they are reaping more than they sow once the volunteer has been trained, even minimally. While things might be fairly hectic for a while, the good results will be worth it.

Independent building-level coordinators who are assistant librarians, aides, or other staff members working under the supervision of librarians must fully understand the extent of their responsibilities. They must be very careful that they and the librarian are agreed on all points.

In the case of such coordinators who are volunteers, these coordinators must be willing to give much more of their time than is usually asked of volunteers. They must be dedicated to the program. Placing volunteers in this position is not usually recommended since they often expect to make a commitment of no more than one year. It is very depressing to watch someone new to a position spend precious time making the same mistakes that the previous person made and mended. While detailed notes could help alleviate this situation, many if not most people new to a job do not spend the time needed to brief themselves on the position before getting so caught up in it that they feel they no longer have the time to review their predecessors' work. While this might be true also of new employees, they would be more likely to establish continuity by their presence in the same position the following year.

Another reason that volunteers are sometimes not a good choice for this position is that some volunteers do not readily understand the nuances of the interactions of different aspects of the library. Selecting such volunteers for the coordinating positions would automatically mean that the librarians would be involved to a great degree in work they had planned for the volunteers to assume. This might disorganize the librarians to the point that their own work would suffer. Furthermore, the work of a coordinator will encompass all aspects of a library. Coordinators must work to some degree in both administrative and supervisory positions (see table 4.4). This entails much practical knowledge in the elements of library service as well as ability in working with people. Thus, it might be much better for the librarians themselves to maintain control or even to designate a staff aide to the position.

A third reason for not selecting a volunteer for this position is that of authority as perceived by other volunteers. While volunteers generally work together very well, they usually react better to someone they consider "the real authority," especially when disciplinary measures must be taken, no matter how mild. Another factor is that coordinators must be taken seriously by the staff, since they will act as intermediaries in many cases between the volunteers and the teachers or office personnel. It is often easier and faster to do this with a peer or at least a paid staff member.

Table 4.4

The Administrative Function in the One-Person Library

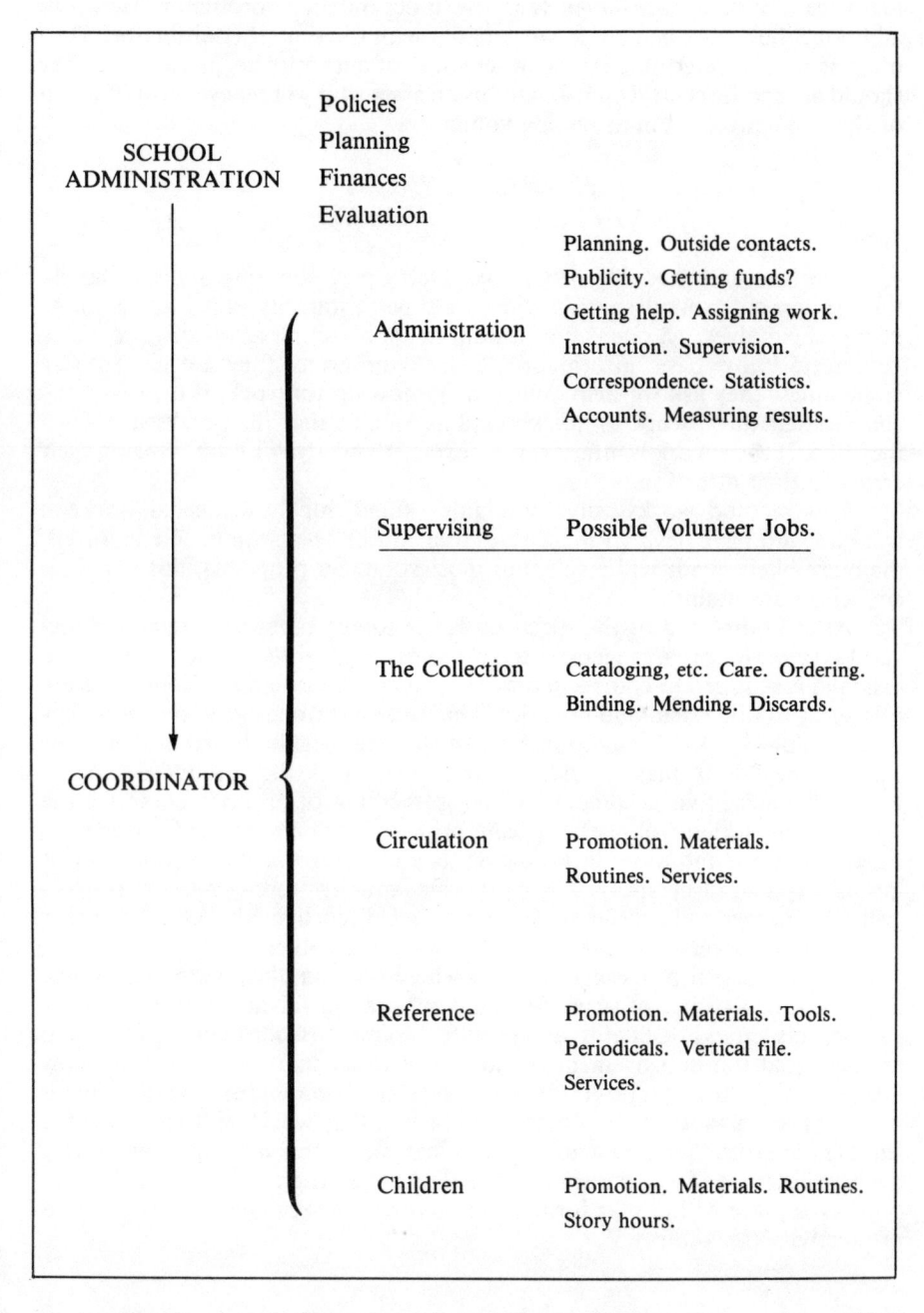

SCHOOL ADMINISTRATION ↓	Policies Planning Finances Evaluation		
COORDINATOR	{	Administration	Planning. Outside contacts. Publicity. Getting funds? Getting help. Assigning work. Instruction. Supervision. Correspondence. Statistics. Accounts. Measuring results.
		Supervising	Possible Volunteer Jobs.
		The Collection	Cataloging, etc. Care. Ordering. Binding. Mending. Discards.
		Circulation	Promotion. Materials. Routines. Services.
		Reference	Promotion. Materials. Tools. Periodicals. Vertical file. Services.
		Children	Promotion. Materials. Routines. Story hours.

From PRACTICAL ADMINISTRATION OF PUBLIC LIBRARIES by Joseph L. Wheeler and Herbert Goldhor. Copyright © 1962 by Joseph L. Wheeler and Herbert Goldhor. By permission of Harper & Row, Publishers, Inc.

LIAISON COORDINATOR

Those selected as liaison coordinators to serve in a library must have many of the same attributes that the independent coordinator needs. In addition, they must be able to work easily with the central coordinator. They must be able to determine exactly where lines of authority begin and end. They should accept the central coordinator as an asset who will relieve them of much of the work involved in attracting volunteers.

ESTABLISHING A STYLE OF SUPERVISION

The first and most important task facing new coordinators is designing their programs around specific styles of supervision. Styles are as varied as people themselves. At one end of the spectrum is complete *laissez-faire*. Once volunteers know basic information about a program, they are left entirely alone unless they ask for help. When they show up for work, if they do, they choose their duty, work as quickly and as long as they like, and leave when they like. If their work is inferior, it is corrected quietly, without bringing their errors to their attention.

This method works only for highly skilled, highly dedicated workers, workers who have devoted themselves to a cause. The more people involved, the more likely chaos will result. For most volunteer programs, this system is eminently unsuitable.

At the other end of the spectrum is the totally organized, tightly supervised system. In this arrangement the worker is arbitrarily assigned to a needed task and is required to come at a time convenient to the library. Volunteers are told what to do, when, and not why. This system, or one close to it, is widely used. Volunteers in an environment like this are usually donating their time because they think they should. Many of them lack the joy and feeling of accomplishment that accompany giving something of oneself. These are the satisfactions which volunteering can bring. Coordinators find themselves becoming more and more inflexible as they discover that few people will fit into this system successfully. These programs usually produce more chaff than grain. Volunteer and coordinator alike become disenchanted. Result? Another "we tried volunteers and they just didn't work out" story.

The successful programs fall somewhere between these extremes. While there must be a degree of structure to any program involving large numbers of people, this should be kept to an absolute minimum. Coordinators must keep as their goal the improvement of library services, and must work in many different ways to accomplish this goal. The more coordinators can individualize their programs, the more likely it will be that they will be able to extract the full benefit from them. Individualization can strike fear into the heart of any overworked supervisor, but if there is form to the program and individualization takes place within that form, time spent will be rewarded with increased productivity (see table 4.5).

Table 4.5

General Principles for the Volunteer Coordinator

1. Continued participation depends upon reward.
2. Volunteers must see the relationship of the job they do, however small, to the total effort.
3. Volunteers must be made to feel the importance of their contribution.
4. The first efforts of a volunteer must be simple enough to insure success.
5. Volunteers must have opportunities to grow and learn.
6. Volunteers must be encouraged to make as many decisions as possible.
7. Volunteers work best in a friendly, warm atmosphere, where their efforts are obviously needed and appreciated.
8. Volunteers must not be taken for granted.
9. Keep volunteers informed about developments in the organization.
10. Care enough about volunteers to learn about their strengths.

Reprinted from *Working with Volunteers* (Chicago: Adult Education Association, 1959), 10-12.

A great deal of individualization will not be needed for some volunteers, since many people thrive on at least some regimentation. To an insecure volunteer, form, organization, and structure may very well provide the best of all possible environments. It is for the creative, the highly motivated volunteer that some elasticity of control is desirable. People who are very successful in their own right can view over-regimentation as a kind of living death. For these people, freedom from scheduling and supervision can be accomplished by guiding them to select activities which are largely self-directional or which require skills that the person might already have developed. These tasks might include such creative work as designing bulletin boards, performing professional storytelling, or developing the art work for a reading program. Rather than supervising every step, the coordinator could meet with the volunteers to discuss the goal of the program, show them similar projects from the past, and ask for a proposal for the present one. Volunteers could work on their own, as long as the results are ready on schedule. At that time the coordinator would approve the plans, making any necessary suggestions, and the volunteers would proceed, again on their own. Many clerical jobs can be done in the same manner. Since former teachers and secretaries swell the ranks of volunteerism, tapping their skills is a very immediate way of benefiting the library. Filling out order forms, checking in new shipments, and typing lessons or handouts are all things which can be done with some initial instruction and a deadline if the volunteer has typing or clerical skills. Former teachers often enjoy designing new lesson sheets or displays. Again, these activities can be done with initial instruction, some samples, and a completion date.

If volunteers are encouraged to volunteer for more than one year in the same job, the number of people who are able to function more or less on their own will increase. Each library has peculiarities of its own, and the volunteer will be trained in the system used and be able to continue in it with minimal instruction.

Once the elasticity of these programs has been established, coordinators will find it easier to establish a system based on their personalities and on the natures of the institutions. For example, a small parochial school will probably have a different type of program from that of a large public school; the atmosphere will be different. Coordinators should strive to establish a program in which they will feel comfortable. Otherwise they will find themselves trying to direct something which "goes against the grain." No one involved will feel really comfortable under such circumstances.

The decision about style can be modified as experience dictates, but it is necessary to begin with a well-considered stance. Both volunteer and coordinator will be able to work with fewer misunderstandings if this is done.

In all cases, coordinators of volunteers must want to work with voluntary help. They must feel that the intrinsic value of a volunteer far outweighs any potential problems. Too many people who work with unpaid workers see them not as people with something of value to offer, but rather as little better than automatons whose functions in the library include only menial tasks. This attitude will be obvious to the volunteer and must be avoided at all costs when selecting a coordinator. Even volunteers who continue to come to work under such circumstances will do so in spite of, not because of, this disparagement. That *joie de vivre*, which is the finest expression of the aesthetic reasons for volunteering, will be lost. Word of mouth will work against a program permeated with this attitude, since the volunteer will lack enthusiasm and loyalty. In selecting a coordinator, the most important factor, after all, is attitude.

5 *Attracting Volunteers*

Locating and getting a commitment from volunteers is a crucial part of any volunteer effort. This task should be approached first by identifying both the people who are to direct the publicity program and the type of program to be established.

In order to achieve a workable volunteer program, coordinators must be aware of and develop expertise in two major publicity areas: motivation and promotion. They must develop skills in assessing people and their reasons for volunteering. Coordinators will find it beneficial to consider the many forms of philanthropy practiced in almost every community and to devise ways to let them benefit their libraries. In order to make publicity work for them, they must search continually for different or better means of promotion, of reaching the ear of the volunteer. Volunteer coordinators will become authorities in the use of the media which best support their particular situations, whether it be the simple but often effective methods which include word of mouth, working with children, club liaisons, and personal contact, or the more complex procedures which involve the use of newspapers, television, radio, and speaking engagements. They must constantly be collecting, evaluating, and implementing information which will help improve their programs. In short, the success of coordinators in acquiring dedicated workers lies in understanding the "market" and in being alert for every opportunity to make their libraries' needs known.

Coordinators must have courage. They should be willing to put a good, well-organized program into action with enthusiasm, rather than test the waters with trepidation. Coordinators must be very aware of other programs which might influence theirs or compete with theirs. They can learn from many sources, but only if they develop the skill of correlating seemingly dissimilar items. Coordinators will want to plan their strategy so that they do a thorough job of what they undertake.

REASONS PEOPLE VOLUNTEER

First, it must be emphasized that while any publicity program should state the needs of the library, it should also make the benefits to the volunteer very clear. There are literally hundreds of organizations available which use volunteer help and many of the best volunteers work with more than one. Anything at all which can be used to encourage a potential volunteer to choose the library should be done. In order to facilitate this, it would be useful to study the flow of benefits in volunteering.

Altruism, role modeling for children, and gaining skills are among the most prevalent reasons for volunteering. In each of these instances, the most important result is the feeling of the volunteers toward themselves and their work. This cannot be emphasized strongly enough. No matter what other benefits exist (letters of recommendation, experience), the feelings of accomplishment and of being needed are the strongest possible motivators. A good coordinator can develop these feelings through a series of positive experiences. An awareness of this should pervade all publicity efforts.

Altruism is the common reason for volunteering. Most people do volunteer, at least in part, in order to help others and to make the world better for themselves or their children. Of course, volunteers will usually consider the position in the light of the questions "What will I lose? Will volunteering hurt me or my family?" Furthermore, the alert volunteer may foresee some possibilities, such as gaining job skills and possibly even being hired by the library in the future. These factors are present whether or not volunteers are perceptive enough to think of them. (While volunteers might enjoy the idea of being future employees, a good coordinator will be sure that they do not sign up with any sort of expectancy.) The fact that people are perceptive enough to be able to identify some possible future benefits does not negate the fact that their reason for volunteering is essentially altruistic.

Many of the people now in the prime volunteer age range (30-40) were involved in high-intensity efforts to form a better world in the 1960s. Although they may have become more conservative in their methods, these people sometimes still care deeply about their society and accept personal responsibility for effecting change and progress. These concerned, caring individuals will probably volunteer their time somewhere. It is the coordinator's job to place his needs before them convincingly enough to encourage a decision in favor of the library.

Another group who volunteer for altruistic reasons are those who were reared in an environment which fostered philanthropy and public service. Members of this group are likely to volunteer in several organizations, so the library would do well to make an effort to reach them. In some ways this will be easier than with other groups since those people will already be associated with service groups through which the library can work. Those people are, themselves, a way of reaching out to others in the community who feel as they do about public responsibility. Through them one can hope to reach not only a new group of people, but a group which is often in a position to help the library in a material way.

A similar example of the way altruism affects volunteerism is in social circles which expect (and sometimes demand) a degree of volunteerism in their members. One well-established method of moving from one social stratum to another is through active participation in local conservation groups, fine arts support groups, and in clubs such as the Junior League. The latter is an especially fine organization which makes rather strict demands on its new members as far as time and quality of work are concerned. Each prospective member is required to spend a certain amount of time fostering the goals of the community. Socially, the new member gains a great deal, but she earns every bit of it. Therefore, it is worth every effort the coordinator can make to attract these people, who are generally dependable, have a good idea of what is involved in volunteer work, and frequently go one step further than required when they see a need.

Other common reasons for volunteering are to provide a role model and to help one's child directly. Parents are highly aware of the emotional needs of their children, and many feel that visibility in the schools is an excellent way to let the child know that the parent cares. People who volunteer for this reason usually want to work with activities directly related to children, for example, summer reading programs, story hours, and craft classes. This does not mean that the volunteers necessarily want to work with their own children, or, indeed, with any children. It means that they want their children to benefit from their work. Thus volunteers may prefer to type catalog cards, knowing that their children will have access to the finished product. Some parents believe that many of those things which raise society above maintenance level are accomplished by people who give more than is required. They try to instill this attitude in their children.

Many libraries have been started by people who realized that they had to fill a need themselves if their children were to benefit. Established libraries have added excellent programs at the instigation and with the help of parent volunteers. Thus a small, one-position library can have a very active film program to supplement classes in history, science, and literature. A film program like this involves hours of time and could not normally be handled by the librarian. Volunteers make it possible. They can pick up films and return them to the loan agencies; they can mail films which were received through the post office; they can handle projection equipment and teach others, including the teachers, how to care for it; they can make out film orders and call them in; indeed, interested volunteers can handle the program, although the librarian must maintain control of it and be aware of developments. In this and many other ways volunteers can help their children directly by broadening their experiences. This is a goal to which many parents have dedicated themselves, and for which they will willingly work: wider horizons for their children.

A growing number of people, notably women and teenagers, are joining volunteer forces in an effort to gain skills, experience, self-confidence, and, incidentally, to acquire letters of recommendation in order to make the transition into their respective careers easier. This is an area which could be made very attractive and which could provide a community service at the same time. High school students could be encouraged to volunteer, with emphasis on real-life experiences. As the Army says, "We don't ask for experience; we give it." The library could be used as a testing ground for students who feel they would be interested in secretarial work, library work, science, history, or any of a variety of other fields in which practical experience is hard to find for the young. Both counselors and teachers can guide the young enthusiast to the library. In addition to special knowledge, the student would gain valuable attitudes and knowledge of the working world.

Widows, divorcees, and any other women who must return to the working force could benefit from volunteering by using this activity as a reentry device. The library can make the experience even more valuable by emphasizing the need to evaluate one's life before a time of trauma and to plan for the future. Many people have forewarning of an impending change in their life styles, and thus, with encouragement from publicity, are able to enhance their assets for job hunting before they have to seek work. Publicity for volunteer programs can emphasize experience, planning, recommendations, and exposure to alternate career fields.

Men and women alike can use volunteer work to investigate careers in library science or in clerical work. Some need a job change, some feel the pressure to assume an additional job. In either case, experience as a volunteer can add to the knowledge and skills which the person will take with him on his search for new or additional work.

A thorough understanding of the reasons people volunteer and of the ways they benefit will help the coordinator to formulate a strong publicity program which will, in the course of a year, reach out to most of the people who might be good volunteers.

SYSTEMS OF AUTHORITY

A decision must be made early in the planning about who will be responsible for publicity. In small libraries there would probably be no problem, but in the case of a program which is centrally run for an entire school system, some definition of authority must be established. Will a central coordinator do all publicity? Will both she and the individual librarian work simultaneously? Will the individual librarian have responsibility? (See tables 5.1 and 5.2, pages 44-47.)

As was noted earlier, while systems may work which exclude principals from the line of authority, they are usually not practical, since the head of an individual school will influence a program whether or not he chooses to take an active part in it, and should retain control.

If there is a central volunteer coordinator, it will usually be best if all media publicity is handled through that person. In this way, the central coordinator can see that distribution of publicity for the participating schools is handled fairly. One coordinator will find it easier than many individual librarians to establish a good rapport with representatives of the different media. This one person would save the time of many in researching the field of mass publicity.

While a central coordinator would be best for mass media work, the building-level librarian should be involved to a degree, if not exclusively, in other types of publicity. The local librarian can appeal to the local populace on a level which a central representative would find it difficult to reach. Thus, school librarians find themselves very effective spokespeople at meetings, with the children, and with personal contacts. Central coordinators may choose to include a great deal of this type of publicity in their work, but they should not

(Text continues on page 48.)

Table 5.1

Systems Suitable for Use of a Central Coordinator

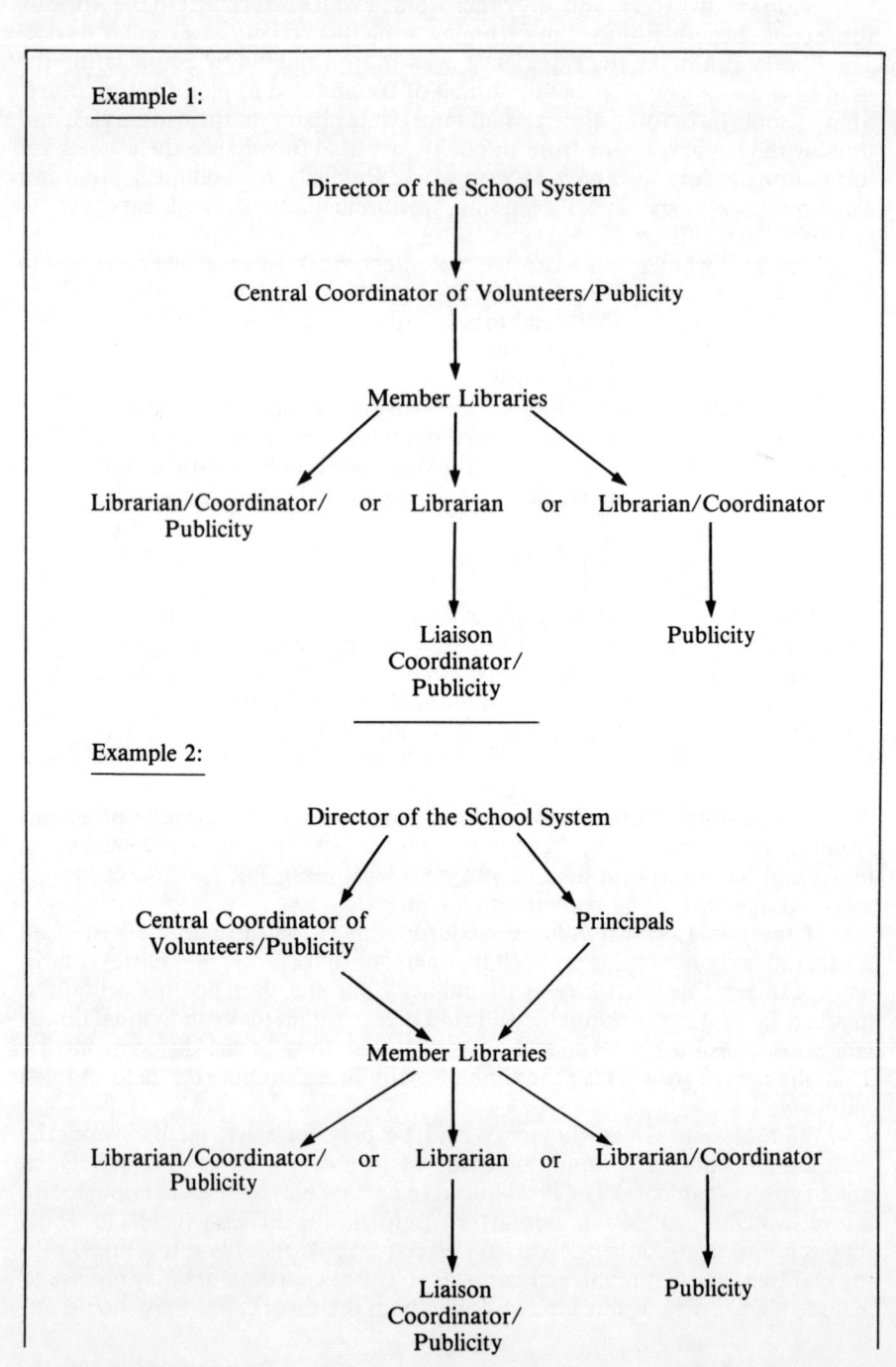

Example 1:

```
                    Director of the School System
                                 │
                                 ▼
              Central Coordinator of Volunteers/Publicity
                                 │
                                 ▼
                          Member Libraries
                     ↙           ↓           ↘
   Librarian/Coordinator/   or  Librarian  or  Librarian/Coordinator
        Publicity                  │                    │
                                   ▼                    ▼
                               Liaison              Publicity
                            Coordinator/
                             Publicity
```

Example 2:

```
                    Director of the School System
                      ↙                       ↘
   Central Coordinator of                    Principals
   Volunteers/Publicity
                      ↘                       ↙
                          Member Libraries
                     ↙           ↓           ↘
   Librarian/Coordinator/   or  Librarian  or  Librarian/Coordinator
        Publicity                  │                    │
                                   ▼                    ▼
                               Liaison              Publicity
                            Coordinator/
                             Publicity
```

Table 5.1 – *Continued*

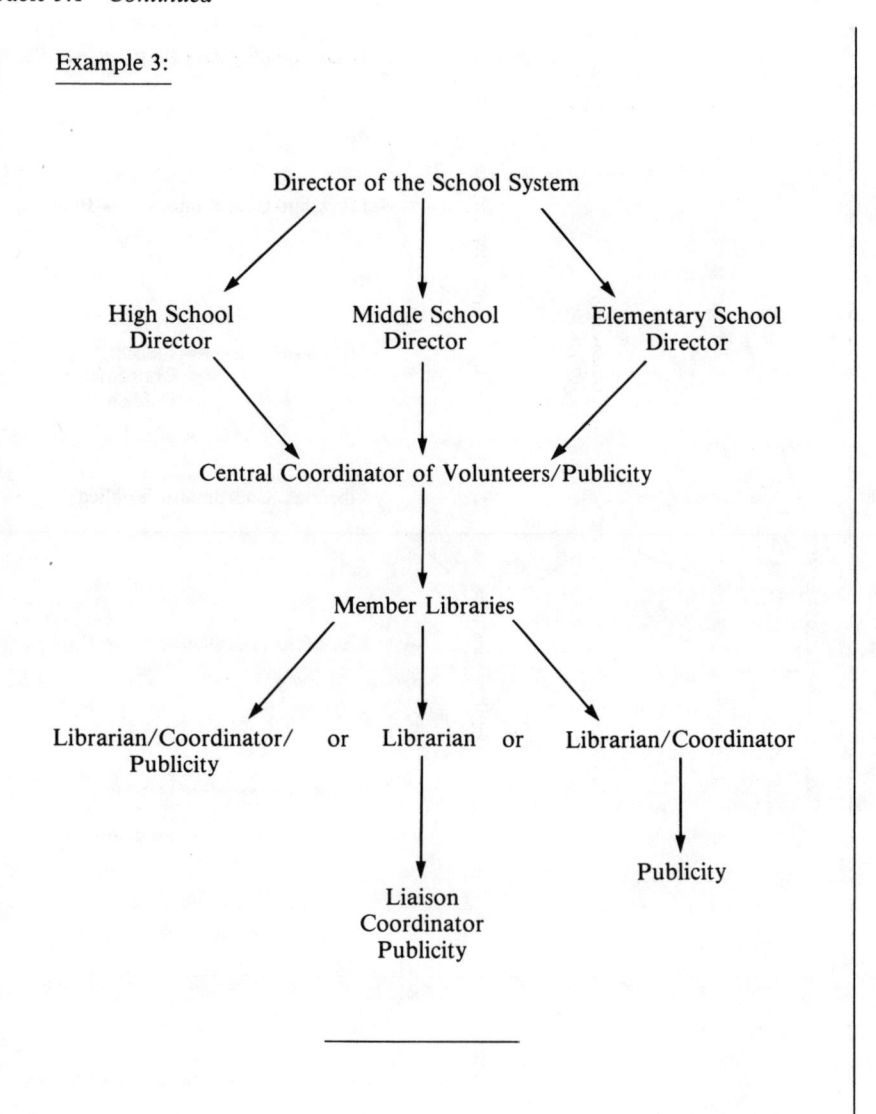

Example 3:

```
                    Director of the School System
                    ↙           ↓           ↘
        High School        Middle School      Elementary School
         Director            Director             Director
                 ↘              ↓              ↙
              Central Coordinator of Volunteers/Publicity
                                ↓
                         Member Libraries
                    ↙           ↓           ↘
  Librarian/Coordinator/   or  Librarian   or   Librarian/Coordinator
       Publicity                  ↓                      ↓
                               Liaison               Publicity
                              Coordinator
                               Publicity
```

(Table 5.1 continues on page 46.)

46 / 5—Attracting Volunteers

Table 5.1—*Continued*

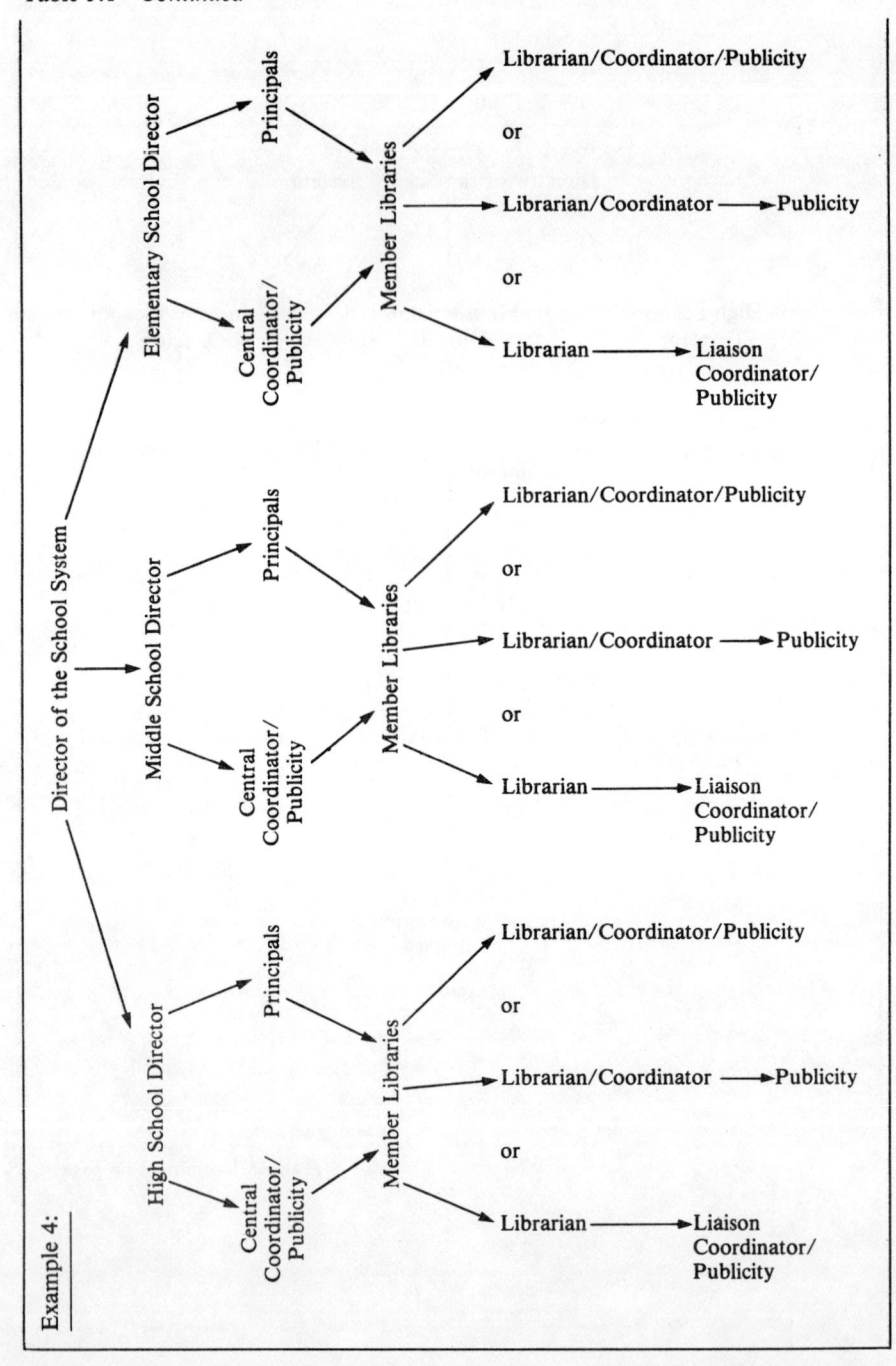

Example 4:

Director of the School System
- Elementary School Director
  - Principals → Member Libraries → Librarian/Coordinator/Publicity
  - or
  - Member Libraries → Librarian/Coordinator → Publicity
  - or
  - Central Coordinator/Publicity → Member Libraries → Librarian → Liaison Coordinator/Publicity
- Middle School Director
  - Principals → Member Libraries → Librarian/Coordinator/Publicity
  - or
  - Member Libraries → Librarian/Coordinator → Publicity
  - or
  - Central Coordinator/Publicity → Member Libraries → Librarian → Liaison Coordinator/Publicity
- High School Director
  - Principals → Member Libraries → Librarian/Coordinator/Publicity
  - or
  - Member Libraries → Librarian/Coordinator → Publicity
  - or
  - Central Coordinator/Publicity → Member Libraries → Librarian → Liaison Coordinator/Publicity

Table 5.2

Systems Suitable for Schools Using Only Individual Coordinators

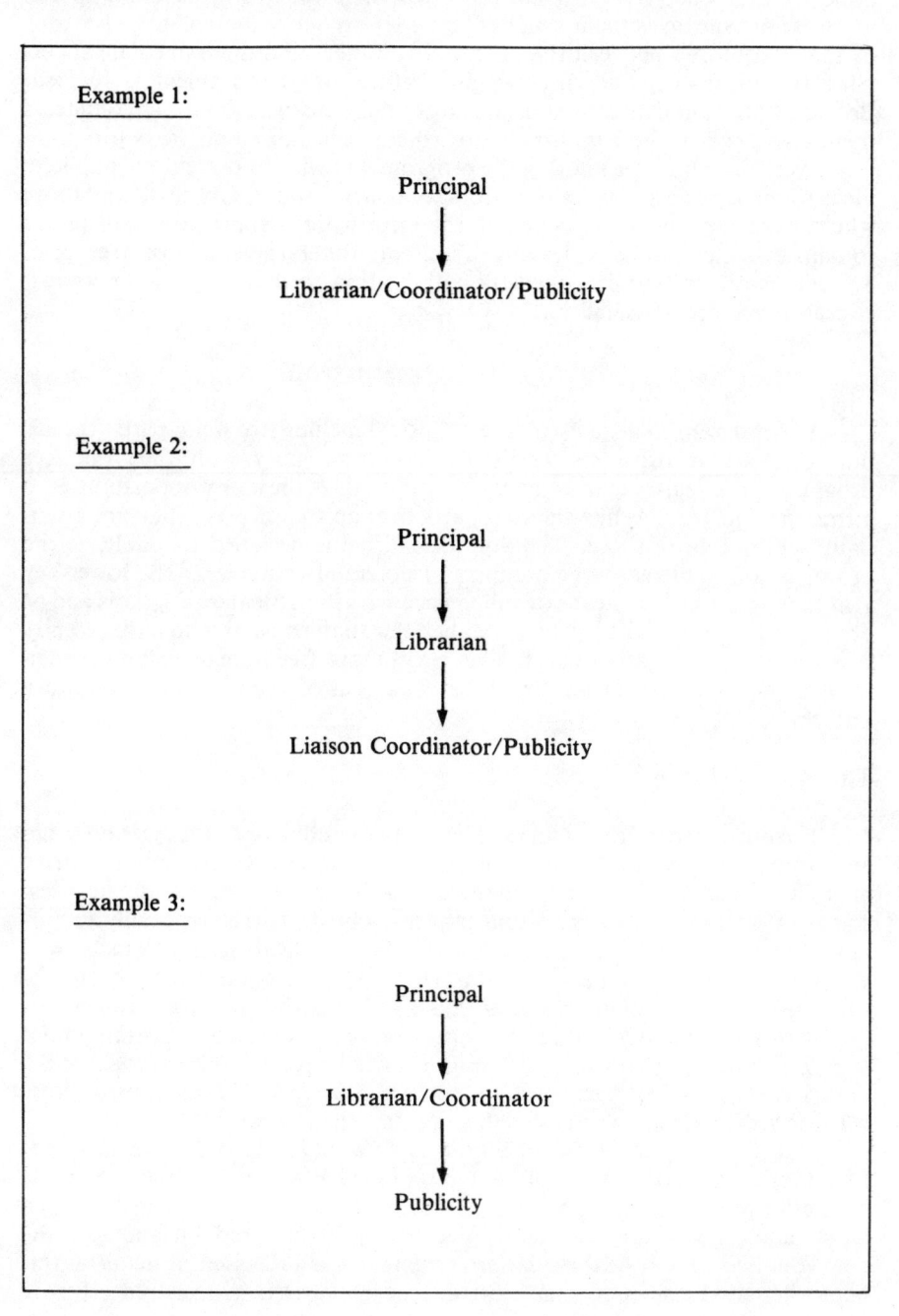

Example 1:

Principal
↓
Librarian/Coordinator/Publicity

Example 2:

Principal
↓
Librarian
↓
Liaison Coordinator/Publicity

Example 3:

Principal
↓
Librarian/Coordinator
↓
Publicity

maintain control of it to the exclusion of a more grass roots representative. To restate this principle briefly, publicity aimed at acquiring volunteers should be done by everyone, reserving certain areas only when they demand special expertise or time investment which is better left to one than to many. The value of the relationship between the potential volunteer and the immediate supervisor is inestimable, and often begins before any commitment is formed. Because of this, individual librarians must retain the right to attract volunteers themselves, even if there is also a more general, centralized publicity program.

Everyone who is promoting the program will wish to present his publicity ideas to the appropriate administrators, of course, and to give them and those who answer the telephones copies of the information. Some principals prefer to approve any publicity leaving a school; others give almost free rein. Secretaries or receptionists need the information so that they can be knowledgeable when parents call in.

TYPES OF CAMPAIGNS

Any program to attract volunteers should include two main parts: the all-out, once-a-year drive to familiarize the community with the volunteer program and a year-round, constant effort to utilize the many opportunities to attract new helpers. While the two parts overlap to a degree, they are essentially separate in purpose. The volunteer drive is designed to publicize the program and to attract large numbers of potential volunteers. The lower-key year long program is a means of filling vacancies in particular programs and of obtaining the help of those who are either new to the area or who have recently had a change of situation which gives them more free time to volunteer than they might have had during the drive. The goal of each is to better library services.

The Annual Drive

The once-a-year drive is an excellent way to publicize a volunteer program and to generate enthusiasm even in those who do not participate. The drive must be planned in meticulous detail, and must include plans for the next few stages of involvement after volunteer commitment. This is especially important, since people who volunteer want to know that their time will be well spent, and resent the appearance of a haphazard operation which, to an outsider, seems to lack cohesion and promises to utilize the volunteer's time poorly. There are too many well-run volunteer organizations in most communities to risk a comparison in which the volunteer will be forced to conclude that the library is poorly supervised—a complaint which is especially irritating to those who view the average library as a bastion of organization.

Thus the components of the all-out drive would include decisions on lines of authority, lines of responsibility, types of media to be used, as well as needs of the library or libraries, volunteer screening methods, a system by which large numbers of volunteers can be placed quickly, and initial training for the new volunteer. Each of these latter components is discussed in detail in this book; it must be stressed that a drive is in jeopardy if it takes place before thorough planning of each phase has been accomplished.

Advertising Skills

Expert knowledge of the potential volunteer must be combined with in-depth knowledge of the publicity field if the drive is to go smoothly. It is astonishing how much publicity can go out about a topic and how few people really hear it. Our society is over-communicated. Americans, who comprise 6 percent of the world's population, consume 57 percent of the world's advertising.[1] Message after message distracts the citizen; advertisements, newspapers, magazines, television, radio—all contribute to a kind of mental numbness which must be overcome if the information is to get through.

Coordinators can best challenge over-communication by avoiding very general messages. Instead, they should simplify, build their campaign on variations of a single message. The message will only get through to a certain number of people, but those people really will have heard. In order to be understood, the message must be designed from the volunteer's viewpoint. Teaching through advertising is a wonderful idea, but it will only work if the recipient is taken into consideration when the message is formulated.

Only by reaching each person at the optimum time with the perfectly phrased message can the organization hope to succeed in communicating its ideas. "In the communication jungle out there, the only hope to score big is to be selective, to concentrate on narrow targets, to practice segmentation."[2]

This idea is certainly applicable to the library. A prominent modern advertising concept explained by Ries and Trout touches on two major points which directly affect libraries: over-communication and the fact that libraries are Johnny-come-latelies in the mass volunteer market. Rather than ignoring the fact, libraries should let it work for them. Libraries can fill a *creneau* a 'hole' in the public's awareness of volunteers. Thus, rather than compete with other agencies, libraries can create a special place in the patron's mind, one which was not available before, where library volunteerism is now accepted. This is termed "positioning."

According to Ries and Trout, the way to position a program in a person's mind is to be first in some category. Libraries cannot be first in people's minds as a place for volunteers; that position was taken years ago by large public-service agencies such as the Red Cross. They can, however, be first with the idea that the library volunteer can acquire both practical experience and knowledge in many fields. The library, as a repository of information on literally every topic in the world, is truly in a unique position.

The general approach to volunteerism is to present only the need of the institution: "We need you." Today everyone seems to need the volunteer. What can the library do for him? The library can position itself in the mind of the volunteer as an organization that the volunteer needs and, incidentally, as an organization which can also use the volunteer's services in many ways, for the betterment of the community. In this way the library can be first in the volunteer's mind as a place in his community where he personally will benefit while he helps others, just as VISTA has been for those with a more adventuresome personality.

The coordinator will want to have a long-term (at least a year) advertising plan based on one positioning idea. It takes time to reach many people, time for them to accept an idea, and time for them to act on it. A brilliant idea is useless if it reaches only a few people.

The campaign should show pride but not arrogance. Certainly any organization which needs (as opposed to "will accept") volunteers is in no position to be arrogant. On the other hand, the organization must make it clear that the use of volunteers is not for survival; it is to make a good organization better.

The campaign needs a sharp, descriptive, memorable slogan and a logo which will immediately swing the viewer's thoughts to the library. The slogan should present the campaign and tell the potential volunteer what the program's major benefit is. The coordinator should try to avoid words with negative connotations, slogans that disguise the nature of the program, and slogans that are too similar to those of other programs. In addition, it pays to make sure that the initials of the slogan do not form an unfortunate combination. The coordinator should also examine prospective slogans for aural qualities. Some words or combinations of words do not sound pleasant to the ear.

A logo should be designed, preferably by a professional. It should be simple and should relate directly to the program. The choice of words and design can influence a person for or against the program.

The logo and slogan will be used on promotional material, bulletin boards, and as a way of describing the program to the volunteers. For instance, Rossmoor Public School uses the acronym VITAL, which stands for their slogan Volunteers in Teaching and Learning. A storytelling group might meet with their PEERs—Partners for Entertaining and Educational Reading. The idea is to help volunteers identify with the program and for the public to identify the program with the library.

Using Media

The use of newspaper advertising depends upon how inclusive a volunteer program is desired. A small private school, for example, might not want to use general publicity as much as a citywide school system.

For the large school system, newspaper exposure will be beneficial not only in recruiting volunteers but also in publicizing the extent and direction of library involvement. This will help alleviate the old bugaboo of no public image which libraries have dealt with for centuries.

The smaller library could advertise in a newspaper whose circulation is limited to people who might have a real interest in the school, or who would if they knew more about it. This would include neighborhood papers and those publications which serve the larger areas or districts of a city. Figure 5.1 shows a sample ad.

The scope of readership of the newspaper and the type of advertisement used will determine to a large extent the quality and quantity of volunteers who will result from running the announcement.

Radio and television have a special effect on volunteers just because they are different. Broadcast advertising should certainly be considered if the organization is a citywide one or one which covers a major portion of the city, such as a large public school system.

Remember, however, that flyers, newsletters, and posters also constitute media.

El Paso Public Library

BE WISE, BE A LIBRARY VOLUNTEER

Become one of our volunteers and have a real job experience this summer. You will be assured of an interesting orientation about the library, on-the-job training, a good work experience, and the possibility of a reference when you have finished your summer with us.

WHAT KIND OF JOBS CAN YOU DO FOR US? The following are just a few of the job possibilities available at the El Paso Public Library:

CIRCULATION ASSISTANT

People are needed to check in and check out books at the circulation desk.

CHECKOUT STAND AIDE

We need someone at this desk at all times to check to see that people have not forgotten to check out their books when they leave the library. Having you there will relieve a regular employee, who will be able to do some other job behind the scenes.

SHELVING ASSISTANT

Hundreds of books need to be put back on the shelves every day as they are returned. You can help us so that customers will find the book they want on the shelf.

TYPISTS

To type overdue notices, booklists, stencils, index cards. You have to know how to type, but speed is not required.

PICTURE AND PAMPHLET COLLECTION ASSISTANT

To select and mount pictures for our picture collections that are used by students, teachers, artists, and many other patrons. To help us weed out old pamphlets and replace them with new ones.

YOU MAY VOLUNTEER FOR AS LITTLE AS TWO HOURS A DAY, ONE DAY A WEEK. A training program will be held from 2 to 4 P.M. on Monday, June 7th. If you are interested, please call Mrs. Goodman at 543-6021 or 543-3804.

RECEPTIONISTS FOR ART GALLERY EXHIBITS ARE NEEDED.

Fig. 5.1. Sample ad. Reprinted from *Library Journal* May 1, 1972. Published by R. R. Bowker Co. (a Xerox company). Copyright © 1972 by Xerox Corporation.

By the time the campaign is put into effect, most of the work will have been accomplished—that of organizing and decision-making. What follows should run smoothly and show real benefit for the library with as little interruption of the regular schedule as possible. This intensive campaign should use all appropriate media at one time so that the community will become very aware that the library has a volunteer program and that there are so many facets that nearly anyone can participate; indeed, nearly everyone is *needed*.

Daily Promotion

As was mentioned above, the annual campaign should not carry the whole burden. The excellent results of ongoing promotion are exemplified by the many fine volunteers who come in individually during the course of a year. These are volunteers who would, in all likelihood, have volunteered elsewhere had they not been reminded of an existing library program. Coordinators' regular efforts at publicity for their activities will ensure more top-quality volunteers, since people must be reached at varying times, due to circumstances which are constantly changing. Daily promotion will ensure that the library can present its needs to people at the optimum time for enlisting their services.

Daily promotion is not difficult and will attract volunteers with specific skills to offer. Frequently the massive yearly campaign becomes just one more thing for citizens to relegate to the edges of their minds. They are accustomed to being bombarded with information. In this situation a low-key, carefully worded statement of immediate need in a specific area will sometimes get through to the patron's consciousness. This is the way to really emphasize specific departments, activities, and projects. People might volunteer only for a specific project because of this type of promotion, but, if they are happy in the work, they will generally stay on to work on other tasks. They then become dedicated library volunteers.

Using Themes

One plan which can be used on a regular basis is to emphasize themes such as the holidays ("Give a gift of time," "Send a valentine to Garner Middle School"). Seasonal themes work well, too ("Children in school? Let us help you keep in touch," "Don't let the dormant season affect you; let us help you blossom"). Items in the news can be used to encourage participation in such areas as bulletin boards and vertical files ("Give our children a lasting record of the royal family," "The making of a President—for now and for the future"). These approaches will appeal to special segments of society, such as Anglophiles or politically active people, who might otherwise be impervious to the pleas of the library. These efforts will educate parents to library services as well as attract volunteers.

Publicity of this nature is useful for another reason: many people have collections on very specialized topics. Awareness of a similar collection in a library might lead to donations or to a collaboration between the collector and the librarian. The average person loves to share his enthusiasms. Some people have spent years of study on a particular topic and have become experts of a sort. Recognition of this fact is one of the surest ways to draw the person into the volunteer community, to the benefit of both parties.

There are many methods of communicating a need to potential volunteers. Almost every library can use word of mouth—publicizing through children, club liaisons, and personal contact to advantage. Most school libraries will want to add speaking engagements, career development programs, interaction with senior citizens, involvement of young people in a multitude of ways, and collaboration with special interest groups. There are also flyers, newsletters, and posters. In addition to these methods, which are either cost-free or relatively inexpensive, larger systems will want to add newspapers, magazines, television, or radio to their list of media, as well as stuffers to be included in utility and store bills. While publicity can be limited initially and branch out, it does need to follow a plan which was devised early in the program. If this is done, a variety of people will be reached; otherwise a great deal of effort might be put into a project which will provide little return.

Coordinators, in planning their publicity campaigns, should consider every possible medium. Some will not be applicable for a given library, and will not be used. Valuable time should be spent on those efforts which will bring in the most volunteers. There will be some areas of questionable return, areas which might produce volunteers, but in which there is some element of uncertainty. Coordinators should, over a period of time, try these, though they should not burden themselves with too many at once, since their time and energy must be used profitably. After each of these methods is used, results must be examined carefully and ways noted in which beneficial changes could be made. A rigid evaluation should follow. All too often coordinators might be attracted to particular methods which, in fact, do not produce enough to justify the involvement of the professional.

Informal Approaches

Word of Mouth

At the top of the list of ways to attract volunteers is the favorable opinion of others. People who participate in any program are in a position to see many things, and these things form the basis for their opinions. Even a problem in the library can be used to advantage if the volunteer understands the reasons behind the dilemma. People enjoy discussing things with which they are involved. A good coordinator must be aware that each positive experience will reinforce the volunteers' good feelings about themselves and their work, and will reflect nicely on the library and on the volunteer program so that it will appeal to more and more people. The coordinator must also be aware that unhappy volunteers will, in all likelihood, unburden themselves to someone. It is wise to consult volunteers who are less than content so that the coordinator can help solve their problems or help them become aware that those problems stem from some factor outside of the library, such as home or children. Often a problem is assigned to the wrong source; a conference will help identify the root of the problem and lessen the chances that the volunteer will speak unfavorably of the library.

If coordinators have a well-planned system of rewards, they will give the volunteer frequent reason to speak favorably of the library. Volunteers can tell their friends of compliments paid them by a variety of personnel, of responsibility entrusted to them, of ideas of theirs which have been used, and of special awards or notice given to them. Everyone likes to be associated with a successful program; volunteers who feel personally successful will reflect that success back to the program and talk about it.

Coordinators can take their volunteers into their confidence about major plans for the program. Coordinators can see that the volunteer is aware that bigger and better things are in store if the program has enough manpower. They can tell the volunteer that they would appreciate anything the volunteer can do to foster the program and encourage more participation. In this way, volunteers will have something invested in the program and will know that they are a vital element of its success. Thus, when volunteers talk with their acquaintances, not only is the message communicated, but it is also supported by people known to the recipients of the message. In a way, the library is being sponsored by the speaker. The people who advocate the program put their own very personal feelings into the discussion. Their enthusiasm and dedication are transmitted easily. They can answer many questions and form a link between the potential volunteer and the coordinator. Such support lends a feeling of authority to the project and makes it stand out above all of the other organizations which are seeking help.

Word of mouth can also be encouraged by being sure that people who work with other volunteer agencies know what the library is doing. A good way of spreading the word is to talk with someone in each organization, asking his opinions on various aspects of volunteer programs. These people have years of experience and are usually pleased to share their knowledge. Effort of this type does two things: it informs a volunteer organization of the library program, since the contacts will usually mention the call to their peers, and it establishes the program as one which is well-organized, as exemplified by the fact that the coordinator is seeking the help of knowledgeable people.

Publicizing through Children

Children can be an effective method of communication, since many parents respond well to the interest of their offspring. In seeking volunteers, coordinators must be very careful that they in no way make children feel inferior if parents cannot or choose not to help. Rather, coordinators should be very complimentary about the parents who do work, and very honest about the need for more participation. Once a program is begun, there should be ample opportunity to let the parents excel publicly. Something as simple as a name in the corner of a bulletin board can be highly effective. Any time children see their parents' names displayed, they are impressed, and enthusiasm is transmitted to their friends, who, in turn, would like to see their parents' names displayed. This method works beautifully when the parents actually work in the library, where they themselves are visible. Direct participation is very compelling. Children love to see their parents drive on field trips, read stories, help with classes, and other things. There is no more effective advertising agency than a child.

Another excellent way of attracting volunteers through children is to establish some activity which is managed by volunteers, or at least allows the volunteers to help in a very visible way. This activity should be one in which the children participate directly, such as a reading club, an acting troupe, or an art club (which would also help with the ever-present need for bulletin boards). Enthusiastic children will not be able to contain their excitement. They will describe their activities to their parents, intermingling the description with lavish compliments for the volunteer who makes it all possible. This kind of activity has another bonus: when the play is ready or the picture painted, the parent of almost every participating child will come into the library for the performance or unveiling, and will be exposed to the excited volunteers as well as the children. For the coordinator who can delegate responsibility, this method requires very little time and will show good results.

Simply put, schools have a ready pool of volunteers waiting to be tapped: parents are interested, eager, dependable, and have their children's futures to consider. Word of mouth, talking with the children, sending home flyers and newsletters are all ways that the coordinator can reach out to the parent. See figure 5.2, page 56 for the sort of handout which attracts parental response.

Liaisons with Clubs

Clubs are a rich source of support for libraries. The alert volunteer coordinator can establish a rapport with different community organizations which will yield excellent public relations and very often many dedicated workers. The coordinator can make initial contact through a personal acquaintance who is a member of the club or by calling the president and arranging a meeting. If this is not feasible, the first discussion may take place over the telephone, although it is usually better for the two to actually meet. The meeting will be more impressive and thus result in a more positive attitude if it takes place in the library. The coordinator can then show the representative specific needs and the work of other volunteers.

The coordinator should work toward having the club "sponsor" a certain area. When this is done, the club will, with supervision from the coordinator, accept responsibility for a particular activity, such as maintenance of the grounds, bulletin boards, bibliographies, inside decor, or story hours. Club personnel would organize members, acquire supplies, and do anything else necessary for the accomplishment of this community service. In this way the club would perform the function of a unit volunteer. Tasks given to such groups should be those which require little training and supervision.

The second type of liaison the library can establish with a club is to develop it as a source of members who will commit themselves to regular library aide status. The club might be willing to commit one member to volunteer in the library, or it might actively encourage participation by as many members as are interested. In either case, the volunteer then falls into the same category as all others, and could be trained to do tasks which take real knowledge or preparation, such as storytelling in the grand manner.

A few large clubs have, in the past, accepted recruitment of volunteers for libraries as a special project. This is usually done in order to start a library program or something else equally spectacular. Most of these clubs will limit their involvement to a one- or two-year period, but this is long enough to establish a program. Among those who may be approached are the Junior League, the Jaycees, and the National Council of Jewish Women.

> **Rossmoor Public School**
>
> VITAL
>
> Dear Parents,
>
> A busy school year is underway at our new Rossmoor School and there are many opportunities for you to be actively involved in the educational program. Volunteers in Teaching and Learning really are VITAL.
>
> What?? You think you're not qualified? Come and learn how easy it is with many resources available!
>
> If you can help, please put a check by your interests and return this form to your child's teacher by Thursday, September 25.
>
> NAME: _____ PHONE: _____
>
> DAYS AVAILABLE: _____
>
> CHILD'S NAME: _____ HOMEROOM: ____
>
> Math Lab
>
> We're planning to continue our fine math lab for all students in grades 1-3. Volunteers work with small groups, usually five or six children, using games, flash cards and written practice activities. Lab will need about thirty-five volunteers, seven per day. The math is easy, and answer keys are cheerfully provided. Come and join us in providing learning with fun.
>
> _____ 9:00-9:40
>
> Library Desk
>
> _____ Assist with book-checking, shelving, etc. This important job keeps the library running smoothly.
>
> Fourth and Fifth Grade Physical Education
>
> _____ Do you like the out-of-doors? Assist with groups at P.E., 8:40-9:55

Fig. 5.2. Sample handout. Used by permission.

The coordinator has an asset nearby in many schools: the PTA volunteer chairman. This person has the task of attracting and assigning volunteers on a school- and projectwide basis. Some groups even have a chairman just for library volunteers. It would be well worth the time to encourage participation if such a group is available. Coordinators will, of course, in defining their role, establish the fact that they are liaisons between the library and any groups which are interested in helping.

Even when the PTA does not have a group of library volunteers available, the publicist would do well to have the PTA accept some phase of the library as its project. In this way the PTA would be responsible for gathering volunteers. Fund-raisers are perfect for this type of involvement. Other parents' groups, such as band parents and tutoring committees, can be encouraged to become involved as a way of publicizing their own work. The library, with its bulletin boards and its books and other resources, would be the perfect springboard for publicity which is good for the library and for the supporting organization.

A library in a parochial school has special resources at its finger tips: groups within the church which sponsor certain aspects of church life. It should not be difficult to interest one of the groups in the library and in forming a special group for support. Many church/school libraries are stagnant, more from lack of leadership than anything else. Once the membership discovers that someone is taking an active interest, participation will follow.

Personal Contacts

Over a period of time librarians talk with many people who, in the course of their lives, have little to do with the library. Every time the librarians mention the volunteer program they will spread knowledge and good will and might gain volunteers. While some groups of people are more likely to volunteer in school libraries than others, a large number of people volunteer there instead of somewhere else simply because they heard a volunteer program was available. The coordinator and the rest of the library staff need to become aware that everyone is a potential candidate. The worst that can happen after broaching the subject is that the contact will not volunteer; the best, an excellent new supporter for the library.

Librarians themselves would do well to volunteer more in areas about which they care. Besides giving themselves all the benefits they are offering to library volunteers, they would also widen their range of acquaintances (potential library volunteers). It would also help support the contention that our public services would be better if each person gave a little of his own time to some cause. Indeed, one of the most rewarding things librarians can do is to volunteer in their own field, but in an area with which they do not usually work. In this way, a school librarian can enjoy the challenge which goes with city library reference desk work, bibliographic work in special libraries, and so forth. Not only is the work exciting, but also the knowledge will carry over into the school position. Factual information and increased enthusiasm can improve everything from bulletin boards to story hours. All of the growth and broadening of fields of expertise that can go with dedicated volunteering can benefit the librarian. One of the most immediate benefits will be that potential volunteers in the school will sense a real dedication to the volunteer system and will view the librarians' efforts to gain extra help for the schools in a new light; their statements about the joys and benefits of volunteering will be absolutely credible.

Another immediate benefit is that fellow staff members, especially teachers, will see that same dedication and might be willing to donate an off period to the library. When this is done, the value is inestimable. Many teachers spend little time in the library during their college years, and many others rarely find time to use it after graduation. Even those who frequent the public library may remain relatively innocent of knowledge of their own school library. Any effort toward increased communication and experience will bear fruit with the students; the assignments given by teachers will relate more directly to materials available in the library, and the range of topics to be explored will be vastly increased. The teacher will have a new appreciation of the problems caused by overdue books and tardiness of classes. This personal contact with teachers can also result in many more volunteers. Parents often know only one person in the entire school: the child's teacher. As he communicates with the parent, the teacher can relay the message: the school library wants and needs volunteers, and, if the teacher works as a volunteer, he can add some personal comments about how satisfying the work can be. The parent will come away from the discussion with more knowledge of the program and with a very positive attitude toward the teacher, who gives some of his rare free time to the school and, by extension, to the children.

Collaboration with Special Interest Groups

College departments and ethnic clubs are excellent sources of people to volunteer for translating, bulletin boards, travelogues, and information on materials dealing with other languages and countries. While many professionals charge for their services as translator, some can be prevailed upon to donate their time for the sake of the community. Their participation might be as simple as allowing their names to be included in a resource file. Foreign-born spouses are a good source, also.

Phone calls to people in the department or organization, flyers at club locations, and requests for referrals will work well with this group of people. Again, once they become involved with the library, they might want that involvement to grow.

Involvement of Young People

College students and young adults of all kinds form a group of highly involved, deeply caring citizens. Many of them are eager to explore new areas and to give; in order to attract them as volunteers, it is usually necessary in speaking engagements to be more specific than "We need volunteers." Rather, emphasis should be on a special group which will benefit (minority groups, children, the disabled) or upon the cause (increasing a specific collection, a new project). These volunteers require more training than some other groups because they lack experience in working for others, but they have hidden assets: enthusiasm, caring, almost inexhaustible energy.

College students can be reached through speaking engagements with campus organizations, through campus newspapers and flyers, and through teachers who know and approve of the volunteer program. It is especially beneficial to let professors of related disciplines know of new projects. For example, if the library is concentrating on its local state collection, the publicist might notify historians specializing in that area, geologists, anthropologists, meteorologists, sociologists, linguists, and any others who could enlarge or better the collection. They might interest their students in working with this phase of the school library or in giving book talks, seminars, and so forth. The professors themselves may become interested enough to join in. Thus, in addition to attracting aides, the library can acquire very knowledgeable speakers on a variety of subjects.

In the same vein, it would be highly advantageous to become associated with a school of library science in order to provide a facility for students doing their practicum. Since many schools of library science do not offer a great deal of opportunity to learn skills in working with volunteers, it would be highly beneficial to prospective librarians to place themselves in situations which give them experience in this area. Publicity coordinators may very well wish to offer their services to the local library school as speakers in order to acquaint students with the program. It would be a good idea to discuss first with the head of the library school the suitability of the school as a practicum resource, so that students can be told of its availability. In this way, many libraries will be affected in the future either by the use of volunteers or at least by an increased understanding of the volunteer system on the part of the librarian. (See table 5.3, page 60 for suggestions on how practicum students might be used.)

High school career development programs offer an opportunity to introduce young people to an area which will greatly affect their lives. Today's student faces a future which almost certainly includes a job, and, in many cases, college. As a speaker, the librarian can offer the library as a place in which students can develop their secretarial, clerical, and research skills. Arrangements may be made with the work-study coordinator to allow students who are willing to work without pay to volunteer part-time in the library. An arrangement of this type would be most interesting to young people who are considering library science as a career area.

There are several benefits which can be used as recruiting points for the young person:

- Librarianship might be very appealing to students; volunteering would give them an opportunity to research the field and to evaluate their interest.

- Students working in a school library would be able to expose themselves to a wide range of knowledge which would support their future work in their chosen fields.

- Practice in research and in the skills needed for research would make school courses much easier and could make some jobs much easier to acquire, since many young people are hired first in support positions, for example young lawyers are commonly asked to do background research on new cases.

Table 5.3

Work Chart for Practicum Student

Date/Time	Duties	Critique

January 6	Regular duties:
	
	1. Call speakers for next week; send note if they don't answer.
	   —Ann Smith, wildlife conservation, 657-9430
	   —Tom Watts, science equipment, 876-0746
	
	2. Put reminder of date and time in teacher's box.
	
	3. Call in film orders. (See film list.)
	
	4. Read story to 2nd grade class.
	
	5. Help teach 2nd grade library skills.
	
	Additional duties:
	
	1. Make bibliography on dinosaurs.
	
	2. Call AV service (435-8776) to pick up 2 tape recorders and 1 16mm projector. Ask if 8mm projector and 2 record players are ready.
		Very organized and thorough
		
		Needs exposure to visual aids in storytelling, especially ones which involve the children.
		
		A natural teacher—discipline is very low-key and effective, which allows for greater emphasis on learning.

In general, high school students are desirable volunteers. While they lack the knowledge and skills of older, more educated volunteers, they do have enthusiasm and time of their own, especially during summers. Often students may be reached through high school teachers and counselors. The coordinator should approach them with the idea of volunteering as a means of gaining skills and experiences, as well as career guidance. Many new recruits for the library field may be garnered in this way. Teachers can mention that the school library needs volunteers in the students' subject areas. A science teacher, for example, can stress the knowledge and familiarity to be gained by working closely with scientific materials and ideas. The business and commerce teacher could suggest that volunteering at the library would result in added experience in typing, filing, and receptionist skills as well as receiving a good letter of recommendation. The important thing to remember is that students also are over-communicated. The teacher or counselor must be really supportive of the idea of volunteering. This belief and the resulting enthusiasm will carry the message, not the words.

Interaction with Senior Citizens

There is no richer source of expertise than our older citizens. People live longer and retire earlier now, which gives them time to explore interests of their own. Coordinators can establish liaisons with retirement communities of various types. They can encourage their staffs and other volunteers to talk with older acquaintances. Elderly people are very dependable and they know what they like to do, which will save a great deal of time for the coordinator. Many like to work with children or with their hands. Some have collections built up over the years which they would enjoy sharing. Some will want to work in the library, others would rather prepare things at their own homes, or arrangements can be made to take projects to a senior citizen center (see fig. 5.3, page 62).

Any program which combines the elderly with children is highly appealing—as was mentioned in chapter 1—and almost cries for a strong publicity program. Even if the senior citizen program is very limited in scope, it is worth having for this reason. The media can be invited to in-house activities involving older volunteers as well as to work days at a home for senior citizens. These work days are especially good ways of attracting volunteers, since the coordinator is on their territory, which would give them a sense of security. In addition, any enthusiasm engendered in even one person would be contagious; close friends could decide that volunteering is something they would enjoy doing together.

Senior Citizen Group Meetings

Volunteer in charge: Anita Gross		Date: January 10
Job assignment:	# Participating	Completed
Alphabetize catalog cards.	10	✓
File catalog cards.		✓
Cut out letters for bulletin board.		Most

Volunteer in charge: Karen Michaels		Date:
Job assignment:		
Cover books.		
Alphabetize cards.	11	
Find volunteers to talk to children about aging.		

Volunteer in charge: Bette Kraus		Date:
Job assignment:		
Make valentine display.		
Plan for Easter party—a few children to go to the home.		

Volunteer in charge:		Date:
Job assignment:		
Mend books.		
Tape memories of the past for history class.		

Fig. 5.3. Sample sheet for reporting senior citizen participation.

Speaking Engagements

In addition to these basic, rather simply accomplished informal methods of attracting volunteers, there are other, more involved ones which can be very productive. An excellent means of informing the public is through speaking engagements which focus on special topic. This can be done with the sorts of groups just discussed: various clubs, senior citizen groups, groups of young people, parent groups, and special interest groups. In each case, the major effort should be toward increasing awareness and establishing communication. To do this, the groups should be consulted about topics which are needed. The form in figure 5.4, page 64 can be useful in surveying groups' interests. The form in figure 5.5, pages 65-66 shows how speaking engagements can be kept track of.

Many librarians already spend some time each month both outside of the library and within doing book talks and educational talks, introducing films, and making presentations. Any occasion is a perfect opportunity to present the volunteer program very briefly. An especially good way is to mention that such talks are made possible by the fact that pressure on the job is alleviated through volunteerism. References may be made to work done by volunteers in the area which is the subject for the talk.

For instance, if a film on gardens and a talk on gardening books are being presented, it would be pertinent to mention a few of the following:

- A volunteer could do a monthly display on flowers or vegetables for that month.

- If the library maintains a mentor file, this might be mentioned along with a request for volunteers who would organize a group of people willing to help students learn more about local gardening.

- Volunteers could acquire information to do a bulletin board on local items of interest in the gardening world (perhaps someone in the community grows a rare plant or has participated in some botanical development); they might even be encouraged to do much of the work themselves.

- Volunteers could be asked to coordinate a seminar on one or more aspects of gardening.

- Local experts could be encouraged to volunteer their time to review materials and suggest especially good ones for purchase. This would be very helpful with films, since most libraries have a limited budget for these expensive items.

- The speaker could suggest that there is a real need for someone with a little time who would enjoy making a bibliography of gardening materials to be found in the library.

- Volunteers could be sought who would act as liaison with local nurseries or garden clubs for use of plants or display items, which these sources are frequently willing to lend.

(Text continues on page 67.)

SPEAKER REQUEST

By _____
Organization _____
Address _____

Topic (check one):

    Art collection _____

    Asian collection _____

    American literature _____

    Business works _____

Group size _____

- -

_____ will be available to speak to your
    (Speaker's Name)

_____ at _____ on _____
    group   time   date

Topic: _____

Length of presentation: _____

_____

Equipment needed: _____

_____

Comments: _____

_____
Name

_____
Address

_____
Telephone

Fig. 5.4. Interest survey and response.

Library Publicity Program

Checklist for Speaking Engagements | Results

SEPTEMBER

Initial PTA meeting 9/2 7:30
Auditorium.
Emphasis: Need volunteers; look what library has for your child.
Contact: Jane Jackson, 483-5967

14 vols., many parents visited library

OCTOBER

Fall Garden Club meeting 10/25 10:00
Annex.
Emphasis: Interesting children in dried arrangements; need for examples of floral art in the library and in books.
Contact: Mrs. Romero, 334-2295

Plans for 1 display/mo. Donation of 5 bks.

NOVEMBER

Handicraft club 11/16 11:00
Methodist Church, Basement.
Emphasis: Need volunteers for demonstrations in library; need displays and books.
Contact: Ida Blenning, 654-8935

Speakers on 5 subjects 2 bulletin boards 4 books

DECEMBER

St. Theresa's Guild 12/3 9:30
St. Anne's Church, Recreation Room.
Emphasis: Teaching children the value of caring through books; need for more books on religion.
Contact: Sister Gregory, 736-5846

JANUARY

Career Day 1/6 10:30
Washington High, Auditorium.
Emphasis: Libraries as a career; benefits of volunteering.
Contact: Jason Rewes, 998-0707

(Figure 5.5 continues.)

66 / 5 — Attracting Volunteers

Figure 5.5 — *Continued*

Checklist for Speaking Engagements	Results
FEBRUARY 　Senior Citizen group　2/5　4:30 　Home Ec. Department. 　Emphasis: Need for volunteers at school or for a workday at the retirement home. 　Contact: Josephine Andrews, 989-5756 **MARCH** 　Aviation Club　3/13　10:30 　Airport Meeting Room. 　Emphasis: Intense interest of boys in aircraft; need for speakers and books on the subject. 　Contact: Adam Renfro, 344-4564 **APRIL** 　Boy Scouts　4/17　3:30 　Gym. 　Emphasis: How the library can support Boy Scout projects, especially in the summertime, need for books, can accept from clubs. 　Contact: Joshua Miller, 345-1937 **MAY** 　Girl Scouts　5/27　3:30 　Auditorium. 　Emphasis: How the library can support Girl Scout projects, especially in the summertime, need for books, can accept from clubs. 　Contact: Natalie Jones, 232-3859	

Fig. 5.5.

Types of Campaigns / 67

- Someone could collect and prepare vertical file material on gardening.
- A volunteer could really help by keeping the gardening collection of vertical file material, books, and periodicals in order.

While it would not be advisable to mention during the speech all the many ways that volunteers could help, mentioning a few could produce several good results:

- Showing the range of volunteer effort possible will prove to the audience that their enthusiasm in their hobby is shared by the library, and thus create good will.
- It will show that the library is constantly trying to upgrade programs which touch them personally without raising their taxes.
- It will acknowledge many of the club members as experts in their field.
- It will be evident that the library is aware that the club is civic-minded.
- It will offer each member an opportunity to grow in his area of interest.
- It will make the club members aware of services offered to their children in their area of interest.
- It will help get volunteers into the library so that they have a better chance to become interested in other areas also.

Getting these volunteers into the library will produce the following benefits:

- It will give members an opportunity to publicly display their successes and share their interests.
- The library will have valuable aid in an area which can become very technical.
- Bibliographies (that all-important area which is too often relegated to the side) will be maintained by people with an avid interest in them.
- It will increase the library collection of vertical file material (also an area which is frequently pushed aside or organized so poorly that it is difficult to use).
- The volunteers will reach out and touch many other people in the community, so the word about the library and its volunteer program will spread.
- Loans or donations of plants would help in library decor, which is expensive to change and so tends to become boring. A garden club might even decide to accept the responsibility for the upkeep of part of the grounds.

Mentioning a few needs will encourage people to ask about other needs after the meeting. At that point a real discussion of potential interaction can ensue. Any gathering that has a focal point of one or a few topics of interest can be a springboard for this type of recruiting. Speaking engagements at clubs are an excellent and very productive method of interesting volunteers.

The library field would benefit in the long run by more understanding from other professionals who typically use library resources. Volunteers who are deeply interested in their work will develop a good attitude. As a result that work will be of higher quality. This poses a positive contrast to the occasional clerical employee who is working because he must but who finds very little joy in his tasks. Indeed, once volunteers intermingle with salaried clerical help, morale and enthusiasm should be increased. Depending upon the situation, the use of volunteers could give the clerical staff an opportunity for leadership for which many are well qualified.

Using the Media

The daily promotion campaign can also take advantage of the news media.

Newspapers and Magazines

In addition to advertisements, newspapers sometimes run free public service announcements. Any group that is sponsoring a special program can submit such an announcement. Remember that is should be brief and to the point.

Another way to use newspapers to market the volunteer program is by creating newsworthy events and inviting the media. Done correctly, almost any activity is worth at least a small paragraph. A few would make a good feature story on the volunteer system itself. When sending in stories, remember to include names of as many volunteers as possible. This sells newspapers, so the editor will be more eager to see the story in print. The article should be typed and accurate. The use of photographs and captions will often help ensure that the story is printed.

The same story can be released to several papers at once, especially those appealing to different groups. (See fig. 5.6 for a useful checklist.) If the school draws children from a military base, it should be relatively easy to be included in the base paper. Church bulletins and newsletters for organizations are other good outlets. These are especially fine because a large percentage of the readership will already be conscious of volunteerism.

Stories in small town papers are especially influential. While school libraries in very small towns will have fewer resources from which to draw, they will be able to derive at least one asset from the limited size of the population: in small towns there are few places to gain experience outside of the home. Many businesses are family-owned and depend upon younger members of the family for extra help. Any person looking for experience will find it difficult to acquire a position under these circumstances. The importance of the library as a skills resource thus increases as the size of the town decreases, just as its importance as a cultural center does. Since volunteer efforts in most small towns tend to be church- or club-oriented, any publicity

Types of Campaigns / 69

Checklist for Newspaper Publicity

	TOPIC OF ANNOUNCEMENT		
	Reading Club	Story Hours	
San Antonio Light David Real Box 161 San Antonio, TX 78291 (512) 226-4271 Deadline 3-7 days before event.	√		
San Antonio Express Cecil Cliff Box 2171 San Antonio, TX 78297 (512) 225-7411 Deadline 3-7 days before event.	√		
San Antonio News Richard Smith Box 2171 San Antonio, TX 78297 (512) 225-7411 Deadline 3-7 days before event.		√	

Fig. 5.6.

in the town paper will be more noticeable due to lack of competition. The idea of improving the limited resources of the town can be utilized, as can the other benefits discussed previously.

Local magazines do not do as much public service work as some other media, but they should be considered because of the impact they have on their readers. The high quality of many of these magazines will be transmitted by association to the volunteer program.

A volunteer could be assigned to write each release, check it with the coordinator, then distribute copies to a preselected group of media. All of this should be done under fairly close supervision, and should result in positive publicity with little use of the librarian's time.

Radio and Television

In the case of smaller libraries it would be possible to use television to cover special events. Many local stations have talk shows which deal with community concerns. It is possible to appear on these and is especially desirable if a volunteer can be included.

Cable television is an excellent showcase for public service announcements. Those interested in certain disciplines regularly tune in to those public access channels which support their interests. There are educational channels, on which might be placed information about volunteer programs in schools and school districts. Minority-oriented access channels can help direct information to citizens who rarely use the library. This would be especially useful for both public and parochial school libraries. Religious access channels can also fill volunteer ranks in parochial school libraries. This communication can be very rewarding to a library, since many parishioners have very specialized knowledge of religion, which is a difficult field, and any extra information can help. (The coordinator must be very careful that excessive religious zeal does not impair the volunteer's usefulness.) There is usually a military access channel which would be excellent for schools serving areas adjacent to bases; there are university and fine arts channels through which libraries could advertise their need for volunteers in special areas.

Network television stations must use a certain number of public service announcements each month. Coordinators may decide to make use of this fact if they have systems which will affect a large portion of the citizenry. See figure 5.7, for help in coordinating this. Public relations firms can help prepare the spot announcements, but a less expensive method would be to ask the station for help. Most stations have someone on staff who renders just this kind of service.

Radio spots also are available at no cost. The station should be consulted well ahead of time for format, length, and other considerations which would affect the announcement. See figure 5.8, page 72 for help in coordination here.

Again, the effectiveness of these audiovisual methods lies in their very sensorial qualities. The manner in which the announcement is made is often as important as the message.

Types of Campaigns / 71

Checklist for Television Publicity			
	TOPIC OF ANNOUNCEMENT		
	Reading Club	Story Hours	
Mail Information to:			
KENS-TV Channel 5 Blanquita Cullum Avenue E & 4th San Antonio, TX 78299 Deadline 6-8 weeks before event.	√	√	

KLRN-TV   Channel 9
Mrs. Olson or Jo Ann Myer
Institute of Texan Cultures
   Building
San Antonio, TX 78291
   Deadline 2 weeks before event.
	√	√	

KMOL-TV Channel 4 Community Service Department Box 2641 San Antonio, TX 78299 Deadline 2-3 weeks before event.	√	√	
KWEX-TV Channel 41 Martha Tijerina 411 Durango San Antonio, TX 78204 Deadline 2 days before event.	√	√	

Fig. 5.7.

72 / 5—*Attracting Volunteers*

Checklist for Radio Publicity

	TOPIC OF ANNOUNCEMENT		
	Reading Club	Story Hours	
Mail Information to:			
KAPE RADIO STATION NEWS DEPARTMENT Box 20107 San Antonio, TX 78220 2 weeks before the event.	√	√	
KBUC RADIO STATION PUBLIC SERVICE ANNOUNCE-MENT Mark Adams 3642 E. Houston San Antonio, TX 78209 2 weeks before the event.	√		
KCCW RADIO STATION & KZZY PUBLIC SERVICE ANNOUNCE-MENT Jerry Franklin GPM Building, South Tower Plaza Level Suite 125 San Antonio, TX 78216 10 days before event.		√	

Fig. 5.8.

FINANCING VOLUNTEER RECRUITMENT

Financing of volunteer recruitment is usually done in a rather fragmented way. In-house facilities will be available to the coordinator for certain promotions, while methods which require a separate budget may have to be funded by donations or money-making activities. Thus mimeographing, copying, stationery, and postage might be supplied by the school, while flyers and paid advertising might not be. It must be remembered that the school or school system as a whole might, and probably does, have a policy toward money-making projects. Heads of schools might want to direct any money-making efforts, or at least approve them. In a few cases they may prefer that the library act alone. If this is the case, every effort should be made to be sure that the good of the library does not cause problems in another area of the school. Cooperation and organization thus become twice as important in the area of financing. Jealousy between departments arises frequently on its own; every effort must be made not to encourage it more than necessary.

Once needs become known, people from the community will probably offer to supply materials and services. To supply any deficit, the coordinator can sponsor any number of fund-raisers, from selling books to approaching service groups such as the Junior League for a limited financial commitment. Service groups have special projects each year, and libraries fall into a category often high on the list of priority projects—that of education. If the library system is citywide, so much the better. Service groups like to feel that their help is reaching as many people as possible, and the idea that a little money can bring in volunteers, each of whom can help many people, is really appealing, as is the idea of working for the future through our children. In truth, volunteer coordinators often find that they have little trouble funding recruitment, since so much of it is done by word of mouth.

School libraries can, of course, interest the parents' council in funding efforts to attract and use volunteers. The success of this venture will depend upon how active the council is and what it sees as its goals. Since this group will have the interest of the entire school at heart, it might be unrealistic to expect it to focus on the library more than once every few years. If this is the case, it might be better to inaugurate a money-making project sponsored by the library itself, in addition to accepting periodic help. In this way the full impetus of the project will be for the library.

Individual appeals for money or equipment will usually prove fruitful. Again, the knowledge that the donation is to be used in an effort to encourage many people to volunteer is immensely appealing. It must be remembered, however, that people who are financially capable of making large or regular donations are usually overwhelmed with "opportunities" to contribute part of their income to various causes. It is up to coordinators or their representatives to present a case for libraries that will make them stand out from the other deserving applicants. Any hint of insistence must be avoided, since this would irritate even the most agreeable person.

In conclusion, it must be noted that many highly educated people have only the vaguest idea of what goes on in a library. The coordinator should look upon publicity as an opportunity to share the many different facets of his library with others as well as a vehicle by which to gain volunteers.

NOTES

[1] Al Ries and Jack Trout, *Positioning: The Battle for Your Mind* (New York: McGraw-Hill, 1981), 11.

[2] Ibid., 6.

6 Screening and Placing the Volunteer

Once the roles of the coordinators have been established, and the initial publicity organized and executed, the program will be in motion. Central coordinators will need to clarify their preinterview strategy so that they can move into their interviews as smoothly as possible. Building-level coordinators will assume most of the responsibilities of the central coordinator if they are acting alone; if they are working as liaison coordinators they must be ready to act as soon as the first new recruits come their way. It is most important that both coordinators be able to go immediately into this phase of the volunteer program as soon as the first volunteer appears. In this chapter it will be assumed that the system employs a central coordinator as well as liaison coordinators at the building level.

THE CENTRAL COORDINATOR AND THE INTERVIEW

The central coordinator can determine to a large extent how new volunteers feel when they begin their jobs. The coordinator can create an atmosphere in which volunteers feel secure, in which they feel appreciated. To assure the success of the initial interview, central coordinators will need to plan their preinterview strategy, which will include assessing the needs of the member libraries, developing a system for immediate contact of new recruits, and organizing a flexible interview agenda. They will then carry out the interviews, at the end of which promising volunteers will be assigned to appropriate schools.

Preinterview Strategy

Central coordinators will probably explore the needs of the various libraries in one of two ways, or with a combination of both. They can send out forms to be completed by the liaison coordinators, (fig. 6.1, page 76) or they can interview each either in person or by telephone. It is much better to interview individual librarians and/or liaison coordinators in person and in

Assessment of Needs

School:

Coordinator:

Telephone Number:

Address:

Assessment of Needs (Listing specifications such as days the jobs are available, number of hours required, special skill requirements or equipment to be used, frequency of need, etc.):

Number of Volunteers Desired:

Comments:

Note: The central coordinator may prefer to make separate forms for some jobs, such as typing or bulletin boards. In doing so, more detail could be used. There will still be a need for the more general sheet, however.

Fig. 6.1. Sample form.

their libraries, if possible, since this will allow the central coordinators to solidify their impressions of the settings and personalities to which they might assign new volunteers. During this interview the central coordinator will offer as many suggestions as possible, and gather as many ideas as possible, so that they can be passed on to others. The on-site interview would not be necessary to repeat every year, although a repeat interview should help immensely when a new librarian or liaison coordinator is hired.

As a result of this survey, central coordinators should come away with written records of the needs of a given library, the number of volunteers needed, and any comments by or about the individual coordinator which would make placement easier. They should be very sure that they know which liaison coordinators are enthusiastic about the program and which are reluctant participants, so that immediate positive results for the latter can be the major goals. They must be sure that they are aware of what is involved in the different tasks so that they can discuss them with the volunteers. Priorities for the assignment of volunteers will be established based on need and potential result. The records gleaned from the interviews with librarians and coordinators should be transferred to a chart so that the central coordinator can see at a glance who is needed where (see fig. 6.2, page 78). Volunteers may become uneasy if there is an excess shuffling of paperwork. They might even feel that it reflects negatively on the organizational abilities of the central coordinator or on the professionalism of the program as a whole.

The central coordinator should set up a system by which recruits can be contacted as soon as they volunteer. This can involve an immediate phone call, thanking the volunteer and setting up an interview time, or a brief thank-you note asking the volunteer to call to arrange a convenient time for the interview (see fig. 6.3, page 79). Calling is preferable, since central coordinators or their representatives will have to talk with the newcomer anyway. This avoids the extra step of the note. The coordinator should not, however, call more than once or twice. If the volunteer is not reached immediately by phone, the note should be sent. The volunteer would be asked to return the call and given times during which the central coordinator is sure to be available. Otherwise the volunteer could get into the frustrating situation of trying to contact a seemingly ephemeral being. If coordinators have secretarial help available, they should leave instructions about interview times. Using volunteers to arrange the appointments is a good idea, since this would immediately expose new recruits to their peers (and their enthusiasm) and it would assure the central coordinator of not having to deal with someone who wants all the facts over the phone. This last must be avoided, since the reason for the interview is not only to give the volunteer facts, but also to allow the interviewer to form an idea about the capabilities and personality of the interviewee. The use of the phone should be limited to making arrangements for a personal interview, since volunteers may well decide that they know what they need to know and would prefer to go straight to the building-level liaison coordinator, sidestepping the important screening process.

(Text continues on page 80.)

Total Assessment of Volunteer Needs

Skill required	No. Desired	School
Typing	2	Garner
	1	Eisenhower
	3	MacArthur
	2	Cleveland
Artwork	2	Garner
	4	Roosevelt
	3	Nimitz
General Clerical	1	Roosevelt
	4	Highland
	4	McNamara
Storytelling	10	Pfeiffer
	12	MacArthur

Fig. 6.2. Sample chart.

Dear Mrs. Johnson,

    Thank you for your interest in our volunteer program. We feel that our efforts make a real difference in the quality of our libraries, which of course influences positively our children's education.

    I was not able to reach you by phone to set up an appointment for an interview. Would you please call me at your convenience? I am eager to meet you as soon as possible in order to find just the right spot for you.

    Again, thank you for your interest. See you soon!

                                     Yours truly,

                                     Margie Wilson
                                     Central Coordinator
                                         (or)
                                     Coordinator
                                     Library Volunteer
                                     Program

Office hours: 8:00 - 11:30
                12:30 - 1:30

Fig. 6.3. Sample letter of acknowledgment.

Before the need arises, central coordinators should prepare agendas for their interviews. This preinterview strategy should include a well-thought-out approach to screening the applicants: on the volunteers' file sheets (fig. 6.4) coordinators should list points they want to cover. The skillful coordinator will probably not want to actually read these out to the volunteer since this would be a very dry way to do a potentially fascinating job. Instead the central coordinator will want to appear spontaneous to encourage the volunteer to ask questions, even though many of those questions must be answered later by the liaison coordinator. As they meet new people and encourage enthusiasm, while helping the library system, coordinators can relax and let themselves respond to the pleasure of the interaction. Agendas should merely be guides for central coordinators who should be sure to include all salient points in every interview but who should be flexible enough to be able to include other points if the situation calls for it.

One of the major benefits of a volunteer system is locating people who have excellent skills in an area not normally used in the library, but which could be used to enhance one or more programs. If coordinators follow their agendas closely and leave no room for exploration, these "gems" will go undiscovered. After these preparatory steps have been taken, central coordinators will be ready for their first interviews.

The Interview

As was mentioned previously, once the central coordinator has attracted volunteers, she will need to interview them as quickly as possible. Doing this will help keep interest high and will help alleviate the lack of assurance which some volunteers may feel initially. The coordinator will find it to her advantage to be friendly and businesslike, conducting the interview quickly. The volunteer must come through the interview with a feeling that her time and skills are valued, that she will gain as much from the work as the library, and that her support will be appreciated. If the volunteer insists on a certain school or type of work, a real effort must be made to place her according to her wishes.

The purpose of the interview is to screen those who are interested so that undesirable volunteers are avoided and those not suitable for library work are sent to other, more suitable areas, to determine the recruit's skills and interests, and to inform the recruit of the facts involved in volunteering at the school. To do this as quickly as possible, central coordinators must not only have an agenda but must have all pertinent information about the volunteer at their fingertips (see application form, fig. 6.5, page 82) and some knowledge of areas other than the library within the school system which need volunteers.

At the end of the interview the coordinator will note on the file sheet general feelings about the volunteer. By that point the coordinator will have made a decision about whether or not the volunteer would be an asset to the library or whether there is some factor which would interfere with the volunteer's performance so much that he would be a detriment.

A copy of the file sheet can be sent to the liaison coordinator who will be responsible for the accepted volunteer. These comments should be very professional, since the records may be legally available to the volunteers.

(Text continues on page 83.)

Volunteer File Sheet

Name: _____ Telephone # _____

Contacted by: Phone (indicate attempts) _____ Note _____

Interview Date and Time: _____

                                                Yes   Emergency only

Skills: 1. Typing
         2. Art
         3. _____
         4. _____

Areas of Interest:
    1. Work with children
    2. Clerical
    3. Social
    4. Driving
    5. Work at home
    6. _____
    7. _____
    8. _____

Comments: _____
_____
_____
_____
_____

Time Limitations: _____

Health records: X-ray   _____
                   T.B.   _____

Insurance policy   _____

Reimbursement policy   _____

Confidentiality   _____

Need babysitter   _____

Recommendations:
    School: _____
    Job Assignment: _____
    Other: _____

Fig. 6.4.

Application for Volunteer Work
Margaret "Peggy" Ross Memorial Library
Hamden Hall Country Day School

Name: _____
          Last   First

Address: _____
            Street

_____
        Town   State   Zip Code

Telephone: _____

Number of Children at Hamden Hall _____

Name(s) and Grade(s) _____

_____

_____

Have you been previously employed? _____

In what capacity? (Explain in detail your responsibilities):

_____

_____

_____

Have you ever worked in a library? _____

In what capacity? _____

_____

Education: (please check)   High School _____

                                     College _____

                                     Graduate_____

Major Subjects _____

Special Training_____

Special Skills, Hobbies, _____

Do you type? _____

Fig. 6.5. Reprinted by permission of Laurence Kingsbury, Head Librarian, Hamden Hall Country Day School.

Determining Interests and Skills

Before plunging into a full discussion of where the volunteer's interests lie, the interviewer will wish to offer babysitting services if they are available. This one service can make more hours of volunteer time possible than any other factor. Either the school can pay for a babysitter or volunteers can stay with children, making it possible for parents to work in the library. If the latter is the chosen method, the interviewer might place some of those volunteers who wish to work with children in this job. Individual situations will determine whether the babysitting service is offered a couple of days a week and all those needing the service asked to work those days, or whether the volunteers are placed first and sitters acquired later.

One of the most effective questions for saving time during the interview is to ask whether or not the volunteer wishes to work with children. An overwhelming majority have a firm opinion, and would not be happy unless that feeling were honored. There are a multitude of jobs for the person who wishes to work directly with children: storytelling, helping as an aide in library skills classes, helping on projects such as making puppets or paper airplanes, helping children locate books or other materials, handling routine questions, going on field trips, running audiovisual equipment, teaching children how to use various equipment in the library, tutoring—the list is as extensive as the coordinator's imagination, and can be a real boon to the professional. On the other hand, the volunteer who wishes to work, but not directly with children, can type, file, mimeograph, telephone, do bulletin boards, prepare displays, do bibliographies, order films, take care of equipment, run errands, work in the teacher's library, or many other things.

Another real time saver is asking whether volunteers can type, and whether they would prefer typing jobs or whether they would type only in an emergency. Many people will have learned to type years prior to any volunteer experience and will not have practiced enough to feel comfortable. Some, on the other hand, would welcome the opportunity to sharpen rusty skills. At the school library which has no paid clerical help, a volunteer who is willing to type will usually be eagerly welcomed. A dependable typist can produce a great many things: catalog cards, book orders, bibliographies, lessons for the library skills classes, notices to be sent to parents, publicity releases, and many others. The typists who volunteer should be carefully assigned so that all individual coordinators who desire this kind of help can receive it. The volunteer typist is one of the greatest resources that a library can have, since he will not only help the existing program and make possible new ones, but he also will be able to directly affect the budget. Costly catalog cards can now be prepared within the library with a minimum of time spent by the librarian, if there is a good, systematic approach to using volunteers to do basic cataloging. The librarian will, of course, maintain strict quality control.

Along the same lines, the central coordinator should ascertain whether or not the volunteer would prefer clerical work. Some people love to file, fill out orders, process books, and so forth. These are time-consuming jobs for the librarian and can be very frustrating for the volunteer who does not really enjoy them. Since these tasks are usually close to the top of the list of things to assign to volunteers, it is wise to identify those people who would enjoy such responsibilities.

Central coordinators should probe gently until they discover whether volunteers want to be challenged mentally or whether they consider volunteer work a respite from their hectic schedules. The person who is seeking volunteer work as a break from tension is a real find. This kind of person can view some of the traditionally boring tasks in a library as very relaxing, such as reading shelves, shelving books, reviewing vertical file material, and locating vertical file material in magazines and newspapers. When placing volunteers with this type of work in mind, the central coordinator should be aware that, while they will probably do an excellent job for a while, they will eventually wish to do more exciting work. Thus they should be placed in a library which needs at least one of their other skills.

Time available for volunteer work is another fact which must be ascertained. The recruit who can only work in the morning should not be assigned to a library in which the liaison coordinator desires only afternoon help. Forcing a change on the part of the liaison coordinator will build resentment which volunteers will soon feel. At some point they will discover that they are "in the way." Needless to say, this will not do much for their self-esteem. In the same vein, the central coordinator must be certain that if there are minimum time requirements, such as two days a week, in the morning or in the afternoon, all volunteers are aware of that fact and can fit it into their schedules. It would be better to place them with another library than to have them quit because they felt pressured by a commitment larger than they wanted to make.

The central coordinator should determine whether or not the people who would like to work with children would like some autonomy or whether they would only like to assist the librarian. For the volunteer who would prefer independent interaction there are story hours (which could involve all kinds of skills), work projects, tutoring, book talks, and so forth. For the recruit who would prefer to work only with someone else, there is helping the librarian work with library skills classes (this will make the class go much faster and be more interesting for the children), work with someone else on story hours, puppet shows, and other programs, and, especially, helping children to locate material in the library. Placing a volunteer who is highly self-motivated with a liaison coordinator who prefers not to delegate much responsibility can be frustrating to both. On the other hand, the person who desires close supervision can feel lost and unsupported when placed with a very casual supervisor.

Some people are very social beings, and would enjoy representing the library as a speaker to clubs, or would enjoy working with a group of volunteers, such as a group in a senior citizen home. Once this is determined, the volunteer can be placed in a library that has or plans such a program.

Some people are party people; some librarians are not. Finding a compatible combination would be a splendid way of assuring a *Green Eggs and Ham* party, a *The Perfect Pancake* breakfast (or lunch!), a *Best-loved Doll* exhibition, and anything else the imagination can dream up. Unless volunteers prefer to work alone, in some cases donating quite a bit of time, they should be willing to work with others on these projects.

There are people who are very eager to volunteer but have no time during the day. The wise central coordinator should find it relatively easy to place them. If there is a library with an evening tutoring program, or if a library is open in the evenings at all, the volunteer may wish to work then. If not, there is a wide variety of things which can be done at home which will benefit the library. Typing, vertical file, bulletin board preparation, working on projects to go with story hours presented by someone else, telephoning, publicity, money-making events: all can be done at home or after school hours with the proper instruction. Again, people working at home will have to be placed with a liaison coordinator who feels comfortable delegating responsibility.

Some volunteers may declare that they are very energetic and do not want to feel "boxed in." The central coordinator could hardly find a better candidate for the role of "gofer." Picking up and returning films, taking audiovisual equipment to be repaired, buying materials needed for a special project—all could be done by a volunteer who does not enjoy long periods in one setting.

For those who plan to volunteer in the library itself, it is wise to ask that a volunteer come at least a morning or an afternoon once a week. Volunteers who come less often than that rarely feel secure in their jobs. They have a difficult time remembering details. They can rarely complete a project and so lose any feeling of real accomplishment. They remain the "new kid on the block" and have a difficult time developing a circle of friends in the library who share something in common.

The central coordinator should discover interests, talents, and skills which might be of use to the liaison coordinator. These will be noted and passed along for help in job assignment. While the volunteer may very well be assigned to a position far removed from that suggested by the central coordinator, still, the suggestions will establish a starting point which will save much time for the liaison coordinator and for the volunteer. The volunteer should never feel that the second interview is a rerun of the first.

Screening

Almost anyone can benefit the library, especially when many libraries are involved, such as is the case when there is a central coordinator. Even so, some people must be dealt with gingerly from the beginning. Those who insist on working every day, all day are a good example. It is possible for some people to do so, but highly improbable. What is likely to happen is that they will realize very soon that they have over-extended themselves and quit. The coordinator should offer to accept such people for a limited amount of time per week, then offer the option of letting them "drop in" at other times after they become adept at their jobs. This can anger the volunteers, after they have just offered their whole week to the library, but it is far better to anger them before hours and hours of training have been invested. Those likely to want this type of involvement are people who are new to town, people who have suddenly realized that they have few friends, and people who have suddenly decided that they are going to "do" something with their lives. All of these are laudable reasons for volunteering, but all are passing situations. After these people feel more at home in the new city, make more friends (some through their volunteering), or decide that it is time to do more for themselves, the backlash will begin. Rather than call in, they will tend to miss work with no warning. They will not feel that they have a justifiable excuse so they will use no excuse. Then they will feel guilty about missing and about not calling. At this point they will start avoiding the library altogether. They will realize that they have not behaved responsibly, and feel further embarrassed. They will become angry with themselves. In spite of conversations which the liaison coordinator will have with the disillusioned volunteer, this anger will soon transfer over to being angry with the library, as the source of the uncomfortable feelings. This reinforces the desire to stay away, and can result in vociferous complaints. The real danger of this is that these complaints can carry great weight with others, since, to the outside world, the former volunteer is in a position to "know."

Thus, central coordinators should convince such volunteers to limit their obligation. Failing in this, initial interviewers would be wise to class those recruits as undesirable, unless there is an individual liaison coordinator who is prepared to deal with a situation such as that described above.

The next two types of potentially unacceptable volunteers are harder to define, since the problem is one of degree. Central coordinators must interview the people and rely on common sense. A person who is volunteering to avoid some deep emotional stress can really hurt the library, especially its atmosphere of friendliness and consideration. While therapists frequently point out the value of becoming "involved" for these people, that involvement might or might not help the people on the receiving end. Central coordinators should have compassion, and, if they feel that something can be worked out so that the library will not suffer, accept the person. Some people, however, are not ready for involvement in a work situation. Hurt is still too new to them; possibly they have not yet learned to turn it off for short periods of time. Using a most exaggerated example (which, extreme as it seems, did happen), a volunteer who comes to work and spends the whole time in fruitless wandering, frenetic activity with no result, literally catching other volunteers by the arm to force them to listen to the terrible situations which are inflicted on the volunteer at home, and bursting into tears almost every day of work is a most undesirable volunteer. Perhaps in several months' time such a person would be a real asset. Central coordinators must carefully evaluate the situation and make a decision, remembering all the while that they are responsible for setting up situations which are not detrimental to the library.

Another type of volunteer who must be carefully considered is the parent who is using the library as a means of watching the teachers or children. While this would be involved to a degree with any parent in a school, it should not be the only or the principal reason for volunteering. Even one volunteer with a motive like this can change the atmosphere of the whole library. While most volunteers will see whatever happens while they work, the volunteer who is constantly watching and mentally judging each teacher or child can make the library an extremely uncomfortable place. Once this begins, it probably will not remain the province of only one volunteer. Suspicion is contagious. Volunteers who see that someone is concerned about an area will naturally observe that area more closely. That is to be expected. What is to be avoided is an attitude of observation with the intent to find something wrong, to incriminate. No school is perfect. More than that, no school can fulfill the qualifications for perfection set up by many different people, since each person would have different standards. The central coordinator must determine as nearly as possible whether a given volunteer might be a threat to the harmony of the library to a degree which would make any help he might give not worth having.

Once the central coordinator has made a decision about the value of a particular volunteer to the system, there are three choices: she can accept the volunteer into the system, she can eliminate him, or she can discuss her feelings with the coordinator of the library to which she would send the volunteer were he to be accepted. In doing this, she would be acknowledging the fact that some coordinators can handle certain situations better than others. Some would like to try to work with the borderline candidate, while others would avoid any potentially uncomfortable situations at all costs. After talking with the individual liaison coordinator, the central coordinator can place or eliminate the new volunteer. In either case the interest of the library will have been served, as well as that of the volunteer.

In eliminating a volunteer, the central coordinator must be sensitive to the feelings of even the most obviously unsuitable person. She must leave all volunteers with a feeling of self-worth, and the knowledge that the library system appreciates their offers of help. The volunteer must not feel rejected or unworthy. This can be difficult, but it is possible to attain a mutual understanding.

One way of alleviating the situation is to guide the volunteer to other areas of the school which accept volunteers. If there are central coordinators for these other areas, they should be given the names of the new volunteers. If, however, the volunteer would go directly to someone who might not be as experienced in interpreting needs and personality, central coordinators may well wish to discuss their feelings with the new supervisor. It would not be a good idea to acquire a reputation for shifting problems off to unsuspecting coworkers.

The screening process will be further refined as the central coordinator establishes health requirements, time requirements, and requirements of location and attitude. Many schools require X-rays or tuberculosis tests of everyone working with children. If so, the volunteers must agree to have these done before their starting dates. The central coordinator must be aware of the school system policy on coverage for accidents. Some schools are covered for anything occurring within the school itself, but are not covered for accidents while driving or supervising children on field trips. Policy toward reimbursement for supplies, driving expenses, and so forth should be covered. If the individual coordinator with whom the volunteer will be placed requires strict adherence to a schedule, with a minimum number of hours worked per week, this should be discussed with the volunteer. The types of work assignments available should be mentioned and described as accurately as possible, although it should be made very clear that actual assignments will be made by the liaison coordinator. Policy toward privacy of information should be discussed, with emphasis on the fact that volunteers are expected to conform to the same standards as the teachers. Deciding on the location of the school may screen out some eager volunteers. If they wish to work only at a particular school, and that librarian does not wish to use volunteers or has enough, the central coordinator can try to guide the new recruit into another location or put his name on a waiting list. Failing that, the volunteer will probably be lost to the system.

Placing the Volunteer

Central coordinators should be very sure that volunteers do not leave the office feeling that they have been assured of a specific job. If the liaison coordinator later finds that the person is really not suited for that job, changing duties might be very difficult if someone else has assigned the task. Rather, a listing and discussion of the various types of work available in specific libraries will build expectation and will make an educated choice of schools possible. If volunteers want to work in only one school, they will see the needs of that library and the task choices they might make.

If desirable recruits seem unwilling to commit themselves, the central coordinator should ask them at least to have an interview with the liaison coordinator before making a decision. Sometimes the reluctant volunteer will find it easier to establish a good rapport with the liaison coordinator than with the central coordinator. Central coordinators should not take this as being a fault in their technique or personality. Instead, they should be aware that they cannot reach every person who comes through the office. The skilled central coordinator will develop the ability to spot this lack of rapport early, before the volunteer becomes disenchanted and decides not to volunteer after all.

The central coordinator should not take into account the various personalities of the different volunteers he assigns to the same school, as long as each is compatible with the liaison coordinator. The liaison coordinator will have the responsibility of devising a work schedule which will allow maximum benefit even from people whose personalities clash.

Actually, one of the most difficult areas with which to work will be that of the possible personality clash between volunteer and building-level coordinator. While central coordinators should not make arbitrary decisions about the personalities of either volunteers or of liaison coordinators, they should use as guides to proper placement any facts that they knows about either. If they are aware that particular coordinators are very rigid in their programs, that they allow very little deviation from a set pattern, they will place in this position a person who would seem to need more guidance and a more structured environment than another might. Central coordinators would place a highly motivated, very self-assured volunteer with a coordinator who can delegate responsibility, who actively seeks out new ideas and innovative approaches. This sort of person might be perceived as a threat to the authority of a person who likes to direct his program more closely.

The central coordinator should make every effort to expedite matters. The time between a volunteer's first making contact to her actual placement in a task should ideally not take more than a week. In order to speed the process the central coordinator should not hold completed file sheets, but rather send them immediately to the liaison coordinators. The exception would be in a case in which the central coordinator held a formal orientation. Even then, the sheets will be handled as expeditiously as possible.

Central coordinators should keep careful records of volunteer placement. They should maintain a copy of all file sheets and any subsequent information pertaining to the volunteers. They should place only as many volunteers as the liaison coordinators requested, but, when this is done, they should contact the individual coordinators to see if they could use more. Once volunteers actually show the quality of their work, the liaison coordinator might get a far-away look in his eyes and envision a wide range of fascinating projects. If, however, an individual coordinator wishes no more, no more should be assigned to that person. Volunteers do not like to stand around waiting for instruction or for something to do. They feel that they are wasting their time, which is true.

THE BUILDING-LEVEL COORDINATOR AND PLACEMENT

The duties of the building-level coordinator at this point will be determined by whether or not there is a central coordinator and by whether or not group orientation will be done. If there are no central coordinators, the building-level coordinators must assume most of their duties, eliminating only those which would be necessitated by a large library system. Once this has been accomplished, the next phase of placing the volunteer can begin. This will include orientation and placement. Again, the assumption in the following discussion will be that there is a central coordination.

Orientation

The building-level coordinator will conduct an orientation, either formal with a group of recruits, or informal, with one or a few. See figure 6.6, page 90 for a sample agenda. The orientation should present clearly the policy of the library concerning dress, use of machinery, confidentiality, relationships between volunteers and students (including discipline) and between volunteers and teachers, reimbursement, eating and smoking in the library, use of staff lounges, and absenteeism. Coordinators may need to talk with their peers on the teaching staff and with the administration in order to have a firm idea of the stance of the school. Once they have sought out and examined the ideas of others, they should put in writing their own feelings about what the volunteers should know. The coordinators should be very sure of policy so that they can convey this to their new volunteers.

The orientation will also include a discussion of universal duties and a tour of facilities. This will be the volunteer's last convenient time to decide not to participate. The liaison coordinator will wish to make orientation as interesting as possible and to maintain complete and thorough honesty in matters which might affect the volunteer.

For a very large program, a group orientation would be better. For smaller programs, especially those in independent schools, small groups or individuals might be better to work with. It is sometimes difficult to get many people together at the same time. The coordinator should be understanding about those who can not make it and arrange a make-up time, but it should be noted that absent volunteers may feel that they began the job with a failure to live up to the standards of the program. An individual orientation might be easier for insecure volunteers, because it would be easier for them to ask questions and clarify things. One way of working this problem out in the most satisfactory way possible would be to offer a group orientation while making it clear that you also offer individual appointments if desired, although it will take a bit longer to interview all the applicants who come in individually.

Orientation Agenda

1. School Policies
    Health records: X-ray
     T.B.
    Insurance policy
    Reimbursement policy
    Confidentiality
    Use of staff lounges
    Use of machinery

2. Library Policies
    Dress
    Food and drink in library
    Visiting with volunteers
    Relationships with staff and students
    Discipline
    Absenteeism

3. Universal Duties (unless covered earlier at district level)
    Checking in books
    Checking out books
    Shelving
    Using card catalog
    Mimeographing
    Requests
    Overdues

4. Tour
    Library — card catalog
     storage areas
     audiovisual equipment
     circulation desk
     files
     supplies
    Bathrooms
    Offices
    Place for coats and personal items
    Lounges
    Machine rooms
    Overview of school
    Special areas (speech therapy, motor development,
     computer room)
    Teacher's collection
    Snack machines
    Janitor's bell
    School supply closet

5. Placement

Fig. 6.6. Suggested orientation agenda.

Policies

If there are regulations about dress, the volunteer should be told immediately. While this area is not usually a problem, volunteers have been known to come to work in bare-midriffed sundresses and tennis clothes. This may not present a problem in some schools, but if it may, it would be far better to address the issue in a general manner before an individual becomes involved.

Using machinery can cause friction unless some sort of understanding is reached very early. A teacher who has a class coming in in ten minutes will naturally be somewhat irked if he has to wait for a volunteer to finish material which does not seem very important to the teacher. About the best arrangement that can be reached is to instruct volunteers both to use machines during times when teachers are normally in class and to offer to let a teacher go ahead if one shows up with work in hand. Unless something is vital to have in the next few minutes (and good planning can avoid most of this sort of thing) the benefits of waiting or rescheduling work will be worth working toward. Teachers will develop a good impression of the volunteers and will lose one common argument against them: that volunteers intrude upon the staff and interfere with their work. Another factor in whether volunteers are allowed to use machinery is the issue of breakage. The more inexperienced people use a machine, the more likely it is to break. This might cause curbs to be put on its usage by the office, in order to lessen repair bills. If this is the case, the individual coordinator should come to an agreement so that at least one or two volunteers would be allowed to use the machines.

If machines are located in an office or other areas where people work, it is mandatory to devise a system which will interfere as little as possible. The office staff can be real friends to the library, and it is useful to cultivate a good relationship.

Wise liaison coordinators will discuss the issue of confidentiality with their volunteers even though it has previously been addressed by the central coordinator. They should press the point that the volunteer will be in a position to see and hear things which should not be discussed with other volunteers or with people outside the library. Volunteers should also be guided to realize that opinions which they may form may be based on incomplete or erroneous information.

The volunteers should be told whether there are any restrictions on their relationships with the students. Some libraries foster an open, easygoing atmosphere, while others lean more toward a scholarly, academic one. Students may form a real attachment to one of the volunteers. This is one of the best reasons for encouraging volunteering; however, the relationship that results should be within the bounds of the goals of the library. In a library which encourages strict attention to duty in the volunteer, a hero-worshipping youngster might be a drawback. It will work far better to set limits early than to have to ask the volunteer and the student to modify the relationship. While the volunteer will probably understand, the student may be crushed, possibly to the point of not wanting to come to the library any more.

Discipline is another area which should be included in orientation. Individual coordinators should thoroughly understand their principals' feelings on the subject of volunteers disciplining students and should impart that understanding to the recruits. If they are expected to discipline students for any reason, they should feel very secure that their actions will be supported.

Relationships with teachers must also be guided. In the case of a volunteer and a teacher who are friends outside of the library, special care must be taken. It is very hard for anyone to tell a friend that he may not borrow a reference book "just for a minute" — volunteers have an added disadvantage in that their role may seem somewhat nebulous. They should know that they will have the full support of the librarian and of the principal if they uphold library rules. If volunteers know this, situations will be rare in which any actual support will need to be given. Once volunteers feel confident, they will do an excellent job of upholding standards and supporting library policy. It will be the person who is insecure in his authority who will vacillate between strict adherence and bending the rules. Volunteers should know what is expected of them and where to find help if they need it. They must be assured of their position and apprised of their authority, its scope and its limits.

If the school policy is to give refunds for materials bought by volunteers, mileage, or other financial considerations, the volunteer should be informed and told of the record-keeping required and the method of payment. A volunteer who turns in a bill for something and expects to be refunded immediately will not react kindly to being told that a check will be put in the mail the first of the month. Many volunteers donate books and other materials, since they are in a position to see a need. They should be told how to get a statement of donation for income tax purposes. It can be very frustrating for everyone when a volunteer who has donated many things over a period of months comes in at income tax time for a receipt. At that point, memory must serve, and the volunteer will almost assuredly come out short, since the librarian must be certain about what has been given. It is far better to do it at the time of the donation.

The question of whether food and drink are allowed in the library will depend to a large extent on whether there is a lounge available for the volunteers. In any case, regulations must be stated before work begins. In addition to food, smoking must be considered. Again, the availability of a lounge may determine the answer.

The issue of whether to encourage or allow volunteers to use staff lounges is a delicate one. On the one hand, volunteers are expected to behave in a professional manner. They must have some place where they can go to smoke, to relax, and to visit each other. Especially for the volunteers who stay all day, there must be a place where they can unwind from their duties. On the other hand, the teachers need to have a place where *they* can relax without feeling that they are "on stage" as they might with volunteers, especially if these volunteers are parents. One way to solve the dilemma is to have separate lounges for the two groups. Another is to ask the teachers to vote on whether or not to allow the volunteers to use the lounge. While this might help to some extent, there will probably be those teachers who voted against the idea who might have to go along because of majority rule. These teachers may feel resentful. If so, it may not take the volunteers long to notice, and, in turn, to resent the fact that their help is not appreciated at least enough for all the teachers to be willing to share their coffee breaks. A third solution is to allow a part of the library to be used for the volunteer's "timeout." This may set a bad example for the children, but it can be alleviated by explaining to them that this is a modification made in order to be able to accept the excellent help of the volunteers. This is a sensitive issue, enveloping as it does a kind of public estimation of value of the workers, both teachers and volunteers. Both groups need to know that their rights and feelings are respected.

Library rules on visiting between volunteers should be made very clear. The atmosphere of the library will influence this decision, as will the types of jobs done by the volunteers.

The coordinator should tell the volunteer of any rules about absenteeism. Some systems eliminate volunteers with two or three instances of absenteeism. Others tolerate practically anything. The new recruit must also know what, if any, limits are set on tardiness. In all cases, the volunteer should be asked definitely to call, since that will offer the coordinator the best opportunity to continue services uninterrupted. Some coordinators wish to have their volunteers find their own replacements. If this is done, each volunteer should have a list of people who are trained in his job, even some who are not on the regular volunteer list. Some coordinators set up a system whereby any volunteer who needs to miss work can call a volunteer whose job it is to find a replacement. The same rule should hold: only a volunteer possessing the needed skills should be sent. To some coordinators having a new or different volunteer come in unexpectedly can be worse than no volunteer.

During orientation volunteers should be told what to do if they have problems with their jobs, a student, a teacher, or another volunteer. They should be familiar with the lines of authority and have a contact person with whom they can discuss problems. This person should be the individual coordinator. Volunteers should be encouraged to come in before problems grow to such magnitude that they are out of proportion. They should also be guided to understand that if they are unhappy and complain to co-volunteers but do not seek to rectify the situation, they can cause a great deal of damage. Volunteers should be left with the warm feeling that their coordinator really cares about their happiness in the work and is willing to do what he can to assure it.

Coordinators should, depending upon their approach to coordinating, encourage new volunteers to offer ideas on programs they would like to see implemented and especially on new ways to accomplish existing ones more effectively.

At the same time, coordinators must establish firmly that any ideas are to be discussed with them before any action is taken, including fostering the idea with other volunteers. The recruit must understand that the coordinator believes in positive change and in growth through the ideas of many different people, but that many good ideas have been tried and discarded in the past because of some negative factor of which the volunteer would have no knowledge.

Universal Duties

In any library there will be some tasks, training for which is universal. These are duties which may be required at any time of any person who works on-site, even those on special projects, depending upon work load and absenteeism. Each librarian will make a decision on these, but some which would generally be required are checking books in, checking books out, shelving, locating materials using the card catalog, mimeographing, maintaining discipline, taking requests, and handling overdues. While all of these would not be taught to the volunteers the first day, they should understand that they will be required to become accomplished in these areas as well as in their areas of specialty. This may seem overwhelming to the new recruits, but with a little sympathy and assurance that they will not be expected to master everything at once, they should adjust to the idea quickly. The coordinator must avoid at all costs letting the volunteers feel that they were tricked into doing more than they volunteered to do. The volunteer should know from the beginning that anyone in the library might have to cover for someone who gets sick or has an emergency. Most people will take this as a real challenge if told ahead of time and assured of proper training. Conversely, the experienced volunteer knows very well that the life of a volunteer is hard; the "once they get your name..." fear will take over if they perceive their job to be expanding from what they had originally agreed to do.

Reassessment

At this point, the coordinator should get the volunteers' responses to what they have heard. Are they eager to volunteer? Mildly interested? Are they disillusioned? Did they perhaps think that they could come in with no training and check books out? If they wish to reconsider, the coordinator should try to clear up any potential misunderstanding, but this is the time to allow reluctant volunteers a graceful exit. There is no need to spend valuable time training someone who does not really want to stay.

The Tour

Coordinators will then arrange a tour of all facilities, whether or not they expect the volunteer to use them. This will make the volunteers feel more at home and will help them when their duties require them to leave the library. Places which must be included on the tour are the different areas of the library, including closets and storage areas; bathrooms; offices; a place to put coats, purses, and other personal belongings; lounges, even if the volunteers are not to use them; machine rooms; general areas of the school (kindergarten, first grade, and so forth); special teaching areas; teacher's collection; snack machines; janitor's bell; school supply closets; and any other places the volunteer might be required to go. After this, even a year later, the coordinator can describe a location rather than having to send an escort with the volunteers if they need to go.

The volunteers must then be instructed in the use of all machines which they might be asked to use. In addition, they should learn where to go if the machine will not work. Volunteers should not be put in a position where they must interrupt person after person to do a task. They should also be instructed about where to find supplies such as paper, fluid, and other items which will need to be replenished.

Selecting the Task Area

After the orientation, the individual coordinator should have a system by which to place the volunteer in a particular job without causing the others to wait an undue length of time. Depending on the number of volunteers, this waiting can turn into a real problem. About the best way to handle it would be to say that the coordinator will interview immediately those who wish to stay. While they are awaiting their turns they can visit with old friends and make new ones. If, however, they prefer, they can choose a time on a sign-up sheet (fig. 6.7, page 96) and come back at that time. The coordinator should have prepared a sheet listing dates and times open for interviews, with a tear-off slip with the same information. This can be done with a sewing machine using no thread. The volunteers would choose times, fill in their names, and take the tear-offs as reminders.

The volunteers should be reminded that there are a limited number of positions for each task, so, if there was something in particular that the volunteers would like to work on, it would be to their advantage to come in as soon as possible, so that the choice of jobs would be greater.

The coordinator will wish to read the volunteers' file sheets before interviewing them. Sometimes a recruit will have skills which are in such demand that placement is almost automatic. Most of the time, however, volunteers will either have several moderately useful skills or no task-specific abilities at all. In the latter case, the coordinator will have to conduct the interview quite carefully, seeking to identify those areas in which the volunteer will be generally helpful.

The individual coordinators can present the volunteer with a few choices or tell her where the library would like to have help. The volunteer should be free to select another area if she really does not want to work in a particular field, but she should be guided to something the library needs. Once this is done, day and time of day can be settled.

In the last few phases, the coordinator will have to make decisions about which areas to discuss first. If a volunteer can only come on certain days, for instance, and the job she wants cannot be done on those days (such as working with a particular class), the volunteer must choose some other field. Volunteers should be encouraged to be realistic about their schedules. They should not volunteer for more than they can handle, nor should they agree to come at a time which is too close to some other obligation. If parents bring their children to school in the morning, they might wish to begin work at that time. If, however, one parent takes the child to school, and the other wants to volunteer, that person might find it unrealistic to agree to come very early. Similarly, if a parent has a child in another school to pick up, he might find his schedule difficult to maintain if he works in the library until 3:00. The coordinator must determine whether it will upset his sytem to have a volunteer who eases out a little ahead of time, or whether this would be preferable to having him come at a time less convenient.

When the volunteer wants to do work at home, the coordinator must set up a system by which materials can be transferred. Instructions can be given over the phone, but materials for bulletin boards, typing, and so forth must be physically passed from one to the other. Depending upon the nature of the material, coordinators may wish to use students to carry home papers and

96 / 6—*Screening and Placing the Volunteer*

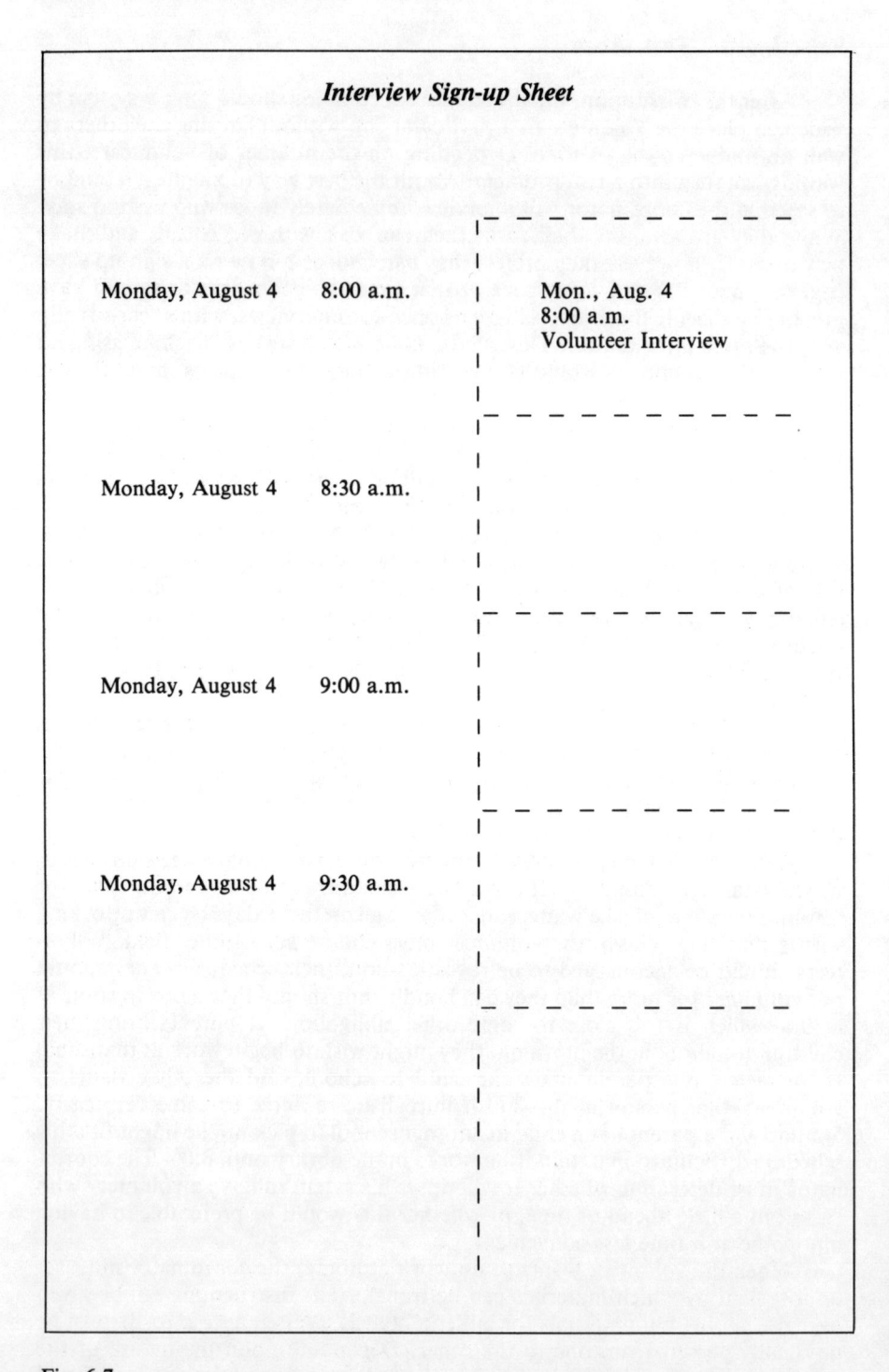

Interview Sign-up Sheet

Monday, August 4	8:00 a.m.	Mon., Aug. 4 8:00 a.m. Volunteer Interview
Monday, August 4	8:30 a.m.	
Monday, August 4	9:00 a.m.	
Monday, August 4	9:30 a.m.	

Fig. 6.7.

other things; they may prefer to find neighbors to act as liaison; the material can be left in a safe place which would be open after the volunteer finishes his regular job; some materials could be mailed. Two criteria must be observed. The safety factor must be directly related to the value of the materials being transmitted and the speed of the system must be satisfactory for the nature of the work to be done.

For the parents who wish to work with library classes, either as storytellers or as aides in teaching library skills, the coordinator should inform them if she feels that it would be detrimental for the parent to work with his own child. It is sometimes better for a parent to work with a class other than the one his child is in. The student whose parent is present every week can feel a great deal of pressure either to be perfect or to act out. Sometimes the child will cling to a mother and make it almost impossible for her to do her job. Sometimes it will become a real distraction (especially when the volunteer is a father, since it is less common to see fathers in the classroom), to the point that the others cannot learn. In a situation which demands that the volunteer maintain discipline, such as a story time, the child can really suffer if his parent corrects the behavior of one of his friends. This can carry over so that a negative feeling exists even at recess or back in the classroom. These problems are easy to deal with, but any involvement on the part of the librarian may embarrass the child or cause resentful feelings in the parent, even if he agrees on the need for such interaction.

The parent can volunteer for a different class, possibly one of the same age. A parent who foresees some problem will usually agree to this once the dangers are pointed out, especially if the coordinator can assure him that there will be a volunteer for his child's class. What parents will generally require is that their children have the same advantages that the other children have. If parents prefer that they work with their own children, it should be done with the express understanding that, at the librarian's discretion, the parent can be changed to another duty. One other way to avoid the drawbacks at least partially is to assign the parent to work during the period when the child is in, but not to work directly with the class. While this may not alleviate all problems, much of the pressure on the child will be relieved.

The need for adaptability and change must be mentioned. Volunteers must feel absolutely free to say that they do not like a task at any point in training. Most volunteers will not abuse this. Rather, they will typically continue in a job they do not like, gather negative feelings, and quit. The coordinator should remain very aware of attitude and be eager to cross-train an unhappy volunteer.

The main goal of placing volunteers is to put them into compatible jobs in which the library needs help, and to let them know enough about what they will be expected to do so that they will not feel later that their willingness to help has been abused. Handled properly, the placement procedure will leave the volunteer with a well-deserved sense of self-worth and eager expectancy, and the coordinator with a feeling of a job well done and the promise of a better future for the library and its services.

7 Training and Implementation

Placing volunteers can usually be done in 30 to 40 minutes by an experienced coordinator. Training them and working them into the program takes much longer. Once the program arrives at this stage, the building-level coordinator assumes most of the responsibilities. This chapter provides pointers and examples which will help the new program take off and the established one improve.

A prime consideration, of course, is to make the volunteer feel welcome. The first tangible sign of the volunteer's value to the library is when he is assigned a place to keep his materials and a location for notes—a "post office." An arrangement such as the one pictured in figure 7.1 can be kept in one cabinet, and provides for materials, schedules, and messages.

Training has a number of aspects including a review of policies and rules, a clarification of lines of authority, a program of instruction in general library tasks, and an introduction to special volunteer program undertakings.

POLICIES AND RULES

The coordinator will wish to have a clear understanding with the volunteer about library policies and rules. These must be discussed so that the volunteer will become aware of the fact that all decisions are made in support of those policies and rules. A rather common view of libraries is that, since it is all so simple, decisions can be made on most topics according to what seems best at the time, by whoever happens to be there. Volunteers, in their training, must be made aware that most issues will be handled a certain way, what that way is, how much leeway, if any, is built into the system, and by whose authority decisions are to be made. An introductory handout such as is shown in figure 7.2, page 100 would constitute a good start.

Although both school and library policies relating to the volunteer will have been discussed during orientation, policies which may be associated with special problems can be covered again during the training sessions.

(Text continues on page 101.)

Policies and Rules / 99

Fig. 7.1. Illustration by Joseph A. Noto

Volunteer Mothers Program

Margaret Ross Memorial Library
Hamden Hall Country Day School

Welcome as a volunteer to the Margaret "Peggy" Ross Memorial Library. Although the librarian offers professional guidance and direction, it is the volunteers who are the backbone of the work done in our library. We welcome your help and hope your experience here will be an enjoyable and meaningful one.

You will be given a schedule of when you will be working in the library. Please post it in a convenient place.

Please be on time to work and please call the head of volunteers if you are unable to work on your assigned date. If you cannot work on your designated day, a substitute should be assigned to your time period.

If you have special interests or talents, please feel free to tell the librarian about them. Typing, story hour, displays, mending, and special projects are just part of the work accomplished in the library.

You will receive the Margaret "Peggy" Ross Memorial Library Handbook. This is a brief introduction to the library. Please read it to establish a basic knowledge for your work here in the library.

Further Notes for Further Understanding:

    a. Please recognize how important it is to be on time. If you are involved with story hour or library skills, plan to be in the library a few minutes early—greeting the students as they arrive at the library is extremely important.

    b. Volunteers should work with the librarian to encourage the students to respect the library for what it is. It is not a recreation center or a student lounge—it is a place where a person can come to study or relax and enjoy our services and materials. A proper atmosphere is important—help the library to remain a library.

    c. Communication between the librarian and volunteers is very important. Ideas, frustrations, concerns should be expressed in a positive way; in this way the library will grow to be an even better place. The librarian/teacher is the professional and the volunteer is available to reinforce and enhance the educational process under the direction of the librarian. If you have questions feel free to ask them!

Laurence Kingsbury, Librarian

Fig. 7.2. An introductory handout. Reprinted by permission of Laurence Kingsbury, Head Librarian, Hamden Hall Country Day School.

A good example of a possible policy problem is that of special privileges being extended to the children of workers. It is unrealistic to say that no privileges will be extended, since, in reality, that is not the way it will work out. For instance, volunteers who process books will usually develop an eagle eye for those which might appeal to their children. The coordinator may have a strict rule that, when books are ready for the shelves, they must all be put out immediately so that each child will have the same opportunity to read them. This system will have built-in failure, however, since the eager processor may put a new book out on the shelves, then check it out. If that does not work, they can alert their youngsters to the book and put it out when their children will see it. Rather than set up a system in which the volunteer is trying to outwit the coordinator, it is far better to have a few perquisites, to let new volunteers know that one of the benefits of the processing job will be that they have first access to any book which does not already have a request on it. In this way, the volunteer will feel special, and the students of the school will have to wait no longer than the regular one- or two-week checkout period. The librarian should remember that, even though the parent has located and checked out the book, its ultimate goal is still a student. The same system may be used with typists. Many fascinating books will pass through their hands; allowing them to put in hold slips will spice up their work days and give them something to look forward to: sharing brand-new books with their children, books which they have prepared for the shelves. This is privilege, yes. But it is practical privilege. It is giving away what the volunteer will take anyway. It is assigning importance to an everyday occurrence, and acknowledging that the volunteer is very special to the library.

Some privileges are not to be extended under any circumstances. These will differ from school to school. Perhaps volunteers would like to have lunch with their children. In a situation in which volunteers must eat in the library due to lack of facilities anywhere else, this will mean a decision on whether children will eat in the library or whether they and their parents will eat with the class. If the library has an open-door policy, in which children are encouraged to come to the library at any time, and if the librarian allows children to eat with parents in the library, a rather serious public relations problem can arise. Once other children see the group lunching together, it would be very surprising if they did not join them. Once this starts, the library can become a cafeteria almost from one day to the next. It is far better to have a policy which can be quoted that no children may eat within the library. If parents would care to join their children for lunch, and if school policy allows this, that will be fine.

Volunteers who lack experience may view the simple request to eat with one's child as an automatic Why not? They must be guided to understand that all such decisions must be left to the coordinator or librarian. What seems simple to the uninitiated can turn into a seething mass of negative feelings as a result of an innocent decision.

Each library will have certain rules which were formulated to satisfy local conditions and foster the program instituted by the current librarian. Volunteers need to know not only what the rules are, but also why they were selected. In this way they will remember them better, show their support to others, and increase the number of those who know and follow the rules.

7—Training and Implementation

Since each library will be different, the use of a few examples will suffice to show how these rules could be handled in more than one way, depending upon the goals of the library.

    A. Interaction of volunteers with patrons: Volunteers are encouraged to become familiar with the different aspects of the library so that they can assist in helping students and teachers locate and select materials. Each volunteer should be able to find the various sections of the library and to use the card catalog. While children are encouraged to work on their own as much as possible, they often need help. Watchful volunteers who see a need should offer their services, and, if they feel they cannot help the student, they should seek out the librarian so that both they and the student can learn. The order of priority should be: students who are checking out books, students who need help in locating books, teachers who need help, and finally, the volunteer's individual task for the day. If someone else is covering the desk, volunteers should no longer consider it their responsibility as they would if there were no one stationed there. Only if there are no patrons who need help are the volunteers to continue in their assigned tasks. Every effort should be made to help children who are allowed to come down from class briefly in order to check out a book; the teacher needs to be able to depend upon their return within a few minutes. The goal of the system is to assure the students of the fastest possible help while still allowing them to experience as much as possible on their own. The library wishes to encourage friendly relationships between the volunteer and the student and to have the children see that adults can and do use the library.

From a different viewpoint:

    B. Interaction of volunteers with patrons: Volunteers are to assist with tasks provided by the coordinator. Unless directed to do so, volunteers will not become involved with the patrons. All reference questions are to be handled by the librarian. Patrons seeking help from the volunteer should be directed to the librarian, or the question noted for a time when the librarian can assist. Both students and teachers should be assured that the librarian will be with them as soon as possible. Priorities of volunteers in the library consist of: Checking books out, working at assigned tasks, and shelving books. The goal of volunteer participation is to assure the accomplishment of the many activities and projects to which they are assigned while at the same time providing patrons with reading material. There must be a clear distinction between professional and nonprofessional tasks.

Or again:

A. Discipline of the students: Volunteers are expected to participate in the discipline of the students mainly by presenting a good model for their behavior. In the event that students need reminding, the volunteer will, using her knowledge of general good citizenship and specific library goals, deal with the situation as gently as possible. Usually a hand on the shoulder or a steady look will suffice to remind the young library user of this responsibility. If more stringent methods are required, a verbal reminder which is kind but firm is in order. The volunteer may, if deemed necessary, use such disciplinary measures as he has seen the librarian take, such as seating a child for five or ten minutes. If the situation calls for stronger methods, the librarian must be consulted. Under no circumstances will a child be removed from the room except by the librarian. The goal is to provide children with a positive model and positive reinforcement for good behavior. Even the more drastic measures must be administered with consideration and the expectation that the misbehavior will be amended quickly. If there is some conflict about the use of certain materials or machines, the child with the greater need will use the item first.[1] If both students wish to use it for pleasure only, the one who began to use it first will have priority, since the library is available to the other child many times each day. The first child should share with the other, however, as much as possible. For instance, if two children wish to use the only record player at the same time, the one who first chose it will take precedence. He must, however, allow the other child to listen to the record if he chooses. The second child must content himself with listening to the record chosen by the first child and coming back at recess or lunch time to listen to his first choice. The goal here is to allow each child some time to enjoy his own selections while at the same time learning to share. Most of the records and tapes are long enough to preclude playing more than one consecutively all the way through during the rather brief periods available to the children. This system will encourage cooperation and the development of planning skills.

And conversely:

B. Discipline of students: Volunteers are expected to report any infraction of the rules to the librarian. They are not to discipline any students. Since volunteers are in the library in an unofficial capacity, it would be very difficult for them to maintain any sort of regularity of discipline. The goal of this system is to assure a consistency and continuity of discipline so that students can feel secure about what is expected of them.

In case of conflict between students over the use of materials, the problem is to be settled by allowing each to use the disputed item for a brief (five to ten minute) period. The objective of this system is to assure a fair distribution of services to all students.

It can easily be seen that possible solutions to problems and methods of avoiding problems can vary widely. Coordinators will familiarize themselves with the problems and determine the solutions and rules, then relay their decisions to the volunteers. In every case the point should be made that the rules are designed to further the goals of the library. Volunteers should be encouraged to ask questions, whether these questions are designed to challenge the value of the rule or to enhance knowledge of it. The result will be a very desirable increase in understanding.

AUTHORITY

The question of authority (who has it, when is it used, and how much) is one that must be settled satisfactorily both for the good of the library and for the security of the volunteer. Volunteers need to be told what authority they have, and then be able to exercise that authority unhindered. If they have the authority to get materials from a supply cabinet when they need them for a project, volunteers should not be questioned each time they open the door. They should have the authority to decide that they need more poster paper or thumb tacks in order to do their jobs. They need to know that they are trusted.

Trust is an issue upon which some volunteer programs fall before they have well begun. In a well-planned program, the coordinator will know the limits of the volunteer's realm before involving that volunteer. Within this realm the coordinator should trust the volunteer as much as possible. Spiral teaching offers an excellent opportunity to see how much the person can be depended upon. To generalize here is to risk either allowing someone liberties who cannot handle them or to be unwilling to accept excellent aid from someone who is most trustworthy. The issue of trust must be decided case by case, and by slow degrees. Responsibility demands trust. Coordinators should not ask volunteers to be responsible for tasks if they feel that they cannot trust those volunteers for everything the tasks require.

When volunteers have been trained in their areas of specialty, and have proven their capabilities, they then add to their own authority, but in those areas only. The veteran of hundreds of checked out books can be relied upon to respond to the novice's questions on that subject, though that does not authorize him to establish the library's position on other questions. Able coordinators will help their volunteers to recognize the difference and to feel justifiably good about the areas on which they are authorities.

Volunteers should certainly be instructed that they are to come to the coordinator if they have difficulty or problems—especially with other workers or with staff. They must be assured that any problem will be dealt with quickly and that they will receive a response as to the outcome. While friendships will develop between recruits, problems should remain the bailiwick of the coordinator. This will limit the mushrooming nature of gossip and will assure prompt attention to problem areas.

TRAINING IN UNIVERSAL TASKS

Choosing the Trainer

Coordinators in setting up their training programs well before they begin work with the first volunteers must decide who will actually teach the necessary skills. In order to allow the program to develop as fully and with as much cohesion as possible, a coordinator should do at least the initial training. At some later point, a well-trained, experienced volunteer might take over.

When initial training is done at the district level, a number of topics can be thoroughly covered, saving the school library staff time and energy. New volunteers may be trained on a districtwide basis on such subjects as general orientation to the goals of the library program, the circulation system and shelving, handling audiovisual equipment and materials, developing a pamphlet file, filing catalog and shelflist cards, preparation of preprocessed materials, processing, mending, storytelling, preparation of reading lists, preparation of bulletin boards, making book games, and many others. Volunteers might attend only those workshops which pertain to universal duties and to their specific duties. Special details which occur in particular libraries may then be taught by the individual coordinators in those schools.

Once outside training is over, at least for a while, the volunteer and the building-level coordinator enter a new phase of their relationship. This period is extremely important in establishing trust and in defining requirements. The coordinator should not pass up the opportunity to institute a lasting relationship with the individual volunteer while firmly delineating what is required from the volunteer in attitude and understanding. The coordinator can use this time to build trust and a rapport which will be demanded if there is a problem later. Without a close relationship, volunteers may well let any small dissatisfaction dissuade them from continuing their work. But once faith is established, the volunteer will usually give the library the benefit of the doubt if necessary, and will actively work to support it.

Initial building-level task training should include the first few jobs in which the volunteer is expected to participate. The fact that these will be relatively simple and could be taught as well by someone else is not the point. The goal is proficiency in the task *and* the beginning of a good relationship, as well as a sense of belonging and a realization of importance. The development of these aspects must rest with the coordinator.

The coordinator will use this time of working closely with the volunteers as an opportunity to discover how well they can follow directions, how much initiative they have, and whether they are becoming part of the group socially. Volunteers will simultaneously be forming an opinion about the work, the coordinator, and the people around them.

After the volunteer feels secure and when the coordinator is assured that rapport has been established, the new recruit may be trained in limited tasks by an aide or another volunteer. While this will save some time for coordinators, they will still need to keep a close check on the training, since any inaccuracies must be caught as soon as possible. Prolonged repetition may embed the mistake in the volunteer's mind to the point that it will be automatic and almost irreversible. In addition, volunteers must be shielded from making mistakes as much as possible, since these will lower their self-image and their trust in the volunteer program, especially the training. They may learn not to rely on the information given by the volunteer or aide, which will lower their estimation of the value of a volunteer program and will, in effect, negate any time spent by that individual in training. If someone other than the coordinator is responsible for training, that training should be specific and of brief duration. The coordinator should review the training at frequent intervals. If any corrections need to be made, they must involve both the trainee and the trainer. In order to lessen the frequency of this problem, the coordinator would be wise not to place new volunteers with volunteers who themselves were trained in particular jobs by volunteers. This way at least every other volunteer will have been trained by the coordinators themselves. Perpetuating mistakes is dangerous because it is difficult to trace the error back to its origin. Unless all persons laboring under the misapprehension are corrected, the mistake will be transmitted to yet another worker, and untold mischief done to the system.

When aides or volunteers are given the task of training other volunteers, they should be told of the limited scope of the assignment. Both they and the volunteer should be completely aware of the fact that all training is being done by the coordinator through the experienced worker, not by the workers themselves. The distinction will become important if there are corrections to be made; new volunteers will need to know that they are not being supervised by two people at once; indeed, using this method, the volunteer will expect periodic review and correction from the coordinator as a sign of interest, and as an outward evidence of a well-run program with built-in immunity from the embarrassment of continued mistakes. Volunteers are thus assured that they will not long continue an action unless that action is indeed acceptable.

Coordinators will find that some of their volunteers are very dependable as trainers, that they quickly comprehend the requirements, that they do not overstep the boundaries of the task, and that they are particularly facile at working with people. These people are worth their weight in gold. The coordinator should cultivate their interest and encourage them to master as many areas of the library as they wish, since they will then be able to teach other, newer volunteers their skills. Consider the suggestions in table 7.1. Unfortunately, the coordinator will also discover some whose talents lie elsewhere. Some people are really adept at their jobs but cannot transmit that adroitness to others. Some are very intolerant of the novice and expect perfection too quickly. Some may not like being involved with others, or not feel any inclination to be put in a position where they have to guide others. Some may simply be reluctant to be responsible for another person. Any reluctance should be honored, since it will provide a negative atmosphere into which to insert the budding volunteer. Since the effect of atmosphere will be felt long after the experienced worker and the trainee are parted, special attention should be given to selecting trainers who are pleased with their work. This will show new volunteers how pleasant their future association with the library can be.

Table 7.1

You and Your Volunteer

---

1. Give him as much of *your* work as he can do, eliminating only professional jobs.
2. Give him experience by doing. (After all, how did you learn?)
3. Let him know *your* job, your values, your goals, your problems.
4. Let him be resourceful on his own.
5. Help him develop his imagination.
6. Let him move the tasks.
7. Teach him to do research and synoptic reports.
8. Insist on follow-through and attention to detail.

CAUTION:

1. Make sure he is courteous and tactful to everybody.
2. Be sure each volunteer understands the scope of his job before he starts.

Adapted from *Finding Time for Success and Happiness through Time Management* by Ivan W. Fitzwater, by permission of Mandel Publications, a division of Management Development Institute. Copyright, 1977, Management Development Institute, Inc.

Covering the Material

Coordinators will probably wish to train volunteers in their own fields as well as give them initially very superficial training in the areas around them. In this way the volunteer will develop a real understanding of the library as a whole and of the way it operates. The volunteer should certainly be made aware of the physical set up of the library (see table 7.2).

Wide-range training will make it possible for volunteers to understand the necessity of some factors of which they would otherwise be critical. Also, in case of emergencies, the volunteer with a good overview could step in and hold the fort if needed. Thus, if the coordinator has a library class in while a volunteer is working on his job of covering books, an emergency need not arise if the librarian needs to leave the room because a child is ill or needs discipline by the principal. Coordinators can be assured as they handle problems that the volunteer can take over to the extent of helping children locate books and check them out. Were the volunteer not trained in these skills, an entire class could lose its library time for the week because the librarian had to be out of the room. Volunteers who feel that their work demands more space than they are allowed will be more accepting of the situation if they have had a little experience with the many other activities sponsored by the library. Storage is a common problem in libraries, and the assignment of it can affect some volunteers' self-images. If they have the experience to know that everyone suffers from the same problem, they will not take it personally when their supplies are assigned to one small shelf.

While general training will be very superficial, especially when a volunteer is still new, training in the areas that the volunteer will specialize in will gradually become more thorough. It is best to give workers more information than they can handle in a limited field of application, while assuring them that they are not expected to remember most of it at first. The benefit of this is that ignorant blunders are rarely made. The coordinator wishes to put volunteers in a position so that they at least know enough to ask questions. The volunteer should be encouraged to ask, and told that the questions will be viewed as a positive sign that information is being assimilated.

Training a volunteer is much like training an employee with one exception: most tasks must be taught in smaller units. Since the average volunteer comes once a week, it will be difficult for even the brightest to become adept at tasks if too much is expected of them at one time and if they are not given sufficient opportunity to master a few skills before going on to others. The following paragraphs take some of the more usual tasks and break them into small units. Depending upon the assiduity of the volunteer and the frequency of visits, the coordinator may wish to teach a small part of a task, allow practice time, then teach another part, and so forth. Only when there is a skilled person immediately available for questions and guidance should the volunteer be taught the entire unit, then allowed to practice it all. Without help right at hand, doing this could force the volunteers to feel either ignorant or mistreated. They should feel at all times that they are being given a fair opportunity to acquire knowledge and skills. Mistakes occur more often when a volunteer is trying to remember many details without having mastered any.

Table 7.2

Library Arrangement

A volunteer should be able to recognize and locate each of the following:

Circulation desk (checkout desk)
Librarian's office or desk
Card catalog
Dictionaries (abridged and unabridged)
Easy books
Fiction books
Nonfiction books
Biographies
Encyclopedias (including those on checkout)
Atlases
Almanacs
Magazines
Newspapers
Vertical file
Microfilm
Filmstrips and projectors
Records and record players
Tapes and tape recorders
8-mm projector
16-mm projector
Conference areas
Shelflist

Some volunteers will be able to assimilate things very easily and quickly; the coordinator will shortly become aware that they can go faster than usual. In the following discussion, a variety of tasks will be discussed and, when appropriate, comments made on aspects which may need to be emphasized with the volunteers. Details are, of course, for illustrative purposes only. Remember that all instructions should be in the volunteer manual.

Checking Out Books

This duty is very effective as a first task, since, in the minds of most volunteers, it is "real library work." From childhood people see mainly this part of the librarian's job. Many people who use large libraries are not aware that those at the circulation desk are rarely professionals. Thus, a great deal of importance is associated with this particular task, and the volunteer's self-esteem will immediately climb.

Coordinators should base their instructions on the situations which volunteers will be faced with on their work days. The checklist in figure 7.3, pages 111-12) demonstrates the sort of set of reminders which the coordinator should carry into any instructional session. In terms of how much to teach: if the school is one which serves preschool as well as higher grades, and the preschool is allowed to check out books, the coordinator will wish to present the systems for both age groups only if the volunteer will need to deal with both immediately. Otherwise it would be better to let one wait until the volunteer has had practice in the other.

The coordinator should go through the entire process, even the part handled by the student, since the volunteer may need to remind the child of the correct procedure. The associated page from the volunteer manual (see fig. 7.4, pages 113-14 for example) should be referred to. In addition to these instructions the coordinator should also instruct the volunteer as soon as possible without overload in how to handle minor problems, such as location of scratch paper, new book cards, extra date due slips, cards for special categories of materials such as periodicals, and how to fill them out. (Some volunteers will not understand until they have worked with overdues the importance of noting the issue on the magazine card.) The question of overdues should be handled without much delay and should be done as a unit, so that the volunteer can see the overall picture. New recruits should be given guidelines on whether to have other students wait while they look into one child's problem or whether to have the one wait while all of the straightforward checkouts are handled. In fact, the entire issue of how to treat the children should be addressed early on. The hints in table 7.3, page 115 might contribute to a good start.

For preschool children, the system is always somewhat modified, since most of them cannot write their names small enough to fit on the average book card. The volunteer will have to give more guidance to the youngsters in order to be sure that they leave the library on schedule, since they cannot tell time. The volunteer should also notice as the children come in to be sure that they return their books to the proper place before they go to the shelves. The small children should be instructed, as should the older ones, about whether they

(Text continues on page 116.)

Checklist for Teaching Checkout Procedures

1. Under no circumstances should a new card be made for a book. If there is a problem, make a note describing the situation and hold the item for the librarian. Tell the student or teacher that the book cannot be checked out without the card, but that as soon as the problem is cleared up, he will be notified.

2. No one is to sign any name other than his own to a card. If an exception is made to this rule for teachers, it should be stated. It should also be pointed out that sometimes parents wish to check out books and use the child's name. In case of overdues, which no one intends to have, the overdue notice will go the child. This, besides being unfair, can be very embarrassing. The children are being taught that a library card is a legal document and that, as with all documents, they are to use only their own names. Some volunteers tend to forget this rule and may have to be reminded that, even when a child is in a rush, he must take a minute to sign the card.

3. Each child should sign his last name at a table and put his class designation on the book card. Then he should put the card back into the pocket. This will make the checkout procedure go very quickly during that last-minute rush before a class visit is over. If a student arrives at the desk with the book card out of the pocket, he should be reminded of the rule and told that it cannot be accepted like that. There is too much chance that the card will inadvertently be lost.

4. When more than two or three students come to the circulation desk, they should get into two lines. Again, this rule is most valuable when many members of a class are trying to check out books. The volunteer will alternate between the two lines so that each moves quickly.

5. When volunteers check out books, they should first look at the child's last name, then check the overdue file. If they have overdue books, children may not check more out. The volunteer should offer to save the new ones for two days, and say that the students may have them if they return the overdue books within that time.

6. If children insist that they have returned the book, the volunteers should ask for help from their librarians, and listen to the way they handle the problem.

7. The volunteer must check to be sure that the child's class designation is on the card.

(Fig. 7.3 continues.)

Figure 7.3 – *Continued*

8. Volunteers must check the card and the pocket to be sure that all essential information is identical. If not, the card is in the wrong book. They should offer to notify the child who is trying to check the book out when the mistake is rectified; they should not make new cards or change information on the incorrect ones. They will, of course, follow up on this as soon as possible, by consulting the librarian.

```
JF                    c.1
Ols              $4.98
Olsen
Come join us in the
    garden.
```

Room	Name	Date
34	Smith, M.	

```
JF                    c.1
Ols
Olsen
Come join us in the
    garden.
```

9. If all information is correct, the volunteer should put the due date in the book and on the card.

10. The child will take the book; the volunteer will keep the card. All cards should be put in front of the checkout file. They will be put in order at the end of the day.

The coordinator cannot stress the perils of making new cards (or changing existing ones) too much. No matter how reasonable such a step seems, it should not be done without the consent of the librarian. Nor can the coordinator overstate the problems caused by not comparing the card and pocket. Both types of problems can be especially painful when they involve a student. As always, the volunteer should be encouraged to ask questions.

Fig. 7.3. Sample checklist for training volunteers.

Checklist for Preschool Checkout

1. Preschoolers may check out one book at a time.

2. After their books have been selected, children will go to the proper file, find the color of card designated for their class. Then each child will locate the card with his name on it.

3. He will then take the card and the book to a table.

4. If the children are in kindergarten, they will sign their names on the colored card, not the book card.

5. The four-year-olds do not sign their names unless they wish to.

6. The children will then attach the colored card to the book card, using the paper clip which is attached at all times to the colored card. In the beginning of the year, some will require help. The volunteer should not do it for them. Rather, he should help the children learn how to do it. The volunteer should show them how to put their fingers on top of the paper clips and slide the book cards under those clips.

7. Both the child's name and the name of the book should show. In other words, the cards should be back to back.

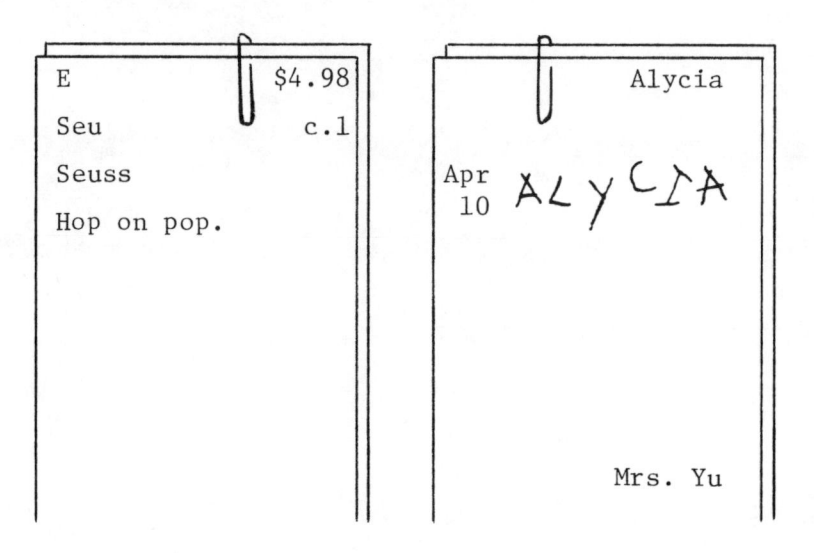

(Fig. 7.4 continues.)

Figure 7.4—*Continued*

> 8. The cards must be in the pocket of the book when the child comes to the desk.
>
> 9. Once the child comes to the circulation desk, the volunteer should be sure that all steps have been taken, put the due date on both book and colored card, give the child the book, and place the card with all other checkout cards for the day.
>
> 10. Since all children have two cards with their names on them, it is not necessary for the volunteer to check in their old books before checking out the new ones.
>
> 11. Since the teachers mark off each book as members of their classes return them to the library, there is not much danger of a child's having more than one book checked out.
>
> 12. If parents wish to let the child check out more than one book, they should sign their own names to the cards. The teacher is responsible for only one book at a time.

Fig. 7.4. Sample process checklist.

Table 7.3

Hints for Volunteers Who Work at the Desk

BE AVAILABLE
Even though you may be working on something while you are sitting at the information desk, people will sense whether you mind their interruptions or not. A smile, a question, "Can I help you" will determine whether your help is needed.

BE A RETRIEVER
When students ask you where a book is located, don't point; if possible, you should walk with them to the section and help them to find the books. Once you have helped, return to your desk so the next student will be able to find you.

BE A DETECTIVE
Many people will not tell you what they really are looking for when they first ask. Usually, by further questioning and conversation, you will find out what they are seeking.

BE A TEACHER
Treat students with the same courtesy you accord to VIP adults, but don't do all the work for them. Find out what they really need, lead them to it via the catalog, help them find it on the shelf once they have call numbers, suggest any further possibilities with materials that they can find in other departments. Follow up and find out if they found what they were looking for.

BE A STATISTICIAN
Write down individual subject requests. These can be used to help with book selection.

BE A STARRY-EYED POLLYANNA
No place is perfect, but always give the impression that everyone in the library wants to do his part to serve. Don't knock another department when material is unavailable. Give the impression that you are proud of your organization and all the people who work to make it go.

USE THE LIBRARIAN
If there is a problem you don't know how to handle, or a question you aren't sure about, talk with the librarian. If you feel that the student needs more information than you can find, go to the librarian. When students come in with research questions, help should be minimal, guidance maximal. The goal here is not the information, but the process of doing the research.

Reprinted from *Library Journal* May 1, 1972. Published by R. R. Bowker Co. (a Xerox company). Copyright © 1972 by Xerox Corporation.

should use a marker for replacing books on the shelves or whether they should leave unwanted books on a table. Older children will be able to reshelve their own books.

Checking In Books

Checking in books can be taught in connection with checking them out, since both require many of the same skills and will thus reinforce each other, and since both may be done by the volunteer at the desk.

The volunteer should understand that books should be checked in promptly, never going longer than one day without being carded. Until then, they are not available to the public. The volunteer should be made very aware that no one is to rummage through books which have been returned but not carded. They are temporarily off limits. If students see books that they want, a request may be taken for them. New volunteers will probably feel that it is reasonable to stop what they are doing to card a book if someone wants it. But it should never come to that. They should be told of the dangers of letting people handle books which are in the return-book bin and guided to realize that students who are allowed to do so under supervision may feel that they may do it at any time. Librarians understand that if a book is inadvertently removed from the library without being first checked in, an innocent patron may eventually have to pay for it if it is lost, since the last name on the card will, in fact, belong to a person who did return the book. Once volunteers become aware that an act of theirs may cause a situation such as that, they will agree most eagerly with the rule.

Coordinators should go through the checkin process step by step with the new volunteer. They should show the arrangement of the file, whether it is kept by class or by date, and the arrangement of the cards within each category. Volunteers should be cautioned not to change the order of any cards in the file. If volunteers suspect that a mistake has been made, they are to call it to the attention of the librarian, not change things themselves. One category which seems to cause repeated problems is the 920 section. Even after an explanation, some volunteers find its placement difficult to accept.

The checkin process can be made simple: the volunteer should find the date due in the book, locate the card in the file, card the book (checking to make sure that the card is precisely the right one, not a similar one by the same author or a different copy), check the book for damage, then put the book on the book truck. Additional steps must, of course, be taken with overdue books if there is an overdue file and volunteers should be instructed to hold any books whose cards had notes attached until they are told how to handle them.

Any special procedures should be made clear. In our school, for example, when checking in preschoolers' books, the volunteer follows the ordinary procedure, with the exception of removing a colored card from the book card and filing it, with the paper clip still attached, with the appropriate color in the preschool tray.

Handling Special Notices

Once volunteers have carded even a few books, they will begin to run into special notices of one kind or another. These books may be set aside or dealt with immediately, depending upon how well the volunteers seem to be doing with their tasks and how available someone is to help them. Notices may include reserve notices, in which case the volunteer will need to write a notification slip, put the date on the reserve slip, and put the book on a special shelf. Another familiar notice is a note saying that there is a problem of some sort. These should all come to the librarian until the volunteer has much more experience.

Volunteers should be told that every note on a card means that something needs to be done, and that the book is not to go out until the problem is dealt with.

Handling Overdues

Volunteers may be asked to write out the overdue notices. If they do, they will quickly become disgusted if there is an excessive number of books out. While those volunteers' children will become exemplary citizens, the volunteers themselves may overreact to the problem. They must be helped to understand that citizenship is being taught, but that the highest priority will go to encouraging reading.

Another facet of overdues which will probably irritate volunteers is the number of books not renewed by the teachers, but allowed to become overdue. Efforts to alleviate this may cause the teachers to stop checking out books as often as they have in the past, or it may cause friction between the volunteers and the teachers. On the other hand, most volunteers find it practically impossible to understand why more responsibility is demanded of their children than of the teachers.

Allowing the teachers a longer checkout period will help this situation but may cause more lost books, which will also irritate parents who are struggling to instill good habits in their children. Perhaps the best method is fostering an atmosphere of mutual cooperation so that small problems such as this can be overlooked.

There are many incentives which can be used to help control overdues. The biggest drawback is that most of them take more time than they are worth. Volunteers who are interested, however, could plan and implement a program to offer recognition to those students who do a good job of returning books. In practice, the librarian may find that an inventive class, upon being offered a contest or some type of reward for the fewest overdues, will elect to stop checking out books as a sure-fire method of winning. This, of course, negates any good done by the contest!

Shelving

Shelving is an activity which most people in a library do at one time or another. It should be presented as one of those things which everyone needs to know about and have some skill in. The coordinator should take special pains to see that the volunteer checks the book card against the pocket in every book before placing it on the shelf. This will help lessen the possibility that a book will be checked out with the wrong card. Volunteers should work with one section at a time so that they will become adept at the little variations. If the library is one which serves a church as well as a parochial school, the coordinator should emphasize the difference between the school and the church collections. They are easy to confuse.

Another area which will call for special attention is the biographies. Volunteers who seldom work at shelving will probably have some trouble if the 920 designation is used. Once they have had some experience in locating the section and in using the subject's name instead of the author's, the volunteers will adapt; some will even come to prefer the biographies.

The coordinator should use care in distinguishing among other sections of the library as well. The volunteer should be instructed to take the call number letter by letter (or number by number) in discovering its correct place, and the coordinator should emphasize the fact that a misplaced book is actually, for all but the casual browser, a lost book.

Some volunteers may wish to organize huge stacks of books on the book cart and spend hours doing so without ever putting a book on the shelf. Such helpers should be guided to organize a group of books, then shelve it. Otherwise, the unshelved books will grow and grow, yet the volunteers will be very busy (and unproductive).

Shelvers should straighten each shelf as they add books. It takes only a minute to do so, and keeps the library looking neat. Once all the books are shelved, the volunteers can stand back and glance over the collection. If they see that a few shelves were not straightened that day, they can briefly do so.

Coordinators may find that some of their volunteers really resent it if anyone "messes up" their shelves. They should be encouraged to realize that a library will be in a constant state of untidiness if it is used well. It is up to caring people to repeatedly straighten it. The students do need to be taught how to use the library, but no one should put so much emphasis on neatness that desire to use the library is lessened.

Using the Card Catalog

Every person who will work around students should be able to use the card catalog and to locate materials in the library. Students should be exposed to adults who constantly refer to the card catalog in seeking a variety of answers. Volunteers should regularly respond to a student's request for help with "Let's go to the card catalog." Once there, they should guide the student to the proper place rather than find it for him. By the end of the first grade, many students will be able to locate anything they can spell. The most frequent problems that a volunteer will have with the card catalog will include alternate subject headings and alphabetizing with numbers and abbreviations. The latter can be overcome with practice. As for the former, when working with students, the volunteer should encourage them to offer their ideas on what subjects to look under, and together they should seek the help of the librarian if they cannot find what they need.

The coordinator will soon find that, just as checking books out is, to many people, what a librarian really does, so the card catalog is a symbol for the incomprehensible, the overwhelming side of a library. Unfortunately, many people grew up without using a card catalog. Perhaps there was one in a library which they used, but they were never encouraged to explore it. For some, the first real exposure was in college, when the experience was surrounded by the feelings of helplessness and insecurity caused by a research paper or by seeing more scholarly people working with assurance.

Even though it may seem unnecessary, the coordinator should mention to the volunteer that cards are never to be taken from the drawer. Some helpful recruits have been known to take the card out in order to locate the book more easily!

If the library is a small one and files the shelflist in the same cabinet as the card catalog, volunteers should be told of the difference. They should be encouraged to remind children who use the catalog when they seem to forget. Some are so intent on alphabetical order that they do not realize that they are in the wrong drawer.

Being able to use the card catalog will not be very useful unless the volunteer can locate different sections of the library and understand the designations on the cards. While this will come with experience, it will help if the volunteer knows where to go for information without interrupting the librarian.

General Instructions

Along with the training in the specific skill, the coordinator should inform volunteers of situations they may face while doing that particular task. For instance, if they are carding books while at the circulation desk, students and teachers may come to them for help in locating books or solving questions about an overdue book or request. The volunteers should know what the coordinator wants them to do both during the learning period and afterwards. Should they call for help? Should they stop carding and help the patron themselves? If so, they will need to be trained concurrently in using the card catalog and in how to find answers to the most common questions.

Training Techniques

Many of the duties typically assigned to volunteers can best be described as a combination of distinctive skills. Taught in this way, volunteers will more readily move from one task to another, and develop a kind of overriding expertise with which they can acquire many more skills in a minimum of time. If volunteers know that they can succeed in most of the segments of a whole, they will have enough self-confidence not only to make a project succeed, but also to overcome any feelings of inferiority caused by minor failures. This can be particularly beneficial when temporary help is needed.

In line with that, when volunteers first begin work, they should be guided to recognize tasks as a series of specific skills which can be combined in many ways. They can thus learn to recognize checking books in as a combination of skills which include alphabetizing (which will be useful in using the card catalog and in locating materials on the shelves), differentiating between different categories of library materials (which will help in locating and shelving them), locating those books needing repair (which will help in mending and in teaching children how to care for books), handling overdues (which will help in awareness of one of the major problems of libraries, in locating request books, and in teaching the students good citizenship), reserving books (which will help in taking requests and in becoming aware of the needs of the library), and putting the books on the book cart to be shelved (which will help with understanding library scheduling and the sporadic need for everyone to pitch in when there is an influx of books). All of these tasks will increase the volunteers' awareness of the problems with which libraries have to deal and with possible solutions. They will develop skills which can be used in other areas and which may give them the incentive to ask for additional or different jobs.

The coordinator must be very sure to give sufficient training and to be available for questions. Many volunteers will be willing to work but remain unsure of themselves even after some practice. One sure way to have problems later is to assume without reason that workers are confident in a particular area and then to leave them in a position to make even minor decisions without guidance. Volunteers will naturally do their best, based on the information they have assimilated. But it is desirable for them to discuss their choices or decisions with the coordinator fairly frequently. If they do not, the coordinator may never locate any mistakes. Some tasks are particularly risky, in that the error will not be obvious until it is very difficult to correct it. Other tasks will provide a situation in which mistakes are easy to spot but hard to correct, such as on a bulletin board or a flyer which has already been printed. The idea is to teach and to be available for questions until the volunteer is very competent. At that time, the closeness of supervision can be lessened. The volunteer will then be in a position to give real help to the library with very little additional time invested by professionals.

The coordinator must watch the volunteer and their work for signals that they are ready for more. "More" will not necessarily mean additional range; it will usually mean a deeper understanding and a wider application of the existing routine. This method of learning and relearning in greater and greater depth is the spiral which seems the best way for most people to gain knowledge. With this system, the volunteer will master each stage before moving on to the next. Most people are familiar with this method, and feel secure with it, since they have used it from birth. Volunteers can relax and know that they have conquered the first curve as they work on the second. Most volunteers enjoy the feeling of being increasingly good at something (see table 7.4); this is more encouraging than it would be to continually add new skills without the opportunity to become better than mediocre at them.

Table 7.4

What Are People Really Like?

THEY ...

1. Grow when motivated
2. Work harder after each success
3. Basically want to succeed
4. Are goal seeking
5. Become committed when involved
6. Want to do more and better work

THEN WE MUST NOT ...

1. Assume their goal is to avoid work
2. Manage by threat
3. Use punishment to motivate
4. Inhibit natural growth by too much control

Adapted from *Finding Time for Success and Happiness through Time Management* by Ivan W. Fitzwater, by permission of Mandel Publications, a division of Management Development Institute. Copyright, 1977, Management Development Institute, Inc.

Volunteer Manual

There should, of course, be a policy and procedures manual for the volunteers. This manual is an important part of any volunteer program. It includes detailed instruction on each phase of work which is handled by volunteers. It is simple and easy to understand. Each volunteer is given a copy and there is at least one available at the library. Volunteers are told that the manual serves two main purposes: it gives a recruit a well-rounded idea of what others are doing and it provides a checklist with which to brush up on procedures when the volunteer is unsure of himself.

Items which are usually included are a policy statement on the use of volunteers in that particular library, a statement of goals, and the description of procedures. Illustrations will help make the manual understandable and visually appealing.

Good manuals are up-to-date. This currency should reflect the state of the individual library, even if it differs somewhat with standard procedure. (See sample manuals in appendix C.)

UNDERSTANDING THE SCHEDULE

One of the best methods of introducing volunteers to the active life of the library is to go over all schedules with them. They will emerge from this training session with a good overview of the functions of the library and the ways in which the personnel interact. They will also have the ability to read the schedules, which is not as easy to do as it sounds.

One essential schedule is the written schedule of library use which notes any group or activity that needs a special area reserved or that would interfere with the use of any area by another group or individual. Volunteers, after having the schedule interpreted, will be told how to schedule classes which want additional movie time or research time. It is wise to tell volunteers that they can tentatively schedule library use for a teacher, but that the librarian will verify it. In this way the teacher can reserve the time as quickly as possible, and there is a back-up system.

The work schedule will also be explained to the volunteers. They will know that they are expected and when, and who their coworkers will be.

Volunteers also need to know who is involved in film acquisition and how the system works, since they may be asked to fill in.

All the guidelines discussed in this section are from a specific library. Other librarians will have slightly different situations and will wish to devise guidelines which are modified for their libraries. While the details may have endless variations, each topic should be covered.

SPECIAL PROGRAMS

At the same time that volunteers are being trained in the general tasks expected of everyone, they can be exposed to their particular areas of concentration. While a few people will wish to handle mainly the secretarial type of tasks, dealing with universal duties and with a multitude of things which come up unexpectedly, most volunteers will prefer to have one or two areas in which they can become very adept and in which they can feel a sense of progression toward a goal. The following discussion will center around some special programs that volunteers may undertake.

Bulletin Boards

The volunteer should be encouraged to view the bulletin boards as a method of advertising the library and its programs and of encouraging participation in both students and teachers.

If volunteers work on bulletin boards at school, they should come on days when they will be able to use a table without interfering with a class or another project. This is a task which can take some space and should thus not be compressed any more than necessary. Volunteers should know that the coordinator is aware of what is involved and that it is important enough to assign a work area. In addition, volunteers should have a place for equipment, such as scissors, tape, pins, and so forth. The object is to allow these volunteers to begin work as quickly as they can with as little of the frustration connected with searching out supplies as possible. In addition, if volunteers will need to get materials from a school supply closet, they should have access to any keys they will need. Some very creative people work on bulletin boards, and they sometimes make use of supplies in strange but surprisingly attractive ways, so the coordinator should encourage a broad range of boards.

The volunteer should be encouraged to design some bulletin boards which inspire student participation. These may be in the form of contests, quizzes, or something as simple as plain paper with the title, "What books did you read during the summer?" Attaching a couple of markers will encourage a deluge of comments.

Another type of bulletin board which the volunteer should be encouraged to maintain is one located in the classroom area of the school. This can be particularly effective if it is one which often has questions whose answers can be found in the library.

One of the more popular projects for a volunteer to come up with seems to be the display of cultural events going on in the community. This project, properly maintained, will reflect positively on the library and will require a small amount of time from one person, or very little from several. The person responsible would need to watch for announcements of coming events, both live and on television. He would need to create a display, one which is attractive and, hopefully, more than just a depository for flyers. For instance, when the ballet is in town, a pair of old ballet slippers combined with a flyer and perhaps a copy of the score or a book jacket of the story would be attractive. An easy project; there is however one cardinal sin which needs to be avoided: leaving material up after the last performance. It is better to have an empty bulletin board than one which is out of date.

Bulletin board volunteers can become as involved as they wish with other school groups, encouraging them to participate in creating bulletin boards which will show the connection of their clubs or classrooms with the library. In this way, bulletin boards will be more varied and will be tied in with the interests of those in the school.

Good bulletin boards will draw many favorable comments, even from people who are just walking through the school. These should be relayed to the volunteer along with a comment about how proud it makes the librarian to hear such nice things. This kind of reward is worth a great deal to most volunteers, but compliments are valueless if the volunteers never hear them.

Doing bulletin boards is one of those jobs which may spill over into the volunteers' spare time. Once they start on a particularly interesting display, they will probably work on parts of it at home. If the coordinator is relying on them to assist with the desk while working at their assigned task, this should be made very clear. Otherwise, the volunteer may feel that, once a given board is up, they need not come to work that week. They should know that time they spend at home is not required, though it is appreciated.

Another way of handling bulletin boards is to have a bulletin board chairman who will make out a schedule and see that members of the committee have new boards up on time. This can work very well or not, depending upon the number of volunteers and the executive ability of the chairman. One library maintained seven bulletin boards schoolwide, changing each one every two weeks on a revolving basis. This rather ambitious schedule could only be maintained by an excellent chairman and many devoted volunteers.

Birthday Donations

One of the most popular and most profitable projects a volunteer can handle is a strong birthday donation program. This will be popular with the children and with the parents, and will bring in money as well as creating positive publicity. The task can be handled by one volunteer who comes frequently or by several who will work in smaller units. A list including each child's birthday can be obtained from the school office. Once a month, a letter should go out to each parent whose child will have a birthday during the next month. The letter should be friendly and caring, and should offer the parent an opportunity to celebrate the child's completion of another year with a book dedicated to him. See figure 7.5 for a sample letter. Children enjoy seeing their names and those of their friends and may encourage the parents to send money or to choose a book themselves. A return card should be included which states the child's name, birthdate, the parent's name and address, and what size donation is being made.

When money is received, thank-you notes should be mailed and/or notes sent to the children telling them of the honor. A book should be chosen, a book plate placed in it, and the title included in the letter. In this way children can locate their books easily. The librarian may wish to hold the donated book so that the birthday child can be the first person to check it out. Volunteers would need to be very sure that records are in good order so that if there is a question later it can be answered easily.

Some parents will wish to select a book themselves or to let the child choose one. This should be discouraged unless it is done after consulting the librarian. Too many times children will select an old favorite, only to find that the library already owns enough copies, or they may want a book that is not suitable in some way for that particular library.

One positive way to solve this problem is to maintain a shelf of books which the library needs from which the parents can choose. Another way is to allow the child to see books which have already been purchased and are in some stage of processing. From these they can choose interesting books.

Dear

    A very special celebration will take place soon. _____ will receive a birthday prayer during the chapel service on (his/her) special day. I would like to invite you to attend the chapel service and celebrate this most important event in your child's life.

    Our school library would also like to offer to you the opportunity to share your joy for the life of your child by giving a book in (his/her) name for the use of all our students at St. Luke's.

    An appropriate name plate, with your child's birthday date, will be placed in a book of your choice ... or our librarian will select a book for you.

    Gifts of $5 to $50 will help us to stock our library with the finest in children's literature.

    Please accept my best wishes on the day that we thank God for the gift of your child.

                                        Sincerely,

                                        The Rev. Chris Jones, Jr.,
                                        Headmaster

St. Luke's Episcopal School   San Antonio, Texas 78209

Fig. 7.5. Sample letter suggesting "birthday donation." Reprinted by permission of St. Luke's Episcopal School.

If the school owns a word processor or if the volunteer has access to one, the procedure of sending out letters will be vastly simplified. This is a profitable program with a minimum of involvement, but anything which can make things go more quickly is highly desirable.

One of the bulletin boards in the lobby area would be a wonderful place to publicize donations of books or money, although it should be general enough that a small donation will not embarrass its donor. One donation will encourage another, and the program will soon be on its way.

These special projects need not be year-long activities. Many are short-term, especially those which deal with the beautification of the library. The establishment of a planter, making a bulletin board, and setting up a teacher's collection are all brief projects which will be effective for years. Many people enjoy volunteering for activities like these, since commitment is brief and results longlasting.

Programs Created by Volunteers

Sometimes volunteers come in not because they feel they can supply a need that already exists in the library, but because they have ideas that they feel would make the library better, ones that they are willing to devote some time to. When this happens, the coordinator must gather enough facts about the scope of the project and the goals of the volunteer to make a wise decision. Many projects are good ideas but would not be feasible in a given library. Coordinators should beware of any projects which would entail using already overloaded volunteers. If, however, there are willing workers with little or nothing to do, coordinators will probably wish to investigate any new proposal. To be a good idea, the project should be one which will in some way, even marginally, benefit the library and its patrons. It must be one which can be accomplished with a minimum of confusion (allowing, of course, for that necessary period of working things through), a project which can be left entirely, or almost, to volunteers rather than demanding precious professional time, and one which will reflect positively on the library.

Many people are "gung-ho" about one thing or another. This enthusiasm should not influence coordinators into making decisions which will be detrimental to the library, or ones which will require that they spend time they really cannot spare. Eager volunteers should be willing to obligate themselves for the length of time that their projects will require.

While coordinators must be wary of overinvolvement and of detrimental projects, they should be open to investigating promising proposals. Many of our finest programs began as the brainchild of a volunteer. The coordinator's approach should be to investigate each proposal thoroughly, then make a decision which will fall into one of three categories: the plan will be rejected, it will be allowed to fail or succeed with little help from the librarian, or it will be actively encouraged and promoted by the library and its staff. Most will fall into the first and third categories. The coordinator should beware of accepting many proposals of the second kind, since, in case of failure, the negative publicity will be attached to the library. The coordinator will wish to foster an image of positive growth and success, not of failure after failure. There may, however, be a time when the merits of a particular project outweigh the fact that the coordinator has little time with which to help.

Once the proposition has been accepted, the coordinator should go over the volunteer's plans or spend some time in helping to formulate those plans. Neglecting to do this will almost assure mistakes in judgment. The average volunteer will not know the school, its goals, and its atmosphere as well as the coordinator, and may, therefore, fail to take into consideration some important factor. A little time spent initially will certainly be worthwhile. After that the project can more or less be turned over to the volunteer, with the understanding that the coordinator will review its progress from time to time. Coordinators should assure the volunteer of their willingness to help should a need arise.

By the next year, the project will either have burned itself out or proved its worth. At that point, the coordinator will decide whether to take it on as a part of the regular program, let it continue as a program sponsored by the volunteer, or eliminate it.

A few examples may suffice to show how varied these parent-conceived plans may be, and how valuable. The range of ideas is as broad as that of the volunteer pool.

Lunch Program

In schools which do not provide any lunches or in those which do not provide any snack foods, a lunch program can be a source of both revenue and favorable publicity. The heads of the program, preferably volunteers, will determine, with the school administration, whether there are any legal restrictions, how frequent the lunches will be, whether monthly, weekly, or daily. They will then contact various fast food restaurants to find one which will provide a popular bill of fare at a price just over cost. To this they will add a profit margin. This project will involve relatively few people, depending upon the size of the school. One person should volunteer to drive to the restaurant to get the food. This person should be very dependable, since the children need to eat on schedule. That person or another should divide the lunches according to classes or grades and hand them out to the teachers. Another person should be available to hand out lunches to visitors, if eating with children is permitted in the school.

Once the chairman has acquired volunteers, an order sheet which will include each child's name (all those in one family can be on the same sheet), the class of each child, whether the order includes any visitors, the cost, and the menu should be designed (see fig. 7.6, page 128). If the lunch occurs more than a couple of times a month, some variety might be appreciated. This may involve dealing with more than one restaurant or simply ordering a different meal from the same one. The sheet should also include a deadline by which all the orders for a month should be in. Compiling orders any more often than that is not viable. Order sheets should be passed out to the classes about a week before the deadline, with a reminder a couple of days later. Absolutely no orders should be taken after the deadline, since, human nature being what it is, people will learn to drift in with new orders even after the total has been called in to the restaurant. Once all sheets are in, the chairman will compile them, call in totals to the restaurant, and make copies of names and orders for the teachers. The chairman should make every attempt to convince the restaurant

St. Luke's Episcopal School
Wednesday Lunches $2.00

	Chicken Day Feb. 4	Hamburger Day Feb. 11	Chicken Day Feb. 18	Hamburger Day Feb. 25
Deadline Date: January 30, 1981				

Child's Name _____

Class _____

Child's Name _____

Class _____

Child's Name _____

Class _____

Visitor's Name _____
(May Be Picked up in the Library)

Visitor's Name _____
(May Be Picked up in the Library)

Visitor's Name _____
(May Be Picked up in the Library)

Total Number of Lunches Ordered _____

Total Amount Enclosed _____

Chicken Lunch Includes: 2 Pieces Fried Chicken (Popeye's)
French Fries
Pudding

Hamburger Lunch Includes: Quarter Pounder Hamburger
Fruit
Cookie
Chips

COME AND HAVE LUNCH
WITH YOUR CHILD ON WEDNESDAYS

Fig. 7.6. Sample order sheet. Reprinted by permission of St. Luke's Episcopal School.

to ship the order in boxes by grade, if not by class. This will greatly expedite handing out the food.

On lunch day, the chairman should be available for questions. The most common will probably be whether there will be a refund if a child is absent, and queries about whether or not someone ordered a lunch. If the chairman decides not to charge if a child misses a lunch, credit rather than a refund should be given. Once the method is decided upon, precise records must be kept. The chairman must be sure that teachers know to return all unused lunches and the names of absentees. Then the volunteer will have extras to sell. This can create a problem with people coming all morning asking to be put on a list for extras, and being disappointed if there are not enough. If orders for extra are taken, there should be a strict rule that they will be sold only to adults, not to students. This will prevent students' learning to come to school without a good lunch, depending on hypothetical extras. No lunch should be sold as a leftover until ten or fifteen minutes after the lunch period begins, since someone, especially a visitor, may be a little late.

Every effort must be made to see that there is no confusion with the number of lunches or their distribution. Anything, such as calling in more than one order, which opens a possibility for mistakes is to be avoided assiduously.

Children will learn to love their special lunch days, mothers will revel in a morning without fixing a lunch, and the library can benefit from the profit made on each meal. Output of energy, after the planning stage, is one day a month to duplicate and distribute order sheets, one day a month to compile orders and call them in, and a couple of hours each lunch day to get the lunches and distribute them. Not a bad outlay for the profit in money and good will!

Newspaper

A school newspaper or literary magazine is something which most schools cannot find time to handle without a journalism class. The idea appeals to so many people, however, that sooner or later someone will probably approach the library coordinator with the idea. The concept is good, the results will be popular, and the experience worthwhile for the children. Unfortunately, working with a newspaper takes a great deal of time from the volunteer sponsor and from the newspaper staff. Most students will find that they have little time during school and little incentive after school. The sponsor may become frustrated when he tries to get good material on important school topics on a regular basis.

If a volunteer decides to sponsor a literary magazine, problems will be lessened. Teachers and students can turn in things written by the students for assignments or for pleasure. In this way there will be no extra burden on the child.

Any time a student's work is published, a decision has to be made about the amount of editing. This decision needs to be supported by the principal, since the product will reflect on his school. Whether the sponsor does no editing, a little, or complete editing, someone will probably disagree. This is to be expected. Whatever the decision, it must be consistent. Unfortunately, mistakes in the writing of first graders are usually viewed as cute, while those of fifth graders are all too often viewed as lack of ability or poor quality of education. The greatest mistake of all would be to edit one child's work and to print another child's of the same age just as it was originally written. Hell hath no fury like the wrath of a parent whose child has been made to look inferior publicly.

If a volunteer is to do a newspaper, she should first work out a schedule of meeting times with the students. If a school does not involve children in after-school activities, this will be difficult. There must be time allowed for assignments and explaining them, there must be time to go over work and reassign it if more information is needed, and there must be time for the students to collate their newly-printed paper and distribute it. Needless to say, the average teacher would view this as too much time to be away from the class.

If, however, the news staff can meet after school, the volunteer will find that his job is much easier and that the students are enjoying their work more. (A sample student application form may be found in fig. 7.7.) One two-hour meeting per week would probably be sufficient to put out a newspaper if there are enough students to share the assignments, or if the size of the paper were kept to a minimum.

However the paper is handled, it must be done with sensitivity and fairness. The paper should not emphasize one grade level to the exclusion of others, or spotlight one child repeatedly. Given a fair chance, a school newspaper can be a rewarding experience. Poorly planned, however, it will probably rank at the top of the list of bad projects, because it will involve everyone in the school.

ST. LUKE'S *SPIRIT*

St. Luke's Episcopal School
11 St. Luke's Lane
San Antonio, Texas 78209
826-0664

JOB APPLICATION

I would like to apply for the job of _____
for the St. Luke's *Spirit*. I would like this job because:

I understand that I will be expected to do my work as assigned and to turn it in on time.

NAME (Signed) _____

CLASS _____

Fig. 7.7. Application for position on school newspaper. Reprinted by permission of St. Luke's Episcopal School.

REASSESSMENT

After several work sessions, coordinators should have an interview during which they make any necessary changes in the volunteer's task area. If they are pleased with the placement of the volunteers, they should make this clear but offer the opportunity to change if the volunteer is unhappy there. Rarely will volunteers choose to alter things. By this stage they will have begun to establish a niche for themselves. They will be feeling more secure about the job requirements. If they do want to change, it will indicate a really important feeling, so the move should be made with all expediency. By this time the coordinator will know the volunteers' capabilities better and be able to select jobs more tailored to the individual.

If the coordinator feels that it is necessary to change a volunteer's designated task, it should be done with tact and kindness. It will rarely be necessary to tell volunteers that they do not seem to be capable of working alone, or seem to have no self-motivation, or do not seem to be able to work well with the current group of volunteers. Rather, the needs of the library can be stressed so much that the volunteer will be honored to be chosen to help in another area which is so obviously in need of quality support. For example, volunteers may not seem to be able to take direction; they may want to reorganize existing systems and seem unable to work without doing so; they may resent interference even from the coordinator. People like this have obvious skills which should be tapped by assigning them to areas over which they can have almost total jurisdiction, and by emphasizing the fact that they will have almost complete responsibility to perform the task for the benefit of the library. Such a volunteer could organize and more or less direct a fund-raising activity, develop a lively request department which can respond almost immediately to all requests and work more closely with both students and teachers in order to discover just what they would like to have in the library, or develop and manage an active donation system. The main goal would be to assign an area which is limited in scope and which could be worked many ways any one of which would be acceptable as long as the desired result is attained. Doing this will have multiple benefits: the volunteer will no longer interfere in established programs, an excellently developed new program will be initiated (or one which had previously been mediocre improved), and, most important, volunteers will develop a sense of self-worth and loyalty to the library which would have been totally lacking had they been left in constant contention over various issues.

The coordinator must keep in mind that as a volunteer becomes more and more familiar with a task, he may decide at that point that it is just not for him. Unfortunately, many people feel that work in a library is very simple. While none of it is insurmountable, some does require repeated effort to master. If at any time a volunteer evidences dissatisfaction with a job, the coordinator should talk with that volunteer. If only part of the task is causing a problem, the coordinator should help the volunteer overcome it. Often the real problem is a feeling that one's efforts are not appreciated enough. This need is easy to satisfy. If, however, the problem lies in the basic nature of the task, the coordinator would do well to move such a volunteer as quickly as possible in order to avoid a real attitude problem. Sometimes volunteers will not realize, in spite of being told, exactly what the implications of a job are. If they have volunteered to read shelves on a day when there is one class after another, only to discover that they cannot bear to see their nice neat books being loved into some disorder, then perhaps a change in schedule would help, rather than a change in task area. Any volunteer will realize that the books will eventually look disarrayed, but some may not be able to cope with actually seeing it happen. Putting a little space between the volunteer and the eager patron will probably solve this type of problem.

SUBSTITUTING

Once volunteers have a good grasp of library policy and can be considered authorities in the general aspects of the library, they will become that most needed of human beings: capable substitutes. In a situation in which there is one staff member in a school library, it is usually better to have volunteers trained in that library act as substitutes rather than the substitutes the teachers use. These people may have degrees in education but relatively little knowledge of libraries, and practically no knowledge of the library in which they are substituting. It is truly awe inspiring to come back after a day's absence and see what has been wrought by someone unfamiliar with a library, even if written instructions have been provided. Volunteers know better than to make unnecessary executive decisions. They know the rules. They know the atmosphere of the library. It is quite a shock to children to have a free, open, friendly library one day, and the next, to be told they cannot come in unless they are returning a book, and to be asked to sit down, and not even to whisper. It can take weeks to develop trust again in a child subjected to that change. That situation would not happen with volunteers. They would support the rules and atmosphere they had learned to equate with that library.

In order for volunteers to be successful in substituting, they must have had experience in most of the things they will be required to do. They must know how to work the desk, how to read and follow the schedule, what the rules are for children and for teachers, and how to conduct the library classes, if necessary. They should know that all decisions based on their knowledge of that library will be supported even if they make some mistakes.

There are few professional librarians on substitute lists. Trained volunteers are the next best substitute. The need would be less likely to arise in libraries with more than one staff member, but when it does, a good second-best is sometimes highly desirable.

Once volunteers have been used as substitutes, the coordinator will probably discover that a remarkable change has come over them. No longer will they wait patiently until the coordinator discovers that they have completed their tasks and are ready for another. Volunteers who have had the sole responsibility of the library for an entire day will henceforward typically be self-assured and eager to branch out. During their tenure as substitute librarians they will have been brought face to face not only with those things which they felt that they knew just how to cope with, how to handle, and how to answer. They also would have had it made very clear, if only to themselves, the issues about which they were not sure, which questions they could not deal with satisfactorily. Volunteers will then begin a quiet campaign to fill in their knowledge, to flesh out their weak areas. They will hope to be asked to do the job again, and will seek to be better prepared for it. All this will help the library in three ways: volunteers will become more capable as substitutes, they will be able to handle more tasks more capably as regular volunteers, and they will have a better understanding of the library as a whole. In addition, volunteers' self-esteem will have been bolstered considerably. Substituting is one more way in which volunteers can help both themselves and the school.

NOTES

[1]Lillian Biermann Wehmeyer, *The School Library Volunteer* (Littleton, Colo.: Libraries Unlimited, 1975), 7.

8 Predicting and Alleviating Problems

Potential volunteer coordinators often look with trepidation upon the mass of information and personalities with which they will have to deal. In truth, problems with volunteer programs tend to range from minor to insignificant. There are very, very few which happen only with volunteers. Most are "people problems" which can occur any time people get together. The special atmosphere surrounding most volunteer programs tends to insulate them from becoming damaged by the problems which do occur. With insight on the part of coordinators when viewing their own roles, with knowledge of commitments and responsibilities, and with a study of the various relationships involved, and the resultant ability to pinpoint problems, coordinators will come successfully through almost any conceivable difficulty.

THE ROLE OF THE COORDINATOR

Coordinators, of course, are in a position to control almost anything which could be considered a problem in the volunteer system. Before attacking the problems caused by others, they should identify and alleviate those problems to which they themselves may unwittingly be contributing.

In their effort to correct unwanted situations, coordinators will probably wish to change those factors in their own behaviors or attitudes which are encouraging poor results (see table 8.1, page 136). Coordinators must concentrate on motivating themselves just as they do their volunteers, and give themselves corrective training just as they do those under them who have failed to utilize prior training in a satisfactory manner. In other words, all the methods which they use with their volunteers can be used with themselves; they should not expect less of themselves than they do of their recruits. Coordinators must rouse themselves to that pitch of enthusiasm at which the best work is done (see table 8.2, page 137).

(Text continues on page 138.)

Table 8.1

Steps in Changing Your Behavior

A. Adopt a goal

B. Open your mind to new possibilities

C. Devise a plan

D. Build in motivation

E. Visualize benefits

F. Retrain yourself

G. Generate excitement

H. Include others (include benefits to them)

I. Have periodic evaluations

J. Modify goals

Adapted from *Finding Time for Success and Happiness through Time Management* by Ivan W. Fitzwater, by permission of Mandel Publications, a division of Management Development Institute. Copyright, 1977, Management Development Institute, Inc.

Table 8.2

The Four Ingredients of Successful Planning

---

1. *Personnel:* You have some. Don't complain about the men you don't have. Ask, "What can I do with the people I do have?"

2. *Equipment:* You usually have it in abundance. Some of it probably has not seen the light of day in the last year.

3. *A place to train:* Just about anywhere if you have enough of the fourth ingredient in abundance.

4. *Knowledge of goals and your own imagination:* This is all mental: what you have learned about your library, what you know of its capabilities, how much you have studied the environment—it's all in the mind. This knowledge, in conjunction with a little imagination, is the critical ingredient in situational training.

Reprinted with permission from COMMON SENSE TRAINING by Arthur S. Collins, Jr., © 1978 Presidio Press, Publisher, 31 Pamaron Way, Novato, California 94947.

Coordinators will soon come to the realization that they control most volunteer situations: lack of foresight, lack of planning, lack of coordination, inability to delegate—a multitude of problems can result, but almost all can be eliminated with a little thinking and a little action.

The coordinator will wish to develop an ability to isolate problems in the volunteer program, study them, and alleviate them, all within the shortest possible amount of time. One method which will help is to learn to categorize problems.

INTERPERSONAL PROBLEMS

The Staff

Relationships surrounding volunteer service will prove to be a rich source of rewards, but will also provide the potential for problems. Friendships between volunteers and staff members will form a caring, secure environment to which volunteers will be eager to return. A special bond will probably be formed with the coordinator, due partly to the reliance the volunteer may feel. Friendships with other staff members will broaden and deepen this feeling of belonging. Coordinators must be observant about the nature of friendships which develop. If they see trouble such as lowered work level resulting, they should direct the participants toward other means of interaction. Friendships must never interfere with work or authority. For this reason, some coordinators might feel they need to be somewhat reserved. While this will help maintain authority, it will also act as a damper on the volunteers' feelings of acceptance and thus on their enthusiasm. A better means is honesty. Open discussions with the volunteer and with any involved staff member will usually bring about desired results. Volunteers are truly remarkable. They really care about their organizations and want to help as much as possible. Making them a part of the overall goal is the fastest way to insure their cooperation.

Disagreements between volunteers and staff members are very rare. When they do occur it is usually through misunderstanding. In order to alleviate possible problems, some issues must be handled before they arise (see table 8.3). Staff members must be very careful not to criticize volunteers. Complaints should go through the coordinator, who should, in their training sessions, be sure the volunteer is told of any rules or preferences of staff members.

While it is important that the volunteer not be subjected to criticism from more than one source, the one exception should be specific information pertaining to a task which is supervised by another. For instance, if a staff member has been asked to teach a volunteer to shelve books, that staff member could correct any mistakes in shelving. In all other matters, the coordinator should deal with the volunteer. If staff members who are up-line in authority have complaints, they need to present them to the coordinator, who will then discuss them with the volunteer. Since volunteers have no established position in the library, they feel particularly vulnerable and must be protected as much as possible.

Staff members must be discreet about in-house information. Volunteers are as interested as anyone else in gossip, and gossip is certainly a means of becoming part of an existing group faster. A volunteer will rarely pass

Table 8.3

Problems

Who Is to Blame?

Problem	Cause
Unplanned interruptions	Failure to delegate
Lack of solutions by volunteers	Failure to train volunteers
Unclear goals in organization	Failure to plan
Volunteer mistakes	Failure to provide wholesome accountability
Excess volunteer personal problems coming to you	Failure to maintain organizational structure

Adapted from *Finding Time for Success and Happiness through Time Management* by Ivan W. Fitzwater, by permission of Mandel Publications, a division of Management Development Institute. Copyright, 1977, Management Development Institute, Inc.

reasonable bounds in asking for information. On the other hand, he will rarely pass up an opportunity to hear gossip when it is freely given. Indiscriminate conversation can do much harm, but this is a problem with the staff, not the volunteer. If a library's staff has frequent problems with gossip, a volunteer program will probably make it worse, since the volunteer will be in a position to decide what to do with the information. If, however, a library is well run by true professionals, any negative conversation will be more in the nature of constructive criticism. This, in turn, will have a salutary effect on the volunteers. They will see people working on problems, not magnifying them. Staff members need to be very aware that they lose control of the way information will be used when they take anyone into their confidence. Many issues simply do not concern volunteers, and it is better not to bring them up.

In school volunteer systems, a special situation exists. Volunteers in the library might be working very closely with their children's teachers. It does little good to tell volunteers not to discuss their private problems, such as children's grades and behavior problems, while they are working in the library if the teacher encourages such discussion. In all ways, members of an organization must work together in establishing the role of the volunteer.

Staff members should not second-guess volunteer motivation. Volunteers do indeed have motives; each person will have one or more reasons for volunteering. Coordinators need to know these so that they can tailor work experiences to satisfy these needs. Other staff members should accept the volunteer's offer of help and let it ease their workload without examining reasons.

The role of the administration should be that of decision-maker and supporter. Principals should, of course, have had power of veto on establishing any volunteer programs. After these have been decided upon, the principals should present them to the staff and issue any guidelines, such as lines of authority, what to do with complaints about volunteers, and so forth. In addition, they need to make the office staff aware of the situation. Depending upon the size of the organization, the office might see a great deal of the volunteers. If so, the staff will definitely be affected. Volunteers in a small school, for instance, will feel freer to go to the office for help and for complaints. The office must be prepared to handle situations which arise.

Most school staffs support volunteer programs; this support must be nurtured through careful staff-volunteer relationships. The result will be mutual growth and enthusiasm.

The Volunteers

The most frequent type of problem is that some volunteers have difficulty working together, either from antagonism or from friendship. This happens even in a salaried situation with staff members and usually results in the resignation of one party or in a long-term strained atmosphere which is unpleasant for everyone. Happily, when this occurs in a volunteer situation it is much easier to solve.

There are many things which can irritate people. Perhaps some volunteers have particularly strong personalities. Those working with them are likely to feel like wallflowers at best and, at worst, downtrodden. Problems will arise if one volunteer tries to establish dominion over another. If ever any human

Interpersonal Problems / 141

beings were created free and equal, it was volunteers. Similarly, sometimes volunteers develop a personal and very strong feeling about their work. This is frequent, since coordinator must emphasize the need for everything they ask their volunteers to do. Some people care so deeply that they lose their perspective and feel that their needs supersede those of other volunteers. This can be very annoying, since the attitude is projected that the second volunteer's job is of lesser value. It is terribly difficult to get dressed, put off things you need to do, and go to a volunteer job, sinus headache and all, when the job is not important. Coordinators must be sure that their programs are run equitably, and that volunteers know the value of their own work and that of others.

Another typical problem is that volunteers have friendships with each other outside of the library which can deteriorate. In spite of great effort on both parts, this can affect their work in the library.

Solutions? Most of them are easy: separate the two people, either by changing the day one of them works (stressing, of course, the fact that you desperately need help on the new day, while ignoring the problem, which will then no longer exist) or by cross-training one in a job which will physically separate one from the other, this time emphasizing the fact that they are now ready for expansion, not of work load, but of responsibility.

If one volunteer tries to establish authority over another, the preceding solution might work, since some people are less easily dominated than others. The coworkers on the new day might be more forceful. If changing the schedule does not work, the coordinator will need to have a conference. A person who is involved in this kind of problem is usually very strong and sometimes very dedicated. The coordinator must work to channel that dedication so that it will not be lessened but will allow others the right to work unbothered.

If one volunteer trains another, there is potential for trouble. Even though some can perform satisfactorily, they cannot necessarily teach. Any miscommunication will cause the second party to look bad; this is not acceptable to most volunteers.

The solution to training problems is for coordinators to train people themselves. Sometimes that is not feasible, but if training is delegated, coordinators should be very sure to supervise it.

Some volunteers are so attuned to "making good on the job" that they will rarely have any problems with patrons. The most common problem that might occur will be that library rules might not satisfy the volunteers' ideas of propriety. They might feel that a limit, a stricter limit, or no limit should be put on checking out materials. They might disagree with the noise level allowed. They might feel that use of materials should be limited (or not limited) by age. These are really problems between the volunteer and the librarian, but they might surface through the patron. The best way to alleviate these problems is knowledge. The coordinator should be sure the volunteers understand the reasons for the rules, and that they understand that they are to work with these rules whether they agree or not. They are not to discuss their opinions with the patrons, as this might encourage dissatisfaction. If volunteers find that they cannot adjust to the way things are, they need either to be put into a job in which the irritating factor is not present or they need to be dismissed. Unhappy volunteers who cannot adjust and cannot avoid the source of their unhappiness will only cause trouble. Once everything has been tried and has failed, it is time to admit failure and go on to other things.

The last main problem directly concerning volunteers is excessive talking. They appear regularly and on time, the work they do is excellent, but volume is low. The best solution is to change the work day of one of the volunteers. The next best is to change jobs. If necessary, the coordinator should discuss the problem with each party, trying to secure cooperation. This solution is tenuous at best, since an artificial restraint will have been erected which will contribute to an uncomfortable atmosphere. It is far better to eliminate the situation which allows the problems.

PROBLEMS WITH RESPONSIBILITY

In examining problem areas, the interested observer will discover the importance of defining spheres of responsibility. Both volunteers and coordinators must have a clearcut idea of their duties. Dissension and dissatisfaction arise when expectations are not met. Since the coordinator's view of the volunteers' responsibilities does not always match their view, and vice versa, it is of paramount importance that these be delineated early.

Some commitments require effort from both the coordinator and the volunteer; for instance, there should be some understanding about the time commitment. If the volunteers must come on a certain day at a certain time, they should be told to do so.

Any requirements for absenteeism (usually prior notification) must be noted. Absenteeism is one of the more frequent problems with volunteers. Coordinators of volunteer programs must expect this and not schedule themselves into a corner. Volunteers make things easier for everyone concerned, but the library should be able to function without them. In the initial interview and periodically after that, volunteers should be reminded that they should call if they cannot come in. Since a large volunteer program will have an overall attrition rate of about one-fourth to one-third, and a hard core of dedicated, dependable volunteers of about one-third, the rest of the program will consist of people who are usually dependable but who sometimes miss. The reasons are legion: babies, illness, car trouble, out-of-town company, business, trips. All are valid to the volunteer. The coordinator must stress the need for advance notice and the need to have the work accomplished as soon as possible. Many volunteers will come in an extra time to make up work, or, if possible, take it home.

If make-up time is required, this should be discussed. Most volunteers will respond negatively to this, since they are being asked to do more than salaried people. It is far better to indicate that, while it is not required, make-up work would certainly be appreciated. If a substitute is required, this needs to be established from the beginning, as well as who is responsible for that arrangement. Most volunteers feel very strongly that they have made a commitment; many even feel that they should perform as if they were working for pay. It is hard to ask for more dedication than this!

Another obligation which involves both parties is initiative. The coordinator must decide whether volunteers should, when they finish one job, begin another that they see is in need of doing. The coordinator might feel that volunteers should finish their jobs and ask for others. For instance, if a volunteer's regular job is to process books, and he finishes those available, he should know whether he should shelve or check in books, if he sees a need, or whether he is to report to the coordinator. In either case, he should be very aware that he should not attempt work about which he knows nothing. It is very unusual to find a volunteer who would even consider that. Initiative in many cases includes being willing to do work which is needed at the moment but is not part of the regular assignment. Volunteers should be asked either to assume jobs or to ask for extra work, not to wait until the coordinator comes to them.

Responsibilities of the Volunteer

Initiative covers a great deal: doing assigned work as well as possible, giving the coordinator necessary information (for instance, if the library has a baby sitter for the volunteer's child, and the child gets sick so the mother cannot work that day), making relationships pleasant, and letting the coordinator know if something is interfering with the completion of a project (lack of materials, perhaps, or lack of instruction).

Volunteers have a responsibility not to volunteer for work they know they cannot do. They also should be realistic about how much time they are able and willing to volunteer. Volunteers have an obligation to follow directions precisely and not to be creative if they are unsure of themselves; instead, they should ask the coordinator to clarify matters.

Another area in which volunteers have a responsibility is discipline. They must, of course, discipline themselves. In addition, they should follow explicitly the organization's policy on volunteer-patron relationships.

Many volunteers expect more from themselves than the coordinator does; others have to be guided. Volunteers should be aware that if they go "above and beyond" what the coordinator requires, they should not project onto that supervisor dissatisfactions about doing too much work.

Responsibilities of the Coordinator

Not only does the volunteer have a responsibility to the library; the coordinator has certain responsibilities to the volunteer. Volunteers deserve to have their coordinators available. They deserve support and encouragement. They deserve all the materials and instructions that they will need to complete their tasks. If they are doing poor work, they deserve a conference, no matter how informal, which is private and as ego-salving as possible. They deserve a stimulating, enriching experience.

Coordinators owe their volunteers a clear understanding of their duties before they agree to them and positive feedback during the course of the program, not all at once at the end of the year. This will have a much more beneficial effect on both the worker and the library.

Some people do not respond at all to arbitrary supervision. Even those who do respond would probably respond better to a leadership which does not depend upon aggressiveness and demands. Under supervision which leads instead of pushes, most volunteers will respond quickly when they are shown a problem. They will probably make an immediate attempt to solve it, using the information given to them by the coordinator. If this does not happen, the coordinator may need to become a bit more specific. It is doubtful that many out-and-out orders will have to be given.

The volunteer has a right to reasonable consistency. Working in a foreign environment four hours once a week is not an easy thing to do. It is much harder if the requirements change from week to week.

Volunteers need to feel that they are needed. The only thing volunteers get from their work is the way they feel; they deserve to feel good.

Sometimes the coordinator will note that a volunteers' work is of poor quality. The reason is usually that he is doing the wrong job. He should be cross-trained into a more compatible area. Occasionally volunteers are not aware of the importance of their work. The coordinator needs to position the job in the volunteers' minds as a part of a whole. Volunteers should understand how their work affects that of others. This will inspire more careful attention to detail. The problem should be solved by the coordinator's tailoring the job more closely to the volunteers.

The coordinator owes volunteers an opportunity to remove themselves from unpleasant situations gracefully. If they would prefer a different task, the opportunity and the changes should be presented as quickly as possible.

Some volunteers feel very insecure for a long time. If there are to be changes in the schedule, it would be thoughtful to notify everyone. Field trips, inspections and other activities can cause anything from curiosity to a feeling of unsureness.

Coordinators owe the volunteer every effort they can make to be sure work is done properly. If everything fails, the coordinator must fire the volunteer for the sake of the others. There are very few reasons to dismiss a volunteer, but when it must be done, it should be done quickly, caringly, and finally.

PROBLEMS WITH TIME MANAGEMENT

Time is the most precious commodity the volunteer coordinator has. It is to gain time more than any other single reason that a person initiates a volunteer program. As has been demonstrated, recruiting free helpers can present the library with a gift of many thousands of hours of time. Poor organization of that program, however, can eat away at any benefits derived from that gift.

In order to utilize every moment to the fullest, coordinators must work diligently to overcome any problems which result in a loss of time. They will be able to attribute some of these losses to themselves, some to their volunteers or staff members. In every case, they must identify the problem, find the cause, and decide how to minimize it (see table 8.4, pages 145-47).

In a very friendly, open atmosphere, for example, volunteers may tend to socialize, often using the coordinator's time as well as their own. This can be the result of one of the main reasons people volunteer: to find friends and to be around other interesting adults. Coordinators will have to decide how much is acceptable in their particular libraries, or with particular tasks. Once this is done, the coordinator will look for a means of changing things without hurting anyone's feelings.

(Text continues on page 148.)

Table 8.4

Rx for Time Wasters

Disease	Cause & Symptoms	Cure
Volunteers socializing in librarian's office Too many visitors	Natural love of socializing Improper office arrangement Ego needs	Volunteer to act as secretary Turn back to office door Go to volunteer's work area Limit conferences Have periodic meetings
Indecisiveness on part of coordinator	Procrastination Insecurity Laziness Lack of planning Lack of accountability	Handle paper once Conquer tendency to be perfectionist Delegate Set deadlines and keep them
Too many meetings Poor meetings in terms of productivity	Fear of making decisions Habit Ego satisfaction Social needs	Review needs for meetings and eliminate unnecessary ones Set agenda in advance Set time limits Control participation
Lack of volunteer initiative	Poor job description Failure to delegate authority Wrong motivators Lack of recognition Poor example	Reward initiative Permit mistakes Delegate and hold accountable Give recognition
Little planning done	Need not appreciated Administer by crisis Lack of delegation Poor scheduling techniques	Give priority to planning Show its value to accomplishment Establish firm schedule Involve others

(Table 8.4 continues.)

Table 8.4—*Continued*

Disease	Cause & Symptoms	Cure
Unclear personal and organizational priorities Lack of commitment by volunteers	No firm goals Lack of involvement Imprecise communication	Reduce targets to writing Place them in time sequence—set deadlines Clarify for volunteer
Executives spread too thin	Poor time analysis Tendency to say "yes" to everybody Broad interests Ego needs	Learn to say "no" Define work capabilities in terms of time Share the glory
Hasty action by coordinator Lack of deliberation	Impatience Lack of organizational input Inability to say "no" Anger	Show how correct decisions save time Emphasize accountability Plan time better
Inadequate delegation	Lack of confidence in volunteers Ego needs Poorly trained volunteers	Select volunteers carefully Conquer your tendencies Train volunteers Do only big jobs yourself
Desk clutter	Waiting to dictate Poor planning Lack of delegation Work image Secretarial inadequacy	Delegate Organize office Touch each paper once Plan every day Overcome work compulsion
Unavoidable waiting periods	Poor planning Habit No materials at hand Failure to group errands Desire to socialize	Group errands Carry work and note paper Plan for time windfalls

(Table 8.4 continues.)

Table 8.4—*Continued*

Disease	Cause & Symptoms	Cure
Reading backlog	Image of stacked desk and long day Compulsion to personally do everything-inability to skim Lack of delegation Improper trash attitude	Don't read everything Delegate reading Eliminate some magazines Discourage unnecessary memos-use telephone Speed read and skim
Telephone and mail	Poor value system Habit Curiosity Fear Poor planning and office organization	Delegate authority Plan the day Group calls Limit time per phone call
Lack of appreciation of time as a resource	Poor planning Unconsidered cost Poor organization Unclear goals Poor organizational discipline	Motivate self Compare time to money Organize and plan Discipline self Set goals, clarify Emphasize accountability
Unclear longterm goals	Procrastination Inability to see today's relationship to future Tendency to be satisfied with generalizations	State probable time span in years, months, etc. Determine specific needs Set high goals

Adapted from *Finding Time for Success and Happiness through Time Management* by Ivan W. Fitzwater, by permission of Mandel Publications, a division of Management Development Institute. Copyright, 1977, Management Development Institute, Inc.

One may decide that a secretary would be an effective shield against interruptions. This is a good solution; there will be many volunteers who would love the position since it would give maximum involvement with a limited time commitment. If this is undertaken, the coordinator will want to make the limits of authority very clear. An officious secretary will irritate anyone, but an officious volunteer secretary will be really unwelcome.

If coordinators have offices of their own, they can physically change the setup so that their backs are to the door. This will automatically result in fewer interruptions, since that eye contact which gives a person permission to enter will be lacking.

In addition to this, a standing rule which limits the length of visits will help. No one will feel slighted, since the rule will stand for everyone. This has the added benefit of giving importance in the volunteer's mind to the few occasions when more time is allowed. If the coordinator is actively involved in supervision, and is up and around, going from volunteer to volunteer, discussing various things on their territory, the need to come to the coordinator's office will not be as great. Volunteers will learn to associate their coordinator's presence in the office with "time off, visiting not encouraged." The use of periodic meetings would help also, but it is often difficult, if not impossible, to get more than one or two volunteers together at a time. If this system is to be used, it should be so stated in the very beginning. Otherwise volunteers may feel offended when they are expected to show up not only at their regular time, but also at additional times.

Coordinators should take a firm stance on their use of meetings. They should think the possibilities through carefully, assessing the temper of their programs and their own ambitions for the projects. Meetings can cause problems or solve them. If held, they must be almost mandatory for at least a small group of volunteers who are working on the same project; otherwise the coordinators' time will be doubly spent: they will have to spend time both at the meeting and in individual conference with those who missed it. The size of the organization will determine whether this is much of a problem. Once meetings have been decided upon, coordinators must plan them so that time wasted will be minimal (see table 8.5).

Another real time-waster is volunteers who lack initiative. This may result from a feeling on the part of the volunteers that they do not really know what to do or that they do not have the authority to do what they have been asked to do. The wise leader always gives authority commensurate with responsibility. Volunteers, like salaried workers, will be hamstrung if they are asked to accomplish something but not given the means by which to do it. More rarely, volunteers' lack of initiative can result from the feeling that they are not appreciated or that they really do not want to do what they know is expected of them. The coordinator must make it clear that mistakes which happen in spite of following directions will be viewed as a symbol of real thinking or of real involvement. The coordinator will, of course, correct the mistake and train those volunteers in the proper execution of that phase of job, but they will not criticize them for it. In addition, the coordinator will wish to recognize any effort at initiative. A little positive reinforcement will go a long way. Lack of initiative can also be the result of unwillingness on the part of the coordinator to delegate, to "let go." This must be overcome or the coordinators will create

Table 8.5

Meetings

Arrange agenda in advance

Set time limit (per meeting and per item)

Outline purpose and activities at beginning

Include only appropriate people

Have meetings only when necessary

Encourage all to be on time (avoid chug-chug starts)

Use meeting only when involvement is needed—otherwise, use a memo

Practice good group dynamics (two-way communication)

Adapted from *Finding Time for Success and Happiness through Time Management* by Ivan W. Fitzwater, by permission of Mandel Publications, a division of Management Development Institute. Copyright, 1977, Management Development Institute, Inc.

150 / 8—Predicting and Alleviating Problems

systems which they cannot handle, ones which will demand too much time for any person to control.

Neophyte coordinators may reach the point where they feel that they are spread too thin, that they cannot handle everything that is required of them. This is a common result of a failure to study time and its control. Coordinators who cannot say "no" will find themselves in this predicament, as will coordinators who demand that all credit go to them. A serious study of time and its uses, a determination to learn the judicious use of the word "no" and a willingness to share credit for things which are being accomplished will combine to eliminate that feeling of being submerged in a vat of good ideas. Tables 8.6 and 8.7, pages 151 and 152 offer some useful tips on time management.

The coordinator will be the standard by which volunteers set their criteria. If the coordinator seems not to value time, neither will the helpers.

In conclusion, time management calls for the ability to manage one's own time (see table 8.8, pages 153-54) and to plan for the use of the time of others. It will not suffice to use one without the other.

A good volunteer program must include an active note-and-resolve approach to problems. This can be done by coordinators who can accept and deal with their own roles in those problems, including their ability to control time. The coordinator must have and be able to share an accurate assessment of the commitments and responsibilities imposed on staff and volunteer, as well as an ability to pinpoint and deal with problems. These attributes will help smooth out problems in an otherwise outstanding program.

(Text continues on page 155.)

Table 8.6

Ways to Save Time for Greater Efficiency

---

1. Don't read everything. Delegate reading assignments.

2. Only send typed memos when: you must confirm, remind or clarify; or to communicate with several people. Otherwise, use the phone. Extra Benefit: Immediate reaction.

3. Always keep a pocket or desk diary at hand for jotting down ideas that come to mind.

4. Establish a uniform filing system. Purge files regularly. Desk organizing and tickler files may be useful.

5. Eliminate clutter. Stacked desks are time wasters. Piles of paper are distracting and retrieval is slow and inefficient.

6. Equip properly, buy the best you can afford to cut back on time-wasting repairs and faulty operation.

7. Use your trash basket.

Adapted from *Finding Time for Success and Happiness through Time Management* by Ivan W. Fitzwater, by permission of Mandel Publications, a division of Management Development Institute. Copyright, 1977, Management Development Institute, Inc.

Table 8.7

Time Management

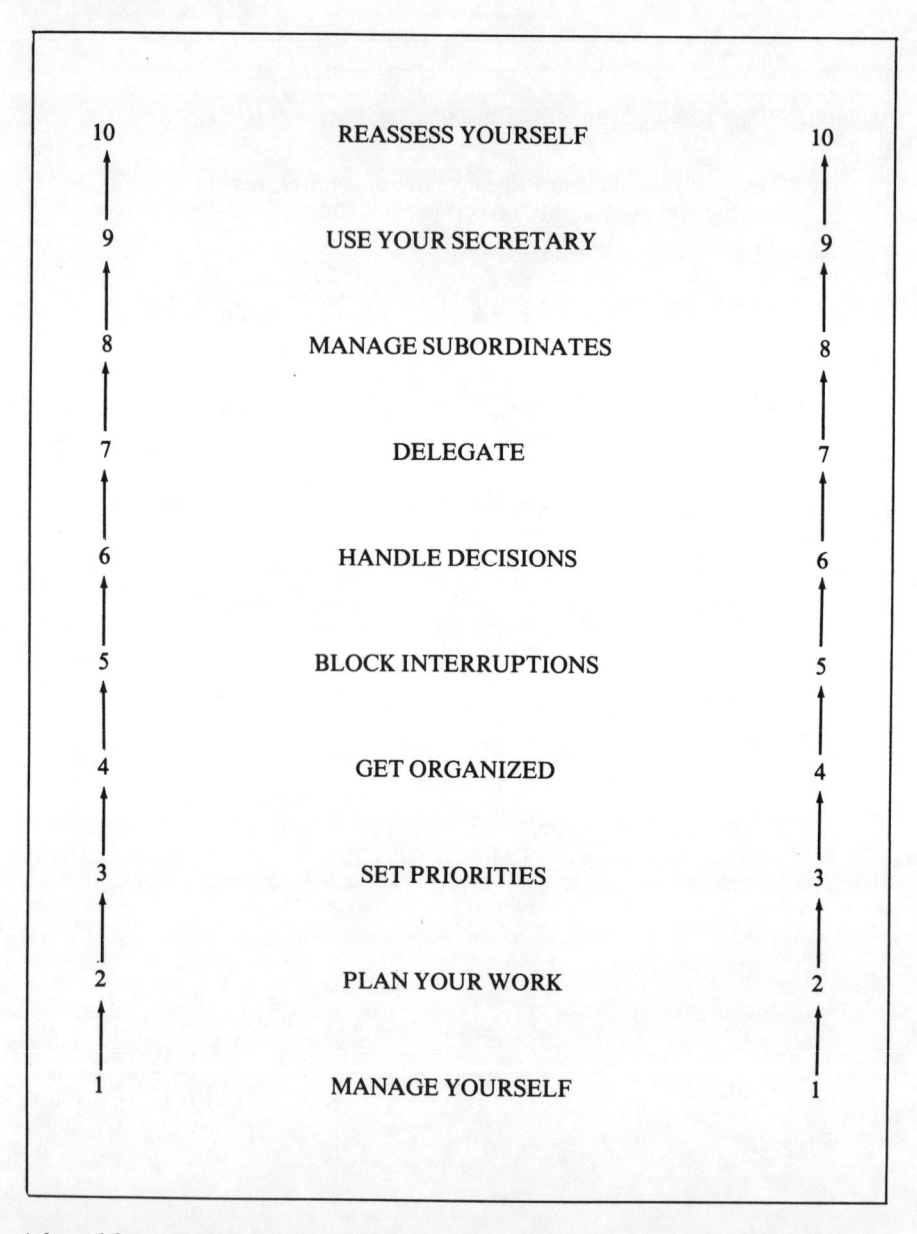

10	REASSESS YOURSELF	10
9	USE YOUR SECRETARY	9
8	MANAGE SUBORDINATES	8
7	DELEGATE	7
6	HANDLE DECISIONS	6
5	BLOCK INTERRUPTIONS	5
4	GET ORGANIZED	4
3	SET PRIORITIES	3
2	PLAN YOUR WORK	2
1	MANAGE YOURSELF	1

Adapted from *Finding Time for Success and Happiness through Time Management* by Ivan W. Fitzwater, by permission of Mandel Publications, a division of Management Development Institute. Copyright, 1977, Management Development Institute, Inc.

Table 8.8

How I Save Time

1. I count all my time as "On-Time" and try to get satisfaction (not necessarily accomplishment) out of every minute.
2. I try to enjoy whatever I am doing.
3. I'm a perennial optimist.
4. I build on successes.
5. I don't waste time regretting my failures.
6. I don't waste my time feeling guilty about what I don't do.
7. I remind myself: "There is always enough time for the important things." If it's important I'll make the time to do it.
8. I try to find a new technique each day that I can use to help gain time.
9. I get up early during the week (and go to bed early).
10. I have a light lunch so I don't get sleepy in the afternoon.
11. I examine old habits for possible elimination or streamlining.
12. I've given up forever all "waiting time." If I have to wait I consider it a "gift of time" to relax, plan or do something I would not otherwise have done.
13. I carry blank 3x5 index cards in my pocket to jot down notes and ideas.
14. I review my lifetime goals list every day and identify activities to do each day to further my goals.
15. I put signs in my office reminding me of my goals.
16. I keep my long-term goals in mind even while doing the smallest task.
17. I always plan first thing in the morning and set priorities for the day.
18. I keep a list of specific items to be done each day, arrange them in priority order, and then do my best to get the important ones done as soon as possible.
19. I schedule my time months in advance in such a way that each month offers variety and balance as well as "open time" reserved for "hot" projects.
20. I give myself time off and special rewards when I've done the important things.
21. I do first things first.
22. I work smarter rather than harder.
23. I have confidence in my judgment of priorities and stick to them in spite of difficulties.
24. If I seem to procrastinate I ask myself: "What am I avoiding?"—and then I try to confront that thing head-on.

(Table 8.8 continues.)

Table 8.8 — *Continued*

25. I start with the most profitable parts of large projects and often find it is not necessary to do the rest.
26. I cut off nonproductive activities as quickly as possible.
27. I give myself enough time to concentrate on high priority items.
28. I have developed the ability to concentrate well for long stretches of time (sometimes with the aid of coffee).
29. I concentrate on one thing at a time.
30. I focus my efforts on items that will have the best long-term benefits.
31. I keep pushing and am persistent when I sense I have a winner.
32. I have trained myself to go down my To Do List without skipping over the difficult items.
33. I do much of my thinking on paper.
34. I work alone creatively in the morning and use the afternoons for meetings, if necessary.
35. I set deadlines for myself and others.
36. I try to listen actively in every discussion.
37. I try not to waste other people's time (unless it's something that really matters to me).
38. I delegate everything I possibly can to others.
39. I make use of specialists to help me with special problems.
40. I have someone screen my mail and phone calls and handle all routine matters.
41. I generate as little paperwork as possible and throw away anything I possibly can.
42. I handle each piece of paper only once.
43. I write replies to most letters right on the piece of paper.
44. I keep my desk top cleared for action, and put the most important thing in the center of my desk.
45. I have a place for everything (so I waste as little time as possible looking for things).
46. I save up all trivia for a three-hour session once a month.
47. I try not to think of work on weekends.
48. I relax and "do nothing" rather frequently.
49. I recognize that inevitably some of my time will be spent on activities outside my control and don't fret about it.
50. I keep small talk to a minimum during work hours.
51. I look for action steps to be taken now to further my goals.
52. I'm continually asking myself: "What is the best use of my time right now?"

Reprinted with permission from the book *How to Get Control of Your Time and Your Life* by Alan Lakein, copyright 1973. Published by David McKay Co., Inc.

9 Recognition

The success of a volunteer program will ultimately rely to a large extent upon how good the coordinator is at recognizing the work of others, of letting them know how much they have helped the library, the school, and the students. The most important paycheck volunteers receive is the way they feel; it is the coordinator's job to be sure that they feel good. In accomplishing this coordinators will probably develop several ways of recognizing volunteers and their work. They will develop the ability to view the successes of their own work with the volunteers as recognition for themselves, and reap from this an emotional reward.

RECOGNITION OF VOLUNTEERS

As has been stressed throughout this book, volunteers need to be "loved" as much as anybody else. If coordinators are the kind of people who notice little things, who have the ability to see the many parts of a whole, they will have a head start in making the volunteer feel good. It will be easier for them to show their pleasure to the volunteers. No one wants insincere flattery, but most people appreciate it when something good that they have done is recognized. The goal is to let people know that the coordinators are aware of who is responsible for even the most minute successes, and that they are proud of the contribution and the product.

There are many ways to recognize the work of volunteers. The most important is continual, daily recognition which is publicly and privately voiced. There are several methods of commending volunteers publicly, both personally and through their work. There are social, epistolary, and honorary methods as well. What is most important is that recognition be given somehow.

Daily Response

There are so many ways of recognizing the volunteer's work on a regular basis that it will suffice to mention just a few here. Creative coordinators will find opportunity at every corner, and should use all methods which do not require much time from their work.

The simplest and best way to praise volunteers is to tell them what you think of their work. This can be done with no lost time, with no expenditure of money, and with almost no effort. The coordinator could make a simple statement, working it in with usual comments. "I would like for you to work at the desk during this next class. The children really respond to you, even if you need to correct them for something." "We need to shelve the nonfiction books before doing anything else today. I am so pleased that the kids are checking them out more now—I think that book talk you did on travel really inspired them." "I like the way the easy books have been looking the past couple of weeks. I've noticed that you straighten the shelves when you shelve books. Even the first graders have noticed the difference." "Mrs. Crist brought down a prospective new parent a while ago. She was really impressed with the library, especially that bulletin board you made about different kinds of fabric."

Almost any method will have excellent results, because the volunteer will sense the sincerity with which the statements are made. Coordinators must be sure, however, not to praise one volunteer to the exclusion of another, especially when comments are made with more than one present. They should beware of saying something nice to one, then "tacking on" a compliment for the other. There will be ample time to recognize everyone's work. It is especially nice to praise volunteers in front of parents or staff members. This can be done more openly, calling the volunteers over and introducing them to the visitor, adding, "John and Marsha are responsible for the display you were admiring." This is more valuable than all the certificates in the world!

Coordinators must integrate a new kind of thinking. They must learn to recognize automatically the good that others do and just as automatically to verbalize that recognition. As this becomes second nature, coordinators will forget that they are doing it, and be able to concentrate on more public methods of recognition.

A helpful factor in daily recognition of worth is the silent statement that acceptance gives. Whenever possible, volunteers should have places of their very own. A shelf, a drawer, a folder—any place in which notes for the volunteers can be put, and in which they can leave half-finished work without fear that it will be disturbed. Since there is no way that volunteers can have their own offices or desks, this is the next best thing. The area does not have to be fancy. The arrangement is an acknowledgement that the volunteer has important business which needs to be protected. This has the added advantage of giving the coordinator a private place to leave comments if prior work was unsatisfactory. Often just a little "Mac and Mc are interfiled" type of comment will help the volunteer without making a bigger issue of it than necessary. The type of space allotted will depend to a degree upon the volunteer's task. Someone who processes books will need more space for plastic covers, tapes, and so forth, than someone who shelves books. Even for volunteers who need no space in which to put their supplies, the coordinator should still arrange some small place to act as a mailbox. There can be a file box with alphabetical folders, labeled with the volunteers' names, or a display on a bulletin board with book pockets arranged alphabetically by the volunteers' names. The issue is recognition as well as practicality.

Along the same lines is privilege. The coordinator can allow special systems to operate for volunteers. Perhaps they can be given the same checkout period as the teachers. Perhaps they could receive overdue notices in their mailboxes. As mentioned earlier, they could be given first checkout privileges. The coordinator will need to think through potential results of any privileges extended, as well as the results if they are *not* extended. Whatever the decisions, they should be imparted to the volunteers along with a statement that they are being given these privileges because the library values their efforts. It should not be assumed that the volunteers will understand that. Some people know so little about the workings of a library that they may not recognize privilege unless it is specifically stated.

Recognizing the volunteer as an authority on certain things is another way that recognition can be given. For instance, a coordinator who has volunteers working on ordering, can refer any questions about the arrival of new books to those people. This is not giving them authority that they do not actually hold, but rather recognizing the knowledge they do have. They would be able to give quick, concise responses to questions such as whether or not the library will soon be getting a new book by a certain author, when such a book can be expected, and so forth. Volunteers who mend books can be asked to give a talk on their art, with emphasis on those things which can be done at home with few special materials. Since the volunteers do have a body of information not held by the general public, all the coordinators are doing is making a public statement that they rely on the volunteers—a very complimentary statement.

Another way to recognize the abilities of volunteers is to turn over a semblance of control to them. For instance, when ordering supplies, coordinators can ask the processing volunteers to turn in a list of things which are running low, instead of investigating for themselves. If there seems to be some discrepancy between what the coordinator feels is needed and what the volunteer asks for, it can be checked into. Rather than ask for too much, volunteers will usually bring up questionable items. This will give coordinators the opportunity to look into actual needs and admire the volunteers' assessment of the situation. Supplies needed by the volunteer in charge of repairs can be handled in much the same way. This is merely a statement that the people working with certain projects probably know how much material they use and can foresee about how much they will need.

Means of recognition can be worked into the projects the volunteers do. The storytellers gain recognition every time they are around the children in their groups. Whether it is on the playground or in the hallway, the children will run to them and cluster around. They tell their parents about the storytellers as well as the stories.

Those who do bulletin boards can be asked to put their names in the corner; soon the students will learn to recognize the work of their favorites. This method can be used with all displays.

It must be emphasized that the need to recognize the work of volunteers is constant. Coordinators must learn to handle it as part of their every activity.

Ceremonies

Ceremonies are not as popular in some areas as they once were. Many of the volunteers do not have the time to spend, and, in one school which had a very active volunteer program in several departments, so many parents got awards that it became almost meaningless. However, there is still a place in many programs for the award ceremony.

Unless there are very few volunteers indeed, awards should not be given out at children's closing ceremonies. This will lengthen the programs almost unbearably. It would be better to have a ceremony on a different day when more time could be spent. That way the coordinator could be fairly specific about how the volunteer helped. The others will be interested, as long as the program does not last more than a couple of hours at most. Certificates or pins can be given. When one considers the ultimate end of most awards of this nature, one becomes unwilling to spend much money on them. They should be dignified, simple, and inexpensive. Giving a pin is the more costly, and most people will not wear them. If the school has an abundance of money, it might consider these methods, but coordinators should not feel the least bit embarrassed if they must have a simple ceremony without a physical token. After all, the purpose of the ceremony is to publicly recognize the volunteers' help. This can be accomplished with words alone if necessary.

The coordinator should be sure that the ceremony is covered as well as possible by the news media. This is the kind of story that many television stations like to include briefly at the end of their news programs. Newspapers may send out photographers. If professionals do not cover the story, coordinators should write it up themselves, take photographs, and send them in before the ceremony so that they can come out in the next day's paper. Coordinators should remember to mention all names. If the volunteer program is one which tallies the number of hours spent, high scorers should be mentioned.

Project Publicity

Coordinators have an excellent means at their disposal for recognizing volunteers. As was mentioned in chapter 1 and chapter 5, almost any activity they are involved in can be the basis for some kind of news story. Coordinators must always remember that, along with the project, they are advertising the volunteer. They should give full credit to the people who made the project work. This will be easy for coordinators who do not feel that they are competing with their volunteers, but feel instead that any accomplishments will reflect on them also and their abilities as coordinators.

In fact, any kind of good publicity will help to foster the school library volunteer program and also recognize those who worked on the project. Even publicity not directly pertaining to the library can give a general impression of the school and can, therefore, affect the likelihood that people will volunteer or be proud of their role as volunteers. Certainly the library needs to publicize all of its activities, since in this way most volunteers will eventually gain some recognition.

Of course, media publicity is not the only means of achieving recognition. The library must maintain good relationships with the staff of the school, especially with the teachers, since their comments will certainly influence the attitudes of the parents. A teacher who sees a lot of value in an active film program will say so, thus complimenting the parents who have worked hard to have films. The teachers who feel that their students receive excellent help in research will be more likely to send their classes to the library for this purpose, and the parents will see the results. The coordinator should be aware that recognition of the library is equivalent to recognition of those who work on its programs, and foster this awareness in the volunteers.

Social Activities

Honoring volunteers at social activities can be fun. Whether the outing be a coffee at the school, treating the volunteers to lunch either at school or at a local restaurant, or a party which includes the volunteers' families (who have given up some "mommy time"), the occasion can be a time for volunteers to meet those whose schedules do not coincide with theirs and compare jobs. It is a broadening experience, and one which can lead to increased participation the following year. The volunteer coordinator should not expect 100 percent participation on anything which demands that the volunteer arrange extra time, even a party. Some will not wish or be able to come. The ones who do, however, will have a really good time.

It would be a good idea to invite school administrators and the school board to the get-together. They will see how many people are interested and hear their positive comments on their work and the school. In return, it will show the volunteers that the powers-that-be are really appreciative of their efforts.

Thank-you Notes

The coordinator can, if necessary, send thank-you letters only. These can stress the importance of the volunteer to the library and to the students. They should not be form letters, and they should mention particulars about each volunteer's work and successes during the year. See figures 9.1 and 9.2, pages 160 and 161 for examples.

These letters can be written by the coordinator or by the principal. They can be sent during the winter holidays or at the end of the year. The important thing is that the volunteer be remembered.

A variation of the letter is to send one to the children of the volunteers thanking them for sharing their mothers or fathers and telling them of the ways that the parents helped (see fig. 9.3, page 162). Parents will see the letters, and will be pleased that their children recognize their efforts.

(Text continues on page 163.)

ST. LUKE'S EPISCOPAL SCHOOL
11 St. Luke's Lane
San Antonio, Texas 78209
(512) 826-0664

June 4, 1984

Mrs. Ira Smith
3731 Briarhill
San Antonio, Texas 78218

Dear Ira:

Please accept my grateful thanks for serving this year as Parents' Council Chairman for Book Fair.

We have had an exceptionally good year at the school. Parent participation in Parents' Council and school activities has been at a very high level. I attribute this to the leadership you have provided which has strengthened the quality of our school programs.

My best wishes for a wonderful summer.

Sincerely,

The Reverend Chris Jones, Jr.
Headmaster

Fig. 9.1. Sample thank-you letter to the volunteer. Reprinted by permission from St. Luke's Episcopal School.

ST. LUKE'S EPISCOPAL SCHOOL
11 St. Luke's Lane
San Antonio, Texas 78209
(512) 826-0664

September 10, 1983

Mrs. Winona Jones
3741 Briarhill
San Antonio, Texas 78218

Dear Winona:

My congratulations to you and your entire committee on your very successful Book Fair. The scope and quality of books available to all age groups and interests far surpassed any previous effort undertaken at our school.

I am well aware of the tremendous personal effort and involvement that you have shown to make our library a model of excellence for our students and our school.

Please accept my grateful thanks.

Sincerely,

The Reverend Chris Jones, Jr.
Headmaster

Fig. 9.2. Sample thank-you letter to the volunteer. Reprinted by permission from St. Luke's Episcopal School.

May 5, 1982

Miss Ashley Malone
Master Michael Malone
1618 Robin Forest
San Antonio, Texas 78239

Dear Ashley and Michael:

We want to thank you for sharing your mother with us this year. She has done a great deal to help our school; we really appreciate it, as well as the times that you were understanding if she was tired.

Most of the new books this year were prepared for the shelves by your mother. You know how much you and your friends enjoy them!

Again, thank you for helping our school through your mother.

Yours truly,

Babette Johnson
Headmistress

Fig. 9.3. Sample thank-you letter to the volunteer's children.

Bookplates

One of the finest ways to recognize volunteers' help is to place books in the library with their names and the year of service on the bookplates. This costs the library nothing, since the books can be any books which have already been approved for purchase. The volunteer will, of course, be notified that this has been done. Those who work in a library will have a special appreciation for this sytem, and will be pleased when their children check the books out and mention the plates.

RECOGNITION OF THE COORDINATOR

The coordinator may well wonder how the perpetrator and organizer of this splendid volunteer program will gain recognition! Everyone, even the coordinator, does need some positive feedback. Coordinators will discover very quickly that everything they do is very public. While others may not know specifically which items the coordinators personally accomplished, they will give them credit for all successes within their domain. Coordinators must learn to enjoy hearing positive comments about their libraries, whether or not those comments are directed at them. They know how much their efforts have affected the outcome of the projects, and so should develop the ability to bask in the pleasures of a job well done, especially when others recognize the quality of the product.

With a good system of recognition volunteer programs will shine. Adept coordinators will plan an active course of recognition for both the volunteers and the library, while maintaining realistic attitudes toward public recognition of their own worth.

10 Evaluation and Modification

No program is perfect. If coordinators waited until they were sure that nothing would go wrong or could be improved, new systems would never begin. Instead, plans must be made, forecasts developed, potentialities planned for, and action taken with faith that the program will be good, but with the realization that modifications will have to be made. Even after a program has proven its value, there will be a steady series of changes. The world of volunteerism is one of constant change and adjustment. There are so many factors to take into consideration that the only one certain to remain constant is the element of change itself. The important thing about change is that it should be thoughtful, never impulsive or arbitrary. It should be based on careful and continuing evaluation of the system.

Central coordinators must evaluate the effectiveness of their public relations programs and their ability to place volunteers in the libraries in which they can do the most good. Both central and building-level coordinators must evaluate not only the personnel who work with the program but also the program itself. However, building-level coordinators will necessarily do most of the evaluating, since they will be the persons in greatest contact with the volunteers and the libraries.

METHODOLOGY AND GOAL SETTING

In designing an evaluation system, both informal and formal methods should be used. Neither will suffice alone.

In terms of informal evaluation, a constant awareness is the coordinators' most effective tool. With it they can catch small problems early and eliminate them, they can foresee situations which will require work and they can watch nebulous situations and plan far ahead of time for a satisfactory outcome.

In order to be aware without being irritating, coordinators will need to listen without prying to comments around them; they will need to observe the work and the attitudes in the library; and they will need to pay particular attention to the results of the interaction between volunteers and students and volunteers and staff.

An open-door policy will allow the volunteers to bring situations directly to the coordinator. If these are viewed as ideas for alleviating problems rather than complaints, the coordinator will hear about things before there is a real need to take action.

Formal evaluation requires preplanning. Before a formal evaluation, program goals must be clarified. These goals should include at least one pertaining to the financial results of the program and at least one dealing with the result in terms of actual work accomplished. Others may be included which further delineate those goals which the coordinator hopes to accomplish with the help of volunteers.

All evaluation will be measured according to how well the results work toward these goals. When coordinators feel that accomplishments are coming at a steady pace, they can enlarge or add new goals to the existing ones, and eliminate those which have been met.

For the formal evaluation, the coordinator will use questionnaires, interviews, or other more formal methods of evaluation. (Appendix B contains a number of sample evaluation forms.) Formal evaluations may be done frequently, or once a year. Since the goal here is to allow (or force) the coordinators to concentrate on a single volunteer or one aspect of the library or their own performances, it would be wise to do this only when the coordinator sets aside some "think time," time which is devoted to an in-depth evaluation. Not allowing enough time to do a thorough job not only limits potential benefits but also can lead to erroneous conclusions and ineffective action.

In any kind of volunteer survey, the coordinator must be sure to include everyone. Otherwise those questioned may feel that the coordinator is looking for something in particular from them, and those not questioned may feel that their ideas have little value.

Once the methods and goals have been established, it is time to begin evaluation of personnel and of the program itself. This can be a time of real growth.

EVALUATION OF PERSONNEL

Evaluation of the Coordinator

Not only the volunteers but also the coordinators must be subjected to evaluation. It is hard to be objective about oneself, but the effort must be made, and, with practice, the task will grow easier. Both central coordinator and building-level coordinator must evaluate themselves and their work, and should, at least once a year, concentrate on an objective self-evaluation. The forms in figures 10.1 and 10.2, pages 166 and 167 might serve here. Alternatively, one might devise one's own form based on the suggestions in table 10.1, page 168.

(Text continues on page 169.)

Evaluation of Central Coordination

Name of Coordinator:

School:

Date:

Telephone Number:

List areas in which you feel coordination was successful:

List areas in which you feel that coordination needed improvement:

List areas in which you would like to see coordination:

Comments:

Fig. 10.1

Rating Supervisory Performance

Any list of qualifications of a good supervisor portrays an impossible paragon. It may be more helpful to list some specific supervisory criteria, adapted from several sources.

1. Do you lead without ordering or being arbitrary?
2. Do you learn to know each volunteer as a person and as a worker?
3. Do you see that each worker understands what is expected of him, at all times?
4. Do you know the details of each job so that you can teach it?
5. Do you plan and assign the work to keep all aspects flowing smoothly and promptly and to keep all hands constructively and equally busy?
6. Do you instruct carefully, clearly and tactfully?
7. Do you explain adequately the reasons for each method and instruction?
8. Do you give responsibilities to each worker so that you are developing his own initiative, thinking and accomplishment?
9. Do you word your requests so as not to antagonize the volunteers?
10. Do you keep close scrutiny over the service given to readers by each assistant to see if it can be improved?
11. Do you look into difficulties, conflicts and errors with care and patience, getting all the facts and viewpoints so as to reach a fair solution?
12. Do you correct, criticize or comment on assistants' work in a manner that will not embarrass or let them down?
13. Do you handle grievances and gripes promptly and impersonally, without sidestepping?
14. Do you treat all with equal fairness and cordiality, without favoritism?
15. Do you respect the confidences of your volunteers?
16. Do you recognize, give credit and show appreciation for good work, while giving kindly and tactful correction and criticism when it will improve the work?
17. Do you keep up with, understand and pass on to your volunteer the library's policies and decisions so that they believe in and share your loyalty to the library?
18. Are your own "on time" habits, your cordial, straightforward but not intimate relations with your workers, and your attention to appearance, neatness, and other daily relations such that you represent the spirit of friendly dignity, helpfulness and sincerity which should characterize the library as a public service institution?

Fig. 10.2. From PRACTICAL ADMINISTRATION OF PUBLIC LIBRARIES by Joseph L. Wheeler and Herbert Goldhor. Copyright © 1962 by Joseph L. Wheeler and Herbert Goldhor. By permission of Harper & Row, Publishers, Inc.

Table 10.1

Self-Rating List of Library Management Skills

A librarian or department head should not feel that "the struggle naught availeth" if he does not become an administrative paragon or genius. The following list of skills and any ratings which may result can be applied in whatever way seems most effective in the local library.

Leadership

Adjusting to difficulties and to situations

Balance, as to objectives and proposals

Awareness of pros and cons of national library developments

Getting adequate information to make decisions

Making decisions that stand up

Admitting and capitalizing on mistakes

Using time effectively, including planning

Ability to see and comprehend what goes on

Delegating work and responsibility

Giving sufficient and understandable instructions

Seeking, evaluating, promoting better methods

Resisting expensive unessential enterprises and paperwork

Building an outstanding staff

Communication with staff

Guiding, encouraging and developing others

Drawing out staff ideas and frank opinions

Ability to listen openmindedly to others

Working happily with the staff for mutual satisfactions in the work

Handling rumors to the library's advantage

Improving and enlarging public service at minimum expenditure

---

From PRACTICAL ADMINISTRATION OF PUBLIC LIBRARIES by Joseph L. Wheeler and Herbert Goldhor. Copyright © 1962 by Joseph L. Wheeler and Herbert Goldhor. By permission of Harper & Row, Publishers, Inc.

In evaluating themselves, coordinators should study their interaction with volunteers and with all other school personnel, including the custodial staff. When called upon to direct people or programs, coordinators should observe their own methods of supervising and compare them with the methods of others.

Good coordinators recognize their helpers as real people with idiosyncracies of their own, and try, within reason, to work around these. Coordinators should judge their attitudes toward their workers. They should honestly review recent problems and evaluate their methods for handling them. Could they have been improved? How? Did they fail to take into consideration some pertinent factor? Were the problems to occur again, how would they handle them?

At evaluation time central coordinators should arrange for input from the various individual coordinators they serve. This should include open-ended questions which offer individual coordinators an opportunity to express their views for and against the work done by their central coordinators, and also give them a chance to proffer ideas for new programs or methods that they would like to see implemented.

There are a number of issues that are particularly pertinent to building-level coordinators. They should assess their abilities to redistribute the work load when necessary and their ability to predict what that work load will probably be.

They should evaluate their communication skills. Is there any evidence that they are being misunderstood? Do the volunteers seem to miss verbal clues and need more obvious statements in order to understand the value of some activities? Coordinators should be sure that the volunteers know why some activities are important and others mandatory. They should investigate ways to discover causes of poor volunteer reaction to some jobs and plan ways to overcome those reactions.

Some volunteers blossom under an opportunity to organize, plan, or create. Coordinators should assess their ability to let go and allow independence when it is desired, and their ability to provide security when that is needed. In discovering these needs, coordinators may inadvertently antagonize a volunteer or make assumptions which have no basis in fact. Coordinators will wish to review each of their volunteers to discover whether or not individual needs are being met.

An important item on the self-evaluation agenda is that of surveillance of patron accommodation. Are coordinators aware of each volunteer's relationship with the children or older students as well as the teachers who use the library? Do the coordinators consciously evaluate the attitudes of these volunteers and how well they fit into the atmosphere of their libraries? Do the coordinators check to be sure that any help being given by the volunteer is of the highest quality? Do they provide remedial training if they find flaws?

Interpersonal relationships between volunteers are very sensitive. Do coordinators approach problems of this nature with the attitude that they care very deeply that the outcome be amicable, and that they are sure that a solution is possible? Coordinators should honestly assess their own reaction to such problems; impatience on their part is a clue to the volunteers that neither they nor their work is considered to be very valuable.

170 / 10—Evaluation and Modification

Coordinators should assure themselves that they are doing the very best job possible when they must correct someone's work. They should strive to see that the volunteer's self-esteem is not damaged in any way. Many problems have solutions which will even enhance the volunteers' views of themselves and their importance to the library.

Coordinators should face bravely their reaction to complaints of all types. Do they handle them immediately without feeling personally insulted? Do they allow for the possibility of more than one solution of equal value? Are complaints handled in a private manner when necessary? Does the coordinator usually allow the wishes of one person and disallow those of another?

An area in which many a coordinator has failed to make a good showing is that of recognition. Volunteers need constant praise. It must become a way of life for the coordinator to notice and mention even the smallest successes. Coordinators should examine their own attitude toward those successes. Do they assume that they should be so? Do they feel overshadowed if others are complimented profusely? Do they feel that they are in competition with some of the volunteers who succeed often and well?

Coordinators should be people who can be looked up to. They should assess their manner of dress, their language, their attitude. No one is perfect. Coordinators should welcome these moments of introspection to pinpoint areas about themselves which they can improve.

In addition to those areas which directly pertain to volunteer programs, all coordinators may wish to increase their own professionalism by attending seminars, workshops, and other activities where they will expose themselves to the leadership abilities of others. They can use these as standards by which they can judge their growing professionalism. They can evaluate their own growth in the area and increase it by reading and talking with others who are interested in the area of leadership. The coordinator should use these periods of evaluation as times of personal growth as well as occasions to further the development of library services. The items in table 10.2 sum up very well the ideal against which the coordinator may evaluate himself.

Some of the aspects which must be evaluated, such as productivity and reliability, lend themselves to formal study. Others, like morale and enthusiasm, do not. It would be a drastic mistake to consider only those factors for which there is empirical data. Other factors can often be even more important, both in themselves and because they can affect output.

Evaluation of the Volunteer

Evaluating the volunteer should be done with finesse and consideration. The main objectives should be to identify strengths and weaknesses which will affect the program or the volunteers themselves.

One method of assessing the work of the volunteers is to keep a running comment beside their assignments. If this is done, it is necessary for it to remain private. Even good comments about a volunteer can have negative results if seen by a volunteer whose comments were less than great. This method is good in that it forces the coordinator to make constant decisions on the quality of the volunteers' work. This cannot take the place of a periodic, overall review, however. In order to gain perspective, the coordinator will need to compare a range of comments and impressions. The drawback of keeping a

Table 10.2

Developing Coordinating Ability

For the coordinator, frequent self-review is stimulating and it helps develop executive ability:

1. The coordinator must have a constant awareness, each day, each week, of the need for improvement as a leader and director. A sure way to trim down one's future is to stop trying to develop one's knowledge and abilities, to adopt either the take-it-easy attitude, or the notion that one is really pretty good.

2. The coordinator should study executive methods by reading selected books and periodical articles, including what is going on today in librarianship and related fields. He should peruse the latest "Library Literature" for articles worth study. If he is close enough to colleges and larger cities he should take management courses. Encourage a nearby library to allow participation in in-service training.

3. He should study improved performance as shown in actual results in the library's progress and in morale. He should observe the methods of various executives within his school, why they are good or poor and how they could be improved.

4. He should deal with people: know his staff and public better; develop his ability to judge and appreciate persons; use fairness in dealing with others and integrity in fulfilling promises. He should give instructions in the most effective manner and use co-operation, appreciation, respect and courtesy toward subordinates and superiors; he should help people work together happily and productively.

5. He should develop specific administrative techniques: he should improve organization and the planning of his own work. Decisions should be made with promptness and accuracy. He should improve correspondence, reports, etc.; provide better supervision and development of workers, effective conduct of meetings, methods improvement, and measurement techniques. He should discuss with colleagues the development of management problems and techniques.

6. He should develop technical knowledge of the work supervised: he should keep up with new developments in the field; he should have continual intimate contact with the operations under one's supervision; and expand his understanding of related fields which bear on one's activities.

7. The coordinator should better his personal characteristics: he should work for better control of emotions; he should try to improve his learning and memory development, his neatness of person, his cheerfulness, optimism, thoroughness, perseverance, honesty and frankness.

Adapted from PRACTICAL ADMINISTRATION OF PUBLIC LIBRARIES by Joseph L. Wheeler and Herbert Goldhor. Copyright © 1962 by Joseph L. Wheeler and Herbert Goldhor. By permission of Harper & Row, Publishers, Inc.

172 / 10—Evaluation and Modification

running commentary is that it works against one of the main goals of using volunteers: to save the time of the professional for more important tasks. This system will create a great deal of bookkeeping.

One way of modifying the task so that the coordinator does not participate in the record keeping until the end of the review period is to let the volunteers keep some records on themselves (see fig. 10.3). For instance, those who process books can keep a record of the number of card sets typed, and so forth. In this way, the coordinator can review the records periodically and see who has improved in productivity and who just never seemed to catch on to a particular job.

Coordinators, of course, must take responsibility for the training of volunteers, and must be able to ascertain when they are failing to do a good job. It is very important that this type of evaluation be an ongoing process, both for the sake of the library and for the peace of mind of the volunteer. In other words, coordinators should constantly evaluate those who work under them. This is necessary for quick modification of trouble areas. They should look at volunteers and their work as an outsider would, with emphasis on quality and quantity of product. This is difficult, but mandatory.

In addition to this ongoing evaluation, volunteer coordinators will probably have periodic formal reviews in which they will sit down and concentrate on each volunteer. They must estimate the volunteer's value to the organization and how that value can be increased. They should consider the volunteer's goals and whether they are being met in the program. They should consider all points, making notes to compliment volunteers on their strong points, and identifying any which need modifying. They must be certain to follow up on evaluations. Identifying positive and negative factors is valueless unless something comes of it. Otherwise it is further waste of the coordinator's time.

The coordinator must be able to evaluate actual accomplishments, especially of new volunteers, both to see what progress is being made and to see whether training has been effective and complete. It is very easy for failure in training to be hidden by more recent activities or glossed over by showier problems. One cannot stress too much that especially in a system in which volunteers themselves do part of the training it is necessary to catch the slightest infraction before it is multiplied and assimilated by many others.

Volunteers should have an opportunity to evaluate their own contributions. This self-study is a good idea to incorporate into the coordinators' methods of assessment, since they may not be really aware of assets the volunteers see as their strongest points. Once these strengths are identified, the program can make better use of them. This self-evaluation may be included with an evaluation of the program, or it can be a relatively brief, separate assessment. If done, it should include all volunteers so that none will feel that he is being singled out for some reason.

Volunteer's Assessment

School _____ Teacher _____ Grade _____

Area of service:

    Tutorial _____   General _____   Clerical _____

    Library _____   Cultural _____   Other _____

1. Did you generally feel your time was well spent?

2. If tutoring, did you notice any improvement in the student's performance during your sessions? Behavior? Attendance? Grades? For specific cases use back of form.

3. If you received any training did you feel it was:

    Adequate _____ Unnecessary _____ Insufficient _____

4. Did the students seem to enjoy having you there?

5. Did the faculty and staff seem to appreciate your efforts?

6. Are you interested in volunteering next year?
   If so, would you like to stay in the same school?
   Would you like to stay in the same area of service?

7. In what ways do you feel our services to the schools could be improved?

Date _____   Volunteer's signature _____

Fig. 10.3. Reprinted by permission from Barbara Carter and Gloria Dapper, *Organizing School Volunteer Programs* (New York: Citation Press, 1974), 137. Copyright 1974.

EVALUATION OF THE PROGRAM

Any effort at evaluating the usefulness of volunteers should include an in-depth study of the program used. This study should cover the organization itself, job procedures, and projects and ideas which are considered for implementation. At all times the coordinator must keep in mind the goals of the library and whether or not the volunteer program is an asset in achieving these goals.

Evaluation of the Organization

Evaluating an organization can be very painful. Most coordinators put some of their souls into their programs, and it may hurt to consider weaknesses. Even concentrating on the strong points sometimes does not help. However, going through the process of evaluating personnel will not suffice. The organization as a whole must be considered. See table 10.3 for a list of the sorts of questions one should ask in evaluating an organization.

In judging a volunteer program, one factor will be outstanding: volunteer loyalty. A good program will develop in its volunteers a sense of loyalty and good will which will help carry volunteer and coordinator alike through any periods of trouble. Good attitude can make the difference between an indifferent program and one with sparkle and imagination.

Loyalty must develop not only between coordinator and volunteer, but also among the volunteers themselves. This bond will make their work more pleasant and will bring out their best, both in quality of work and in ideas. Mutual understanding will help alleviate any budding antagonisms which might otherwise develop. It will also provide a sounding board for ideas and a medium of exchange for praise and commendation, which will reinforce good feelings.

Job Procedures

Improving job procedures is so important that many people make a living by identifying better procedures for large industries. While the average library will not find it worthwhile to employ such a person, some may find it imperative to have existing personnel do the task themselves. The steps for such a task are listed in table 10.4, pages 176-77. In order to improve effectiveness, coordinators must first examine tasks as they are presently done, questioning every detail and examining all alternate courses. Once that is accomplished, they should formulate new methods, ones which will probably be a composite of the existing methods and some of the alternate methods. After testing the new methods briefly, if possible, coordinators should put them into effect, being sure to train all personnel in any changes. The final step is to evaluate all results. Some new ideas look wonderful on paper, but fail to satisfy in a real working situation.

(Text continues on page 178.)

Table 10.3

Evaluating the Volunteer Organization

A library's organizational self-rating may be aided by considering the following points:

1. The strength of volunteer loyalty to and identification with the library's objectives, as to quality and quantity of work done, concern for cutting waste and costs, and improving service to the students, and improving process methods.

2. The degree of mutual confidence and teamwork among volunteers.

3. The extent to which each person knows just what he is to do and where he fits into the organization and is free from antagonisms and frictions with associates and with other departments.

4. The extent to which delegation is effectively achieved, and the extent to which volunteers feel their ideas, knowledge and experience are appreciated.

5. The degree of competence among various volunteers to help in solving library problems, and effectiveness of communication up and down and across the volunteer system.

6. What records of performance are available from each person, especially from recent volunteers, to show from time to time whether quality is improving or may be deteriorating through unfavorable turnover?

7. The extent to which readers are getting the materials and services for which they come to the library, and the proportion who do come.

Reprinted, by permission of the publisher, from Barbara Carter and Gloria Dapper, *Organizing School Volunteer Programs* (New York: Citation Press, 1974), 183-84. Copyright 1974.

Table 10.4

Improving Job Methods

Step I. Break down the job

1. List all the details of the job exactly as done by present methods.
2. Be sure details include all material handling, and movement from one point to another, decisions that affect the flow of work and the work itself.

Step II. Question every detail

Why is it necessary? See if other libraries haven't discontinued it; for example, perforating a mark of ownership (rubber stamp on edge of book is quicker, inerasable and more effective). Do not start any new record, paper form or procedure, unless to simplify or combine present ones, without estimating objectively the cost in future continuing paperwork.

Where should it be done? This question is usually overlooked. For example: placing typists, pasters and markers close enough to the individual new books or small piles of them coming from the hands of cataloger-classifiers and typists so that no book trucks are needed, and the books move from person to person.

When should it be done? Example: taking catalog department statistics so as not to delay books even an hour or cause them to be moved to some counting point.

Who is best qualified to do it? This means also at the least cost. By analyzing the work and separating out the elementary and repetitive steps, these can be learned, handled and much of it supervised by clerical workers.

How is the best way to do it? This means finding the new, simpler, stream-lined route, the minimum of things left to do, the promptest way to get through at the least cost of time, in terms of the per-hour work of each person involved.

Have a priority for operations, the essentials first, a daily, weekly or monthly schedule of what's required. Low-priority jobs that languish can often be delegated and cleaned up. All this means that someone, usually the department head, has to plan the work, just where the job is to be handled and by whom, what supplies and instructions are needed, keeping an eye on how it goes. Within a year some factor or need will have changed, and the carefully arrived-at new method may need another shakeup.

Table 10.4—*Continued*

> Step III. Develop the new method
> 1. Eliminate unnecessary details.
> 2. Combine details when practical.
> 3. Rearrange for better sequence.
> 4. Simplify all necessary details: pre-position materials, tools and equipment at the best places in the proper work area; use devices to move a number of books from here to there with least travel.
> 5. Work out your ideas with others.
> 6. Write up your proposed new method.
>
> Step IV. Apply the new method
> 1. Sell your proposal to the boss, if necessary.
> 2. Sell the new method to the volunteers.
> 3. Get final approval of all concerned on safety, quality, quantity, cost.
> 4. Put the new method to work and use it until a better way is developed.
> 5. Give credit where credit is due.
>
> Step V. Measure the result
>
> When a task has been simplified, the benefit may be obvious. The time used to measure just how great the improvement is, often is better spent in improvement elsewhere. For if it needs to be measured, there must have been a measurement before the change, as well as after. Measuring involves quantity, quality and cost. Production, such as books charged, letters typed, cards filed can be recorded for three or four brief sample periods. Quality must be defined and then either counted, as for typing and filing errors, or rated, as for cataloging and book processing, or floor cleaning, for a few sample periods. Costs need only involve direct labor (staff time expressed in hourly pay) and possibly the materials if they involve much difference in cost. Comparing the old method and the new under otherwise comparable conditions, one then will have something more definite than a conviction as to how much of an improvement has been made.

Adopted from PRACTICAL ADMINISTRATION OF PUBLIC LIBRARIES by Joseph L. Wheeler and Herbert Goldhor. Copyright © 1962 by Joseph L. Wheeler and Herbert Goldhor. By permission of Harper & Row, Publishers, Inc.

Projects and Ideas

The evaluation of potential projects and new ideas is mandatory, since the entire program will revolve around developing and accomplishing these. An enthusiastic crew will come up with a multitude of ideas, each with its own proponents and opponents. No library can do all things, so an ability to assess each idea and its value to the local library, resulting in a conclusion which is the most satisfactory under the circumstances, is no light accomplishment. Coordinators must be aware of those factors which form criteria for decisions on projects and ideas.

In order to make a decision about an idea, it must first be stated succinctly and precisely. If this is not done, any attempt to put the idea into action will result in a start-and-stop process which may develop into a haphazard product. Each project should have a firm identity. This may form the core of a much larger project, but still it should be identifiable and the goal of initial efforts. Sometimes the peripheral aspects of a project are developed first, and the project grows and grows without ever realizing its true potential.

Coordinators must always keep in mind their own libraries and their goals. Each library has a different ambiance which will help determine the things it will accept as projects. For instance, a small religious school library might take on as one of its projects a nearby nursing home, taking a group of children over to read and talk with the patients. The library in a school which leans toward the technical might take on the project of developing a rotating showcase for science projects designed by the students. Perhaps it might even develop a cassette program written by students to explain their work. A high school library might develop a resource file listing jobs available for teenagers in the local community, from babysitting to working in a garage, as well as listings of library materials which could help. In accepting ideas for consideration, the coordinator should select only those which seem in accordance with his library. This is not to say that a broadening of goals would not be good, but an abundance of unrelated projects will produce a sense of chaos.

Coordinators of volunteer programs are encouraged to adopt new programs, but they must always keep in mind that they should not overtax their personnel resources. Volunteers only stretch so far, and a new program might take people away from an already-existing program to develop a new, not-really-necessary one. Coordinators should assess whether or not they can draw in new volunteers to handle the program or whether they would have to use those already present. If the latter, they would be wise to tread carefully and be absolutely sure that the new program is worth potential loss to existing ones. If, however, the program is an exciting one or one which might be interesting to a different group of people, the decision can be made more easily.

Another thing which may interfere with the realization of a project is its similarity to another already being done within the school or community from which the volunteer pool comes. If this is the case, the coordinator would be wise to avoid duplication for two reasons: the volunteers who are interested in such a project are probably already involved, and the presence of competition may irritate those who "got there first." Public relations is important, and coworkers deserve consideration.

The coordinator must determine what kind of priorities the project will have. Will it supersede those already in progress? Is it a good project to have when the volunteers can get around to it? When should planning start? Should this planning be done by a volunteer or by the coordinator?

Coordinators will wish to review established methods of evaluation and select from them those which they feel will best reveal the true status of the situation in their libraries. They must gather data, either by themselves or by assigning certain tasks to others; they must use information from the volunteers and from literature on volunteers or pertinent topics; they must probe for ideas and opinions of other staff members when needed; and they must predict possible results or ramifications of the issues.

Before involving volunteers in a new project, coordinators must consider cost, consequences, and objections. Above all, they must keep in mind the constant alternative: to take no action. They must never feel that they must take on an unwieldy project because of enthusiasm, even their own.

If a project passes this rigid evaluation, coordinators must satisfy criteria for putting their plan into effect: they must predict, project, plan, and put into action on a well-prepared basis. If the potential project fails to meet evaluative standards, the coordinator must inform those concerned. Included should be the reassurance that the idea was valid, but would not work for that particular library or at that time.

In conclusion, wise coordinators will utilize constant evaluation and reporting and will periodically look objectively at the broad range of the volunteers' work and at the program. In this way the programs will constantly be improved.

Appendix A: Guidelines

from *Guidelines for Using Volunteers in Libraries*

. . .

ALA Report

The use of volunteers in many types of services and programs may expand in the foreseeable future. The trend toward earlier retirement by professional and skilled workers, the increased need for wider public services, the earlier maturity of young people, the time and labor saving devices which bring more leisure, and the limited financial support of many agencies or institutions, all suggest an increased use of volunteers.

Principles for Success

The following principles should be borne in mind by libraries in using volunteers:

1. Basic to the success of a volunteer program are prior planning and approval on the part of the staff and the governing body of the library.

2. All the principles and good practices that relate to sound manpower administration, such as planning, training, evaluation, and development, must be applied to volunteer workers.

3. Planning for the use of library volunteers must include clarification of their status regarding such items as compensation for work-related injuries, insurance coverage when operating a library vehicle, and related benefits.

4. Library volunteers may have work-related expenses which are to be paid for or reimbursed by the library. The library's policies and procedures regarding such expenses should be established and made known to the volunteer before he begins library service.

5. If it is essential that a minimum or basic library program be initiated or developed by volunteers, this use of voluntary persons should be considered as a temporary measure pending the employment of staff.

6. Volunteers should not supplant or displace established staff position spaces.

Reprinted by permission of the American Library Association.

7. Recognition and appreciation of every volunteer and of all voluntary assistance is imperative. As volunteers receive no salary, other forms of appreciation and recognition are essential.

8. Volunteers should be assigned to meaningful work which makes use of their own talents, experience, training, and interests.

9. Volunteers should be assigned to those jobs which they feel competent to do and for which they have been trained and given orientation.

10. Volunteer assignments should generally be for specific time periods to enable the library and the volunteer to review, evaluate, and reassign duties.

11. There should be a staff coordinator of volunteers.

12. Continued orientation and training is essential for volunteers to keep them informed of procedures, policies, etc., just as is the continued training of regular staff members.

13. The staff should have training on the use of volunteers and should share responsibility for the success of the volunteer program.

14. Written, detailed job description[s] for volunteers are necessary.

15. Realistic scheduling of volunteers is essential; this may mean some overlapping or duplication of personnel schedule, to cover emergencies and absences.

16. Programs and services must be planned bearing in mind the possible termination or unavailability of volunteer help.

17. Friends of Libraries, parent-teacher associations, and other groups occasionally provide volunteer services and programs. Some kinds of volunteer assistance may best be provided through such organizations.

. . .

Appendix B:
Sample Evaluations

Oklahoma City Public Schools
Progress Report on the School Volunteers Program

Volunteer Reaction

Date _____

Sign your name if you wish _____ School served _____

Length of service   From _____ To _____

Total number of hours served _____

RATING SCALE: Check column 1 if the service has been excellent; column 2 if it has been good; 3 if it needs improvement; and 4 if not applicable.

A.   1 2 3 4
1. The purposes and procedures of the program were explained in the Volunteer's Handbook.
2. The general orientation program which I attended helped me understand the volunteer's role.
3. Orientation at the school where I served was adequate.
4. I was willing to work under the direction of the principal and teacher.
5. I was regular in attendance at school.
6. I was able to work harmoniously with students.
7. I enjoyed working in the school.
8. There was evidence that my services were helpful.
9. There was evidence that the children enjoyed working with me.

B. What aspects of your volunteer service did you enjoy the most?

C. What aspects of your volunteer service did you enjoy the least?

D. What suggestions can you make for improving the program?

E. Do you wish to serve as a volunteer during the next school year?

This and the following evaluation forms are all reprinted by permission from Barbara Carter and Gloria Dapper, *Organizing School Volunteer Programs* (New York: Citation Press, 1974), 138-53. Copyright 1974.

Washington Technical Institute
Volunteer Self-Evaluation Form

HOW AM I DOING? ? ? ?

1. Do I plan for the activity which I have been assigned to, not hit and miss or just doing something?
2. Do I make myself helpful by offering my services to the teacher when there is an obvious need for help?
3. Do I have a plan for getting children into groups?
4. Do I observe closely so as to know children's or adults' likes, dislikes, preferences, enthusiasms, aversions, etc.?
5. Do I find opportunities for giving students choices or do I tell them what to do?
6. Have I given some individual help in writing?
7. Do I observe closely the techniques used by the teacher and follow through when I am working with the group?
8. Do I emphasize the times when they fail to do so?
9. Do I really listen to what students have to say?
10. Do I evaluate myself at intervals?
11. Do I accept criticisms and suggestions without becoming emotionally upset?
12. Do I follow directions of the teacher?
13. Do I try to develop a friendly attitude with all of my co-workers?
14. Do I give the teacher adequate notice of absences by reporting them to the office before the day begins?
15. Do I realize that my whole purpose for being in the classroom is to assist the teacher in order that the students might progress more rapidly?
16. Do I give too much help to students rather than allowing them time to think?
17. Do I refrain from interfering between another teacher and student unless called upon for assistance?
18. Do I avoid criticism of the student, teacher, and the school or agency?

(This self-evaluation form can be used at any point during a program. It can be used to suggest areas in which joint volunteer-professional training is needed.)

Washington Technical Institute
Volunteer Evaluation of Program

School or site: _____

Volunteer: _____

Teacher or staff member: _____

1. How many hours did you work weekly? _____
2. Briefly describe what you did as a volunteer _____
   _____

3. Were you placed according to your interests and abilities?
   Yes _____ No _____
   Comment _____

4. Did you have good rapport with the children (adults)?
   Yes _____ No _____ How was it evidenced? _____
5. Did you have good rapport with the teacher?
   Yes _____ No _____ How was it evidenced? _____
6. Do you think you received adequate training before your assignment? Yes _____ No _____

7. Did you receive satisfactory training during your assignment?
   Yes _____ No _____
   Comments _____
8. In what areas were you the most help to the teacher? _____

9. What skills and techniques were most useful during your assignment? _____

10. In what areas were you the least help to the teacher? _____

11. What additional skills and techniques do you need? _____

12. Was your on-the-job supervision satisfactory?
    Yes _____ No _____
    Comments _____

13. Do you plan to continue as a volunteer?
    Yes _____ No _____ Why _____

14. How do you think the program can be improved? (Please be specific) _____

190 / Appendix B: Sample Evaluations

National School Volunteer Program

Annual Evaluation by Unit Chairman or Coordinator in a School

DATE: _____

SCHOOL: _____

UNIT CHAIRMAN OR COORDINATOR: _____

1. Involvement of personnel:
    a. Number of volunteers serving in classrooms _____
    b. Number of volunteers giving general school service _____
    c. Number of volunteers giving general school volunteer office service _____
    d. Number of volunteers giving services to individual children or small groups outside of classroom _____
    e. Number of volunteers added to the program during the year _____
    f. Number of volunteers who dropped out of the program during the year _____
    g. Total amount of man hours during the year _____
    h. Number of volunteers who wish to continue serving next year _____

2. Service:
    a. List the types of service the school volunteer performed for the classroom teacher.
    b. List the types of general service the school volunteer performed for the school, outside of classroom activity.
    c. List the types of service that were given to individual children or small groups of children outside the classroom.
    d. List the types of general service the volunteer gave to the school volunteer office.

3. Training and supervision:
    a. Did members of the school staff participate in the training of volunteers? _____

    In the supervision of volunteers? _____

Sample evaluation form—*Continued*

    b. Was in-school training done through individual conferences? _____

       group conferences? _____

       printed materials? _____

       demonstration of techniques? _____

       observation of experienced volunteers? _____

       other? _____

    c. Were arrangements made for volunteers and teachers to confer on individual children? _____

4. Books and materials:
   a. Do you have a satisfactory collection of text books? _____

      library books? _____

   b. Do you have an adequate supply of instructional materials in the school volunteer office? _____

   c. Does the school supplement your own supply of books and materials?

                     Not at all _____

                     Adequately _____

                     Generously _____

5. Teacher reaction:
   a. Number of teachers on staff _____
   b. Number of teachers using school volunteer classroom service _____
   c. Number who have requested continuation of classroom service _____
   d. Number who have indicated they do not wish continuation of classroom service _____
   e. Number of new requests for classroom service _____

Progress Report on the School Volunteer Program

Principal Reaction

Date _____

School _____   Principal _____

Number of volunteers used _____   Types of services performed:

_____   _____

_____   _____

RATING SCALE: 1 if the service has been excellent; column 2 if it has been good; 3 if it needs improvement; and 4 if not applicable.

A. Administration of the Program

   1. The procedures for screening volunteers have been satisfactory.   1   2   3   4
   2. The procedures for assigning volunteers to schools have been satisfactory.   1   2   3   4
   3. The general orientation programs provided for volunteers have been adequate in number and content.   1   2   3   4
   4. Lines of communication between coordinator and the principals have been open.   1   2   3   4
   5. Orientation of teachers and volunteers at the school has been adequate.   1   2   3   4
   6. Our school has as many volunteers as needed.   1   2   3   4
   7. There was evidence that the use of volunteers improved school-community relations.   1   2   3   4
   8. The time spent in the school per week by the volunteers was adequate.   1   2   3   4

B. In what respects is the volunteer program most commendable?

C. In what respects is the volunteer program in greatest need of improvement?

Washington Technical Institute
Principal or Administrator Evaluation of Volunteer Assistance

School or site: _____
Principal or administrator: _____

1. Would you like to have volunteer assistance continued at your school next year?
   Regularly _____ Occasionally _____ Never _____
2. What kinds of services would you like to have volunteers provide?
   _____

3. What has been the general reaction of the staff to the volunteer?
   Good _____ Fair _____ Poor _____
4. Have the volunteers established sound working relationships with the staff?
   Yes _____ No _____ How was it evidenced? _____

5. Has volunteer service appreciably relieved your staff of nonprofessional tasks?
   Yes _____ No _____ Comments _____

6. Has the help given by volunteers been a factor in improving the achievement of those who received it? (If possible, please cite specific statistics.)

7. Have the pre-service and on-the-job training of the volunteer been satisfactory?
   Yes _____ No _____ Comments _____

8. What additional skills or techniques do you feel the volunteers need?
   _____

9. What suggestions do you have for improving the training or efficiency of volunteers? _____

10. Has the on-the-job supervision of volunteers been satisfactory?
    Yes _____ No _____ Comments _____

11. Has the liaison between you and the total volunteer program proved satisfactory?
    Yes _____ No _____ Comments _____

12. What additional comments or suggestions can you make to improve the quality of the volunteer program? _____

National School Volunteer Program
Principal's Annual Evaluation

School: _____ Principal: _____

1. Would you like to have the school volunteer service continued at your school next year? _____

2. What kinds of service would you like to have? _____ _____

3. Has the general reaction of the staff to the school volunteer been

    Good _____

    Fair _____

    Poor _____

4. Has the liaison between you and the school volunteer unit in your school been satisfactory? _____

5. Has the liaison between you and the central school volunteer office been satisfactory? _____

6. Has the on-the-job training of volunteers been satisfactory? _____

7. Has the on-the-job supervision of the volunteers been satisfactory? _____

8. Has the help given to individual children or small groups of children in the special program tended to improve their achievement level? _____
(If possible, please attach statistics)

9. Have the services of school volunteers appreciably relieved your staff of nonprofessional chores? _____

We should greatly appreciate any comments or suggestions you might care to make.

School Volunteers for Boston
Principal's Evaluation Sheet

School:

1. Was the School Volunteer Program profitable to your school this year?

2. In what ways can our service to your school be improved?

3. Which of the following school volunteer services do you wish next year:

   Reading helps

   English as a Second Language Tutoring

   Classroom Assistants

   Enrichment

   Art

   Music

   Social Studies

   Other

   Library

4. If you had a school chairman, were her services helpful? (We hope to have a chairman in all schools next year.)

5. In what ways could she be more helpful?

6. Would you like volunteers to assist during the opening weeks of school in September? How many?

7. When do you want volunteers to report to your school for regular services?

8. We welcome any suggestions or comments you wish to make about the program.

Please return in the enclosed envelope.

Appendix C:
Sample Manuals

Selected from
Los Alamitos School District Manual

Volunteer

Although this is not an official position, the volunteer is an indispensable member of every library media center staff. This person may work with children as well as perform a myriad of clerical functions and, if appropriate, technical functions as well. Tasks may vary from school to school.

Suggested volunteer activities:

- Replace circulation cards in books and other media.
- Shelve books.
- Read shelves.
- Process overdue notices.
- Read aloud to individuals or small groups.
- Operate or supervise operation of audiovisual equipment.
- Stamp and file cards, under the direction of the media teacher/specialist.
- Sort and file daily check-out cards.
- Mend books and other materials.
- File publishers' catalogs.
- Prepare materials for picture files or vertical file.
- Type lists, bibliographies, etc.
- Assist students in locating materials, as appropriate.
- Assist in the preparation of bulletin board displays or exhibits.
- Assist in performing clerical tasks, operating duplicating equipment, etc.
- Assist in the preparation of instructional materials by lettering, laminating, dry mounting, etc.

Reprinted by permission of the Los Alamitos Unified School District.

Margaret Ross Memorial Library
Hamden Hall Country Day School

MANUAL

CIRCULATION:

There are two libraries within the Ross Memorial Library building: a lower school library (pre-K thru 6) and an upper school library (7-12).

At the upper school library desk books are circulated for a period of 2 weeks. Books may be renewed unless they have been requested by someone else. The date stamp is set at the beginning of the school day by the librarian. With permission from the librarian, magazines and pamphlets are circulated for a period of 2 weeks. Reference books, cassettes and microfilm do not circulate except with special permission from a faculty member.

Reserve books are shelved by faculty member on the shelves next to the librarian's desk. These books are to be used in the library. A student can only check these books out with written permission from a teacher. The book(s) can then be charged out for one night and the book(s) must be returned to the library or the librarian's mailbox before classes next day.

When helping a child check out a book, observe the following guidelines: Have the student sign LEGIBLY his or her name on the circulation card. The volunteer should then stamp the card and the date slip at the back of the library book. Glance at the card to be sure that you can read the card. The student should also provide the grade (*not* the home room number) on the card. Then give the books to the student. It is a general practice not to allow a student to take more than 3 books on the same subject.

Put the upper school circulation cards next to the file box on the librarian's desk—the cards will be arranged and filed by the librarian at the end of the school day.

In the lower school library the circulation system is somewhat different. One person should handle the circulation when the class is in the library. When the class arrives take the returned books and find the circulation cards for these books. The cards left at the end of this process will indicate the books still in circulation—these children with outstanding books cannot borrow another book. This is a difficult moment for some children (as well as the librarian and volunteer) but it is part of the learning process and will actually help the child be more responsible.

At the end of story hour the children will browse and choose a book. The child will then bring it to the desk. Ask the child's first name and write it on the circulation card with the child's grade (this is very important)—then stamp the book card and date slip and BE SURE TO PUT THE CHILD'S GRADE ON THE DATE SLIP. Lower school books circulate for one week and except with special permission a child may choose one book at a time. Lower school library magazines also circulate for 1 week but filmstrips do not leave the library. Even if an upper school student is borrowing a lower school book, the circulation period is still 1 week.

Lower school circulation cards are filed by GRADE. Within the grade slot the books are filed by easies (jE), fiction (jF) and then non-fiction (j + a number). Please adhere to this system so that we can be consistent even though we are many in number.

There are no fines charged for overdue books but a library notice is sent out to students a week after the material is due. In all, 2 notices are sent to the student and then a letter is forwarded home. If there is no response to the letter, a bill follows.

Reprinted by permission of Laurence Kingsbury, Head Librarian, Hamden Hall Country Day School.

CATALOG:

There are two *public* catalogs in the library—the lower and the upper school catalogs. The cards are filed in one alphabetical order by AUTHOR—TITLE—and SUBJECT cards. Each title in the library is represented in the card catalog. You will notice in the upper school catalog that there are cards with colored lines on the top. The red lined cards designate holdings in our cassette collection. The blue lined cards indicate our holdings in the microfilm collection and show what periodicals we have on microfilm. The card catalog is the center or nucleus for our library collection—introduce it to the students as often as possible.

CLASSIFICATION AND ARRANGEMENT:

Physically, the library is basically a circle with halls off the circle. The collection is divided in two with lower school and upper school materials being separate. A map is available indicating the location of materials and equipment. The best way, however, to learn the location of books and materials is to tour and investigate.

The library uses the Dewey Decimal Classification System. The lower school books all have a "j" before the classification symbol.

In the upper school there are 4 areas where books can be found. FICTION (designated by an "F"), REFERENCE BOOKS (designated by an "Ref." with the classification number), the oversize collection and the non-fiction collection. Notations on the bookcases help indicate the subject area you are looking for.

NON PRINT AND NON BOOK MATERIALS:

In the upper school library we have a) MICROFILM. The microfilm collection consists of issues of magazines on microfilm. As mentioned, the card catalog lists the periodicals on microfilm including the dates covered. The microfilm is kept in a gray cabinet near the librarian's desk. b) CASSETTES. These are also listed in the card catalog and the cassettes are filed numerically in the gray cabinet next to the librarian's desk. A list of the cassettes can be found, too, above the gray cabinet. Remember, microfilm and cassettes do not circulate. c) FILMSTRIPS. These are kept in the lower school library on special racks. These do not circulate but are shown to children during story hour. d) PAMPHLETS (and maps) are filed in the gray vertical file located at the foot of the stairs in the upper school library. The pamphlets (using the Abridged Reader's Guide) are arranged according to specific subject headings in alphabetical order.

EQUIPMENT:

There is a DUPLICATING MACHINE in a special room in the lower school library. Students are asked not to run the machine by themselves. Volunteers who feel comfortable with this equipment should feel free to operate it—instruction concerning operation will be provided. Otherwise, please refer requests for copies to the librarian. There is no charge for duplicating pages in reference materials, but the library does charge a nominal fee for all other materials—no i.o.u.'s are permitted; we operate on a cash only basis.

There are a number of TAPE RECORDERS available for student use and they are housed in the upper school supply closet. Students using tape recorders must use earphones (only with special permission will group listening be allowed). Tape recorders and cassettes should be returned at the end of the class period and should not be left on the tables. Be sure the OFF button has been activated and that the machine is no longer running—otherwise the batteries will go dead. Recorders and cassettes only circulate with special permission from a faculty member. When a cassette and/or a recorder is being borrowed please make a note of the faculty or student member borrowing, the time, and the date.

The library also has a FILMSTRIP PROJECTOR which is used for our special programs. The machine is simple to operate and is often used with a tape recorder for our sound/filmstrip programs. The library also owns a FILMSTRIP PREVIEWER for individual or small group viewing.

The library's MICROFILM MACHINE is used for viewing past issues of magazines on microfilm. Instructions will be given to volunteers on how to operate this machine. Students, once taught, can operate this machine by themselves—emphasis should be given on the fact that the microfilm machine should be handled with care—it is expensive.

Again, group instruction is not practical on the operation of library equipment and individual instruction will be provided where it seems appropriate.

SKILLS:

One volunteer mother will be appointed to be head of PROCESSING and she will train the new volunteers on the techniques of preparing a book for circulation. This is an operation that requires much attention and thoroughness. It is not being too dramatic to say that there is a real sense of satisfaction when a book has been prepared with care and is fresh and beautiful and is ready to captivate a reader.

DISPLAYS: There is a definite need for displays in the library. Displays create a warm, bright atmosphere, displays educate, and they are obviously a form of public relations. If you are artistic and have creative ideas that can be worked into our space and budget, please feel free to volunteer your services.

SPECIAL TRAINING SESSIONS will also be provided for cataloging and typing procedures.

STORY HOUR: This is probably one of the most rewarding moments in the library—volunteers who have a real desire to participate in the oral tradition should feel free to assist. Personal training will be provided with basic guidelines so that there will be a successful relationship between the storyteller, the material and the children.

Manual for Library Tasks

*Ethical Culture School
33 Central Park West
New York, N.Y. 10023*

TABLE OF CONTENTS
---

1. ARRANGEMENT OF LIBRARY

2. HOW TO LABEL AND SHELVE BOOKS

3. HOW TO RETURN AND RENEW BOOKS

4. HOW TO ASSIST WITH LIBRARY CLASSES

5. HOW TO FILE CATALOGUE CARDS (with illustration)

6. HOW TO PROCESS NEW BOOKS (with illustration)

7. HOW TO INVENTORY BOOKS

Reprinted by permission of Howard B. Radest, Director, Ethical Culture/Fieldston Schools.

1. ARRANGEMENT OF LIBRARY

1. *Junior Books*—Arranged alphabetically by first letter of author's last name.
2. *Fiction*—Arranged alphabetically by author's last name.
3. *Non-Fiction*—Arranged numerically by subject matter.* (See below.)
4. *Biography*—Arranged alphabetically by first three letters of *subject's* last name.

*Non-Fiction Call Numbers and Categories

000-099 .... Reference and General Works

100-199 .... Philosophy and Psychology

200-299 .... Religion

300-399 .... Social Studies (Includes Government, Transportation, Holidays, etc.)

400-499 .... Language

500-599 .... Science

600-699 .... Technology (Includes Farming, Medicine, Space Travel, etc.)

700-799 .... Fine Arts and Recreation

800-899 .... Literature

900-999 .... History, Geography, Collective Biography (920)

* * * * * * * * * * * * * * *

2. HOW TO LABEL AND SHELVE BOOKS

		Sample Labels
a.	*Junior Books*—Labelled with E and shelved alphabetically by the first letter of the author's last name.	E A
b.	*Fiction*—Labelled "FIC" and shelved alphabetically by the first three letters of the author's last name. If there is more than one book by the same author, shelve alphabetically by title.	FIC ALC
c.	*Non-Fiction*—Labelled with Call Numbers and a letter and shelved sequentially, first by number, then by letters. If the numbers and the letters are the same on more than one book, shelve alphabetically by the first three letters of the author's last name.	398.2 JOH
d.	*Biography*—Labelled "B" and shelved alphabetically by the first three letters of the *subject's* last name.	B WAS
	Collective Biography—Labelled "920" and shelved alphabetically by first three letters of author's last name.	920 DOL

NOTE: When shelving, remember to:

1. give first priority to non-fiction books,
2. reshelve any book that has been incorrectly placed,
3. relabel book if label is missing or incorrect.

* * * * * * * * * * * * * * *

3. HOW TO RETURN AND RENEW BOOKS

All books that are returned to the library are placed on the book cart behind the desk. The following procedure for carding those books and preparing them for reshelving is also applicable for book renewals:

a. Locate the book card in the circulation drawer file for the book to be carded. (These cards are filed alphabetically by author's last name, then by title.) Be sure the book number is the same on the book card and the book pocket. This is important because the library may have several copies of one book.

b. Insert the book card into the book pocket and place book on cart to be shelved — or return to student for renewal.

c. To renew book, student signs book card and stamps date due slip a second time.

* * * * * * * * * * * * *

4. HOW TO ASSIST WITH LIBRARY CLASSES

There are many ways to assist the librarian during class time. Much depends on your own predilections and talents as well as the librarian's needs in a particular class situation. Discuss with her which of the following ways you can be most helpful.

a. Remove books from tables to cart and replace with books appropriate for the next class.

b. Assist students in using card catalogue and in selecting books.

c. Read story to class.

d. At the end of class collect and alphabetize the book cards of books the students have just signed out. Locate the class card file and on each student's card, list the author's last name and title of each book he has signed out.

e. After class cards have been recorded, file book cards in circulation drawer.

* * * * * * * * * * * * * * *

5. HOW TO FILE CATALOGUE CARDS

The Card Catalogue contains three types of cards which are *inter-filed* and arranged alphabetically:

1. *Author Card*—Filed alphabetically by author's last name, then by first name. For an author with more than one card, file alphabetically by title.

2. *Title Card*—Filed alphabetically by title. (Disregard "A" or "The.") For cards with the same title, file alphabetically by author's last name.

3. *Subject Card*—Filed alphabetically by subject, then by author's last name.

There are many old catalogue cards with no call numbers. These books are always fiction. Thus the call numbers should be FIC and the first three letters of the author's last name.

NOTE: See sample of interfiled catalogue cards on next page.

Appendix C: Sample Manuals / 209

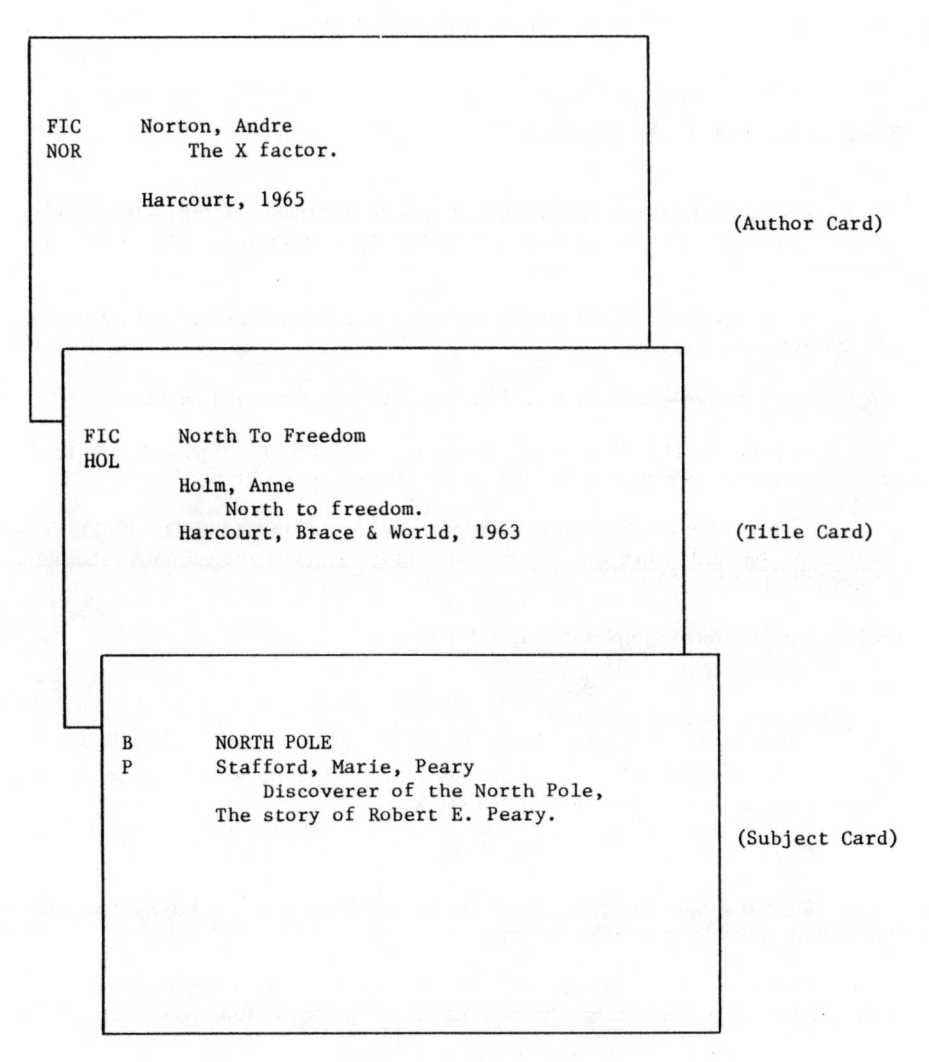

```
FIC      Norton, Andre
NOR           The X factor.

         Harcourt, 1965
```
(Author Card)

```
FIC      North To Freedom
HOL
         Holm, Anne
              North to freedom.
         Harcourt, Brace & World, 1963
```
(Title Card)

```
B        NORTH POLE
P        Stafford, Marie, Peary
              Discoverer of the North Pole,
         The story of Robert E. Peary.
```
(Subject Card)

Read from Bottom to Top

210 / Appendix C: Sample Manuals

6. HOW TO PROCESS NEW BOOKS

There are two parts to this procedure

    1. *Processing Cards for New Books* — Using the information listed on the sample catalogue card given to you, process a minimum of four cards for each book as follows:

    a. *Shelf-List Card* — Type information exactly as it appears on card you are given; add the Accession Number.

    b. *Author Card* — Same as Shelf-List card, but omit Accession Number.

    c. *Title Card* — Title of book appears on top line (in regular type with only first letter of each word in capitals). The rest of the card is like the Author Card.

    d. *Subject Card* — Subject of book appears on top line in CAPITAL LETTERS. The rest of the card is like the Author Card. (Type separate subject card for each subject indicated.)

(NOTE: See illustrated samples on pages 211-12.)

    2. *Processing the Book Itself*

    a. Check to see that label is on spine of book. If not, copy Call Number from sample catalogue card on label and affix to spine.

    b. Cover book jacket with plastic cover.

    c. Glue in book pocket on front fly-leaf of book unless it covers essential information, in which case affix to next page.

    d. Assign an Accession Number from Accession Book by crossing out the next number listed in the book. Copy this number in four places, as follows:

        1. in upper right hand corner of book pocket,
        2. on 3rd line of white book card,
        3. on sample catalogue card,
        4. on the reverse of Title Page

    e. Stamp book pocket and reverse of Title Page with Ethical Culture Library stamp.

    f. Copy call number, author's name and title of book on white book card and on the pocket itself.

    g. Remove sample catalogue card and file in Librarian's Work File under "To Be Typed."

    h. Place book on Librarian's Work Shelf to be checked.

SAMPLE CARDS TO PROCESS FOR A NEW BOOK

1. <u>Shelf-List Card</u>

973.5   Jones, Kenneth M.
JON   War with the Seminoles: 1835-1842

        Franklin Watts, Inc. N.Y., 1975

        1. Seminole War, 1835-1842   I. Title.

---

2. <u>Author's Card</u>

973.5   Jones, Kenneth M.
JON   War with the Seminoles: 1835-1842

        Franklin Watts, Inc. N.Y., 1975

        1. Seminole War, 1835-1842   I. Title.

(Sample cards continues.)

Sample Cards — *Continued*

3. <u>Title Card</u>

```
                 War with the Seminoles: 1835-1842
    973.5    Jones, Kenneth M.
    JON          War with the Seminoles: 1835-1842

             Franklin Watts, Inc. N.Y., 1975




             1. Seminole War, 1835-1842    I. Title.
```

4. <u>Subject Card</u>

```
                 SEMINOLE WAR, 1835-1842

    973.5    Jones, Kenneth M.
    JON          War with the Seminoles: 1835-1842

             Franklin Watts, Inc. N.Y., 1975




             1. Seminole War, 1835-1842    I. Title.
```

7. HOW TO INVENTORY BOOKS

a. Carry the shelf list drawer to the appropriate shelf.

b. Check to see if the book matches the Shelf List card in every respect—i.e., author, title and Accession Number (#).

   1. Put a small check and the year next to the # if everything matches, e.g., k0456 (√ 76). Each # on the Shelf List represents a different copy of the book and must be checked.

   2. If there is no book on the shelf to match the number on the card, put a paper clip on the shelf list card and go on to the next book.

   3. If there is no card in the drawer to match a book on the shelf, hold the book aside to be brought to the shelf marked "NO SHELF LIST CARD."

c. Follow this procedure until you encounter about ten irregularities. Then:

   1. Bring problem books to the special shelf and

   2. Check the clipped cards against the circulation file. If the copy of the book in question is in circulation, put a check and the year next to the #, just as if the book were on the shelf. Remove paper clip. If the book is not in circulation leave paper clip on card. (Several months later there will be another inventory and check of clipped cards. If book still cannot be found, the # is crossed off the Shelf Card List.)

* * * * * * * * * * * * * * *

Appendix D:
Responses to Survey of Volunteers

The experiences and opinions of volunteers are always worth considering. The responses to a 1982 survey of volunteers from all over the United States are abstracted below. Opinions that were expressed more than once are mentioned one time only, since the purpose of the survey was to get an idea of the range of concerns, not their frequency. (As you will note, not all of the responses are based on school library experiences.)

In what types of organizations have you volunteered?
- doctors' wives' clubs
- women's clubs
- neighborhood clubs
- various school projects
- multiple sclerosis projects
- Red Cross
- parents' groups
- church committee work
- nursery groups
- officers' wives' clubs
- Vacation Bible School
- aides in the classroom
- census bureau
- scouts
- room mothers
- Brownies
- Sunday school
- charities which give style shows
- those requiring volunteer clerical work

Why did you volunteer in these organizations?
- they couldn't find anyone else
- wished to see an activity started
- had prior knowledge not held by others
- desired to become involved with the child's school
- felt I was in part repaying a scholarship
- saw a need in an organization
- was asked directly

218 / Appendix D: Responses to Survey of Volunteers

- felt sympathy for someone who was working on a worthwhile project
- as a favor for a friend
- had an interest but no desire to enter the field as a career
- wanted to participate in order to have more in common with my husband or with my child
- enjoy doing things for the children's benefit
- wished to do things so that children could see I was involved
- had free time
- the organization needed the help
- to help my child have a good experience
- from a sense of obligation

How were you asked to volunteer?
- directly since someone knew of my special skills
- posters
- announcement of critical shortage
- teachers asked
- newsletters
- supervisor asked in person
- asked how I could be used
- was called on phone by chairman
- overheard a need
- asked by a friend
- need was announced at a meeting
- people come to me because I have a reputation for being dependable
- had a background of volunteering
- other people seeking a leader because the project would fold unless someone assumed responsibility
- husband said to use my talent
- went in and asked if I could help
- flyer
- "Put a net over my head at the door!"
- sign up board outside library

How much volunteer time do you spend per week?
- two days
- twenty hours
- one morning
- two mornings
- six hours

- really couldn't calculate since time was erratic
- four hours
- one and a half days per week
- twenty-four plus hours per week
- two to three whole days per week
- four hours per week at least
- eight hours per week
- three days per week

What do you feel you owe the organization?
- to be there or find a substitute
- to be responsible for what I take on
- same as salaried workers
- use my own initiative
- remember and use training
- dependability
- doing my best
- always come on time or make up the time

What does the organization owe you?
- proper training
- to let me know exactly what is wanted
- nothing
- to make areas in which volunteers can help known
- the same things it owes salaried workers, except money
- a good training program
- to be positive while I am working on the job
- need to understand the value of sincere critique
- describe everything involved in a job beforehand so a volunteer will know what he is getting into

What duties have you performed in any of your volunteer work?
- having responsibility for a program every week
- directing games
- overseeing the earning of badges
- chaperoning hikes and field trips
- running meetings
- visiting nursing homes
- preparing refreshments

- acting as treasurer
- helping beautification committee
- doing Christmas projects
- cataloging
- performing secretarial duties
- calling committee
- arranging slate of officers
- distributing flyers
- collecting money
- entertaining at lunches, teas, and so forth
- dispensing information
- doing bulletin boards
- ordering materials
- doing classroom talks
- compiling information
- organizing projects
- chaperoning
- caring for patients alone
- working in intensive care
- organizing parties for children
- scheduling
- writing
- teaching crafts
- teaching
- guiding social development
- grading papers
- reading stories
- cooking
- mimeographing
- purchasing materials
- making games
- giving tests
- taking census
- organizing and working booths
- typing
- shelving

Who selected your duties?
- the teacher
- sometimes I saw a need and stepped in
- I did
- I chose based on what the organization needed most
- took whatever came with the job

How much has volunteering cost you?
- gas money only
- $30.00 per year
- $150.00 at least
- $5.00 a week
- nothing
- $1109.00 per year
- $5.00 per month
- $55.00 for three years
- $126.00 per year
- "I got more out of it than it cost me."

Every volunteer but one said he intended to volunteer for the same organization for several years.

Who trained you?
- the outgoing officer
- gathered ideas from other people
- the teacher
- leaders in the organization
- paid staff (not trained by the immediate supervisor)
- nobody
- librarian

How could training be improved?
- provide more input as far as responsibilities go
- be more specific
- be sure the worker knows enough to do a good job
- have guidelines for aides

- think things out beforehand
- new people should be encouraged to participate
- leaders should be willing to try new ideas
- don't let the desirable jobs be taken perpetually
- better organization

Every volunteer questioned had done some volunteer work at home. One indicated that most of her work has been done there.

All but one volunteer indicated a willingness to do some volunteer work at home even with a full-time job.

Most of the volunteers preferred to involve their families in at least some of their volunteer efforts.

What jobs have you done in libraries?
- shelving books
- teaching classes
- checking books in and out
- running inventory
- publicizing movies
- acting as Book Fair chairman
- typing
- mimeographing things
- creating learning centers for classes
- reading stories
- phoning
- taking charge of money-making activities
- filing
- processing
- cataloging
- cleaning films
- putting on leads
- running microfilm machines
- shelving periodicals
- running a film fair
- organizing and labeling periodicals
- labeling audiovisual machines
- cleaning out closet
- ordering, receiving, and returning films
- maintaining vertical file

- organizing teachers' collection
- reading shelves
- handling overdues
- acting as secretary-receptionist
- picking up and returning films
- working the desk
- labeling filmstrips
- telephoning
- storytelling
- alphabetizing
- doing bulletin boards

What did you enjoy least?
- shelving (boring)
- when shelves were disorganized
- working with people who were not compatible
- people who would say they were coming and didn't
- people who didn't do their jobs
- people who knew more than the librarian
- people who made decisions without checking it out
- people who did not follow directions
- times when no one was available to answer questions
- cleaning storage room
- cataloging
- working with periodicals
- inventory

What did you like most?
- typing
- cataloging
- organizing
- the personal relationship with the librarian
- being around adults
- getting back into the school environment
- a feeling of self-worth
- the fact that my children saw that I was interested
- I could help the school without hurting my preschooler
- it gave me some time without my children
- doing something constructive

- through library work I discovered that I like projects which are self-contained
- the good feeling of finishing projects
- like having an assortment of jobs
- like to be busy
- checking out
- working the desk because I was so involved in many different things
- bulletin boards

How could training have been improved?
- give more training on use of card catalog
- have someone always available for questions
- tell volunteer what does not work in his job
- nothing
- closets should be *kept* clean; libraries shouldn't have messy closets
- provide an outline for each job
- eliminate some of the talking between teachers and parents
- have outside school projects in the library
- have more time allowed between classes for spur-of-the-moment training

What problems did you have with students?
- when volunteers corrected them, they sometimes looked sassy
- didn't know how to approach some youngsters when they needed discipline
- students don't respect anyone
- high noise level outside the library
- students who are unable to find P.E. teacher coming into library for key and supplies
- wanton breaking of pencils
- playing with each other's lunches
- teachers who send children to the library for punishment
- interruptions of volunteers who are working by undisciplined students

Did you feel that there was a problem with teachers?
- had negative opinion of teacher who was in library too much
- teachers talk in the library

Did you have problems with other volunteers?
- none; I just ignored things if I didn't like them
- did not like to work with too many people at a time

- felt more work could have been done
- personal relationships between volunteers can make work relationship more difficult
- no
- disapproved of occasional topics of conversation, especially if volunteers talked about children

Did you have any problems with the librarian?

- none
- if asked to do something she did not like the volunteer would do a little, then switch jobs or leave
- not always available for questions
- failed to deal with a bad situation immediately
- failed to be very honest with a volunteer if there is a problem
- failed to support detailed instruction with periodic reminders

Do you feel that you had any authority?

- yes, indeed; as much as needed
- yes, if librarian was not there I felt free to use my judgment
- definite yes, with students and teachers; not over other volunteers
- within job limitations, did not have authority to overreach boundaries

What responsibility to the volunteer do you think the coordinator has?

- to make the work interesting
- to involve the volunteers
- to show that he is needed
- to show that she is being depended on
- to ask people if they wish to do something else
- to see that work goes smoothly
- to see that relationships are compatible
- to make the volunteer comfortable
- to praise him
- to show that she is wanted and needed
- to explain the job thoroughly beforehand
- to be sure he knows the scope of the job
- to be understanding if she can't come in
- to let the volunteer know if work is not done satisfactorily
- to give the same consideration a paid person would get
- to keep the volunteer abreast of the schedule
- to give training

- not to take advantage of the volunteer
- to give clear instructions
- to have a reasonable consistency

What responsibilities do the volunteers have?
- to understand that the librarian is not the volunteer's "mother"
- to follow through with a commitment
- to offer punctual completion of a project
- to do their jobs
- to be willing to do other jobs if needed
- to call when unable to come in
- to show up
- to work
- to ask for additional work
- to cancel babysitter if necessary (when provided by school)
- not to volunteer for work they can't do
- the same things paid employees would be expected to do
- to follow directions, not make up new ones
- to be dependable
- to look on the volunteer work as a job
- to learn as much as possible
- to try to get along with other volunteers and not create an uncomfortable situation
- to let the coordinator know if they don't like a job

Why did you volunteer in the library?
- there was a need
- enjoy people
- enjoy being at school
- to learn more about the school
- to keep busy
- to feel good about myself
- not to waste my life
- to repay scholarship
- friend told how librarian helped her to feel good and how she felt about the librarian
- good experience for job hunting later
- like books
- wanted to know what it was like to work with books and youngsters in a library

- show my children that I was interested
- adult time out
- liked the people in the library
- for my own satisfaction
- to keep abreast of school events

What compensation does a volunteer receive?
- good feeling
- knowledge that he is contributing to something worthwhile
- feeling that what you had to give was valuable
- knowing that you were helping the library
- giving the librarian more time to work with the children
- gratitude
- appreciation from the librarian and the administration
- knowledge that you have helped the librarian and the school
- self-satisfaction for a job well done
- it's a nice feeling not to be selfish
- learned a lot
- more aware of services for children
- pleased with the library
- felt good that even little children learn how to use the library
- feeling of being useful
- responsible for my going back to school
- exposure to a new career
- learned to like precise things so much that will get a degree in accounting
- new friends

In understanding what a volunteer program is all about, it is wise to take into consideration the opinions of the volunteers. This, together with planning and some time, will produce results far beyond those the librarian can hope to attain himself.

Bibliography

"ABC's—A Handbook for Educational Volunteers." Washington, D.C.: Washington Technical Institute, n.d.

Berry, John. "Listen to the Delegates." *Library Journal* 194 (1979): 1093.

Carter, Barbara, and Dapper, Gloria. *Organizing School Volunteer Programs*. New York: Citation Press, 1974.

Chruden, Herbert J., and Sherman, Arthur W. *Personnel Management: The Utilization of Human Resources*. Cincinnati: South-Western, 1980.

Collins, Arthur S. *Common Sense Training: A Working Philosophy for Leaders*. San Rafael, Calif.: Presidio Press, 1978.

Fitzwater, Ivan W. *Finding Time for Success and Happiness through Time Management*. San Antonio, Tex.: Mandel Publications, 1977.

French, Wendell L. *The Personnel Management Process*. 4th ed. Boston: Houghton Mifflin, 1978.

Freund, Janet W. *Coordinator's Guide: Volunteers and Volunteer Services in School*. Winnetka, Ill.: Winnetka Public Schools, n.d.

Goodman, Helen C. "The Library Volunteer—III: Volunteers in El Paso." *Library Journal* 97 (1972): 1675-77.

"Guidelines for Using Volunteers in Libraries." *American Libraries* 2 (1971): 407-8.

Haendle, Connie. "The Community Link: Libraries and the Literacy Volunteers of America." *Wilson Library Bulletin* 50 (1976): 731-33.

"How-to-Do Handbook for Coordinators of Volunteers in Education." Washington, D.C.: Washington Technical Institute, n.d.

"Interviewer's Guide: A Manual for Interviewers of Prospective Volunteers." New York: School Volunteer Program, n.d.

Jenkins, Harold. "Volunteers in the Future of Libraries." *Library Journal* 97 (1972): 1399-1403.

Lakein, Alan. *How to Get Control of Your Time and Your Life*. New York: New American Library, 1973.

"Letters." *Library Journal* 106 (1981): 83-84.

McCauley, Elfrieda. "Volunteers? Yes." *School Library Journal* 22 (1976): 29-33.

"Manual for Trainers." New York: National Commission on Resources for Youth, n.d.

Matley, Marcel B. "Harnessing Volunteer Energy in a Community Library." *Wilson Library Bulletin* 46 (1972): 828-33.

Needle, June. "Peace Corps Librarians in the Developing World." *Special Libraries* 68 (1977): 206-10.

Phillips, Nina. *The Chairman: A Handbook for School Volunteer Chairmen*. New York: School Volunteer Program, n.d.

Plotnik, Art. "Library Life on the West Coast. Part II: The Why-nots and the Have-nots." *Wilson Library Bulletin* 48 (1974): 812-20.

Ries, Al, and Trout, Jack. *Positioning: The Battle for Your Mind*. New York: McGraw-Hill, 1981.

Sannwald, William W., and Hofmann, Catherine N. "Practicing Librarian: Volunteers in Ventura County." *Library Journal* 107 [i.e., 105] 1980: 681-82.

Savage, Noel. "News in Review, 1980." *Library Journal* 106 (1981): 109-24.

Savage, Noel. "Special Report: Volunteers in Libraries." *Library Journal* 101 (1977): 2431-33.

"School Volunteers: Districts Recruit Aids to Meet Rising Costs, Student Needs." Arlington, Va.: National School Public Relations Association, n.d.

Smith, Carl B., and Fay, Leo C. *Getting People to Read: Volunteer Programs That Work*. New York: Delta Books, n.d.

Stenzl, Ann K., and Feeney, Helen M. *Volunteer Training and Development: A Manual for Community Groups*. New York: Seabury Press, n.d.

Trainer, Leslie. "Metro Workshop on Volunteers in Libraries Sparks Controversy, Offers Practical Advice." *American Libraries* 7 (1976): 666-67.

"Volunteer ABC's." Washington, D.C.: U.S. Office of Education, n.d.

Warner, Alice S. "Voluntarism and Librarianship." *Library Journal* 97 (1972): 1241-45.

Wehmeyer, Lillian Biermann. *The School Library Volunteer*. Littleton, Colo.: Libraries Unlimited, 1975.

Wheeler, Joseph L., and Goldhor, Herbert. *Practical Administration of Public Libraries*. New York: Harper & Row, 1962.

Winslow, T. "Volunteers Enrich." *Library Journal* 104 (1979): 2250-51.

Working with Volunteers. Chicago: Adult Education Association, 1959.

Index

Ad, sample, 51
Administration in one-person library chart, 35
Advantages of program
  for budgets, 1-3
  for coordinator, 5
  for librarian, staff, and children, 3-5
  for services, 3
  for volunteer, 5
ALA report, 183-84
Apprehensions about program
  costs, 12-13
  exploitation, 11
  job insecurity, 7-9
  lack of control, 10-11
  problem masking, 9
Attracting volunteers. See Publicity program; Recruitment
Authority systems charts, 44-47

Behavior modification chart, 136
Birthday donation sample letter, 125
Budgets, impact on, 1-3, 13
Building-level coordinators. See Coordinators, independent building-level

Campaigns. See under Recruitment
Checkout procedures, sample checklist, 111-14

Clubs
  publicity through, 53, 63
  as source of volunteers, 55, 57
Coordinators, 40. See also specific types of coordinators. See also under Evaluation of personnel
  and control of volunteers, 10
  evaluations by, 164, 165, 169, 170, 171, 172, 174, 178, 179, 190-91
  general principles for, 37
  justifying costs of volunteers, 12
  preplanning committee and, 20
  problems controlled by, 135, 138-40, 141, 142
  and problems with time management, 144, 148, 150
  recognition of, 163
  and recognition of volunteers, 155, 156, 157, 158, 159
  and recruitment publicity, 49, 53, 54, 55, 57, 59, 61, 70, 73
  responsibilities of, 21, 142, 143-44
  selection of, 24-25
  style of supervision, 36-39
  and training of volunteers, 98, 101, 104, 105, 106, 108, 110, 116, 118, 119, 120, 123, 124, 126, 127, 132, 133
Coordinators, central, 24, 36. See also under Evaluation of personnel
  characteristics of, 29-30
  duties of, 28-29, 32, 33

234 / Index

Coordinators, central (cont'd)
    evaluations by, 164, 165, 169
    and the interview, 75, 80-87
    and placement of volunteers, 88-89
    preinterview strategy of, 75-80
    systems of authority, 25-28, 43, 44-46
    value of using, 30
    volunteer impact on, 5
Coordinators, independent building-level, 30, 36. See also under Evaluation of personnel
    characteristics of, 34
    duties of, 32-33
    evaluation by, 164, 165
    and the interview, 75, 77, 88
    placement of volunteers by, 89-97
    systems of authority, 31-32, 47
    training of volunteers by, 98, 105
Coordinators, liaison, 36, 75
    duties of, 29
    and the interview, 77, 80, 84, 85, 86, 87
    and placement of volunteers, 88, 89, 91
    system of authority, 25, 28
Costs of program, 12-13

El Paso Public Library ad, 51
Ethical Culture School manual, 203-13
Evaluation of personnel
    building-level coordinators, 165, 169
    central coordinators, 165, 166
    coordinators, 165, 169, 170, 171
    forms for, 193
    self-rating forms for, 166, 167, 168, 171, 173, 188
    supervisors, 167
    volunteers, 170, 172, 173, 188, 193
Evaluation of program, 174, 178-79
    forms for, 175, 176-77, 187, 189, 190-91, 192, 194, 195
    methods and goals for, 164-65
    preplanning for, 20-23
Evaluation of purposes and ideas table, 22-23

Funding for libraries
    sources of, 73
    for special services, 3
    volunteer impact on, 2

Gallup Poll on volunteers, 11
Greenwich Public School system
    advantages of volunteer program in, 13
    volunteer impact on budget, 10
"Guidelines for Using Volunteers in Libraries," 183-84

Hamden Hall Country Day School. See Margaret Ross Memorial Library

Impact of program. See Advantages of program
Interview for volunteers, 48, 80
    application for, sample, 82
    and assessment of volunteer needs, 78
    determining interests and skills, 83-85
    letter of acknowledgment, sample, 79
    and preinterview strategy, 75-80
    and screening, 85-87
    sign-up sheet for, sample, 96
    volunteer file sheet for, 81

Job application form for students, sample, 131

Librarians
    apprehensions of, 7-13
    as coordinators, 31, 32, 34
    publicity role of, 43, 48
    self-evaluation form for, 168
    as sources for volunteer programs, 17
    volunteer impact on, 3-4, 7-9, 14
    as volunteers, 57-58
Libraries
    administrative function in the one-person, 35
    hints for working the desk at, 115
    needs assessment form for, 76
    needs of and program planning, 18, 19
    physical arrangement of, sample checklist, 109
    publicity program for, sample, 65-66
    wide-range training in, 108-19

Los Alamitos School District manual, 199
Lunch program order sheet, sample, 128

Magazine publicity. *See* Publicity program: media
Manuals for volunteers
　description for, 122
　samples, 199-213
Margaret Ross Memorial Library, Hamden Hall Country Day School
　sample manual, 200-202
　volunteer mothers program at, 100
　volunteer work at, application for, 82
Media. *See under* Publicity program
Message and project center, sample, 99
Metro workshop in New York, 8, 9, 10, 11. *See also* New York Metropolitan Reference and Research Library Agency
Modification of program, 172, 174
　form for, 176-77
　projects and ideas for, 178-79

National School Volunteer Program evaluation form, 190-91, 194
Need assessment. *See under* Preplanning of program
New York Metropolitan Reference and Research Library Agency, 2. *See also* Metro workshop in New York
Newspaper publicity. *See* Publicity program: media

Objectives of program, 19-20
Oklahoma City Public Schools evaluation form, 187
Orange County, Florida, program, 3

Parents
　as source for volunteer program, 16, 57, 58, 63
　volunteer handout for, sample, 56
　as volunteers, 54-55, 97
Partners for Entertaining and Educational Reading. *See* PEER
PEER, 50

Placement of volunteers, 88
　orientation agenda for, sample, 90
　orientation for, 89, 91-94
　selection of tasks for, 95, 97
Planning successfully chart, 137
Preinterview of volunteers. *See* Interview for volunteers: and preinterview strategy
Preplanning of program, 16
　committee for, 17, 18, 19, 20
　evaluation format for, 20-23
　and formulating the program, 19-20
　and needs assessment, 18-19
Principals
　evaluation forms for, 192, 193, 194, 195
　lines of authority with, 25, 26-27, 31, 48
　recognition of volunteers by, 159
　role in program, 140
　as source for volunteer program, 17
Problem/cause relationship chart, 139
Problems with program
　control of, by coordinators, 135-38
　interpersonal, 138-42, 169
　responsibility, 142-44
　time management, 144-54
Publicity program, 40, 41, 43
　advertising for, 49-50, 51
　informal approaches to, 53-59, 61
　media, 40, 50-52, 53, 59, 68-72, 158
　speaking engagements for, 63-68
　system of authority for, 43-48
　with themes, 52-53

Radio publicity. *See* Publicity program: media
Recognition of volunteers, 155
　with bookplates, 163
　ceremonies for, 158
　daily response for, 156-57
　project publicity for, 158-59
　social activities for, 159
　with thank you notes, 159-62
Recruitment, 40-43
　campaign ad, sample, 51
　campaigns, annual, 48-52
　campaigns, daily, 52-72
　financing, 73
　of parents, handout, 56

Rossmoor Public School
  parent handout, sample, 56
  slogans, 50

St. Luke's Episcopal School
  job application form, 131
  lunch form, 128
Screening volunteers. *See under*
  Interview for volunteers
Self-evaluation. *See* Evaluation of
  personnel: self-rating forms for
Senior citizens
  publicity through, 53, 63
  as volunteers, 4, 61, 62
Sources of volunteers, 4, 16, 17, 54-55, 57, 58-61, 62
Speaker request survey form, 64
Speaking engagement, sample checklist, 65-66
Special interest groups
  publicity through, 53, 63
  as source of volunteers, 58
Staff
  and building-level coordinators, 32
  needs of, and program planning, 18
  volunteer impact on, 4
  and volunteer relationships, 138-40
  as volunteers, 58
Students
  needs of, and program planning, 18
  publicity through, 53, 54
  as source for volunteer program, 17
  volunteer impact on, 3, 4, 5
  as volunteers, 58-59, 61
  work chart for practicum, sample, 60
Survey of volunteers, 217-27
Systems of authority charts
  for building-level coordinators, 31
  for central coordinators, 26-27, 44-46
  for individual coordinators, 47

Teachers
  needs of, and program planning, 18
  publicity role of, 158-59
  relationship with volunteers, 92
  as source for volunteer program, 17
  as volunteers, 58
Television publicity. *See* Publicity
  program: media
Time management. *See under* Problems with program

Time management charts, 145-47, 149, 151, 152, 153-54
Training volunteers
  authority for, 104
  policies and rules for, 98-104
  and reassessment of tasks, 132-33
  for special programs, 122-31
  as substitutes, 133-34
  in understanding the schedule, 122
  in universal tasks
    choosing the trainer, 105-7
    covering the material, 108-19
    with training techniques, 119-21
    with volunteer manual, 122

Ventura County, California
  advantages of volunteer program in, 13
  cost of volunteer program, 12
  impact of volunteer program on budget, 10
  volunteer program, 2
VITAL, 50
Volunteers. *See also under* Evaluation of personnel
  advantages of using, 13-14
  as central coordinators, 30
  file sheet on, 81
  as independent building-level coordinators, 34
  interrelationships of, 140-42
  needs assessment of, 77, 78
  needs of, and program planning, 19
  problems with using, 7-13
  program impact on, 5
  programs created by, 126-30
  reason for being, 41-43
  responsibility of, 142-43, 144
  and staff relationships, 138-40
  time management for, 144, 148, 150
  as trainers, 106
Volunteers in Teaching and Learning. *See* VITAL.

Washington Technical Institute evaluation form, 188, 189, 193
Workshops, 2, 8, 9, 10, 11

Young people
  publicity through, 53, 63
  as volunteers, 58-61